500

LET JUSTICE BE DONE

LET JUSTICE BE DONE

New Light on the Jim Garrison Investigation

William Davy

Jordan Publishing
Reston, Virginia, U.S.A.

Copyright © 1999 by William Davy

ISBN 0-9669716-0-4

Published in the United States by
Jordan Publishing
11654 Plaza America Drive #369
Reston, VA 20190-4700

for Karen

Fiat justitia ruat coelum. *

* This Latin maxim has been ascribed to Lucius Calpurnius Piso Caesoninus (d. 43 B.C.) and translates literally as, "Let justice be done, though heaven should fall." The Hungarian King of Bohemia and Hungary (1558-1564), **Ferdinand I**, adopted it as his motto in the form of, *"Fiat justitia et pereat mundus."* (Let justice be done, though the world perish.) In 1967, this became the guiding principle of the New Orleans District Attorney's office as they investigated the murder of President John F. Kennedy.

Contents

Foreword

On October 1, 1998 the Assassination Records Review Board closed its doors and issued its Final Report to both congress and President Clinton. Thus ended the efforts first begun four years ago to declassify the secret record about the facts concerning the murder of President John F. Kennedy. This monumental, unprecedented process was brought about by Oliver Stone's film, *JFK*.

The reception given the conclusion of the Review Board's four year odyssey into the new frontier of declassifying records that the intelligence community wanted closed, met with a queer reception by the mainstream media. Commentators like Tim Weiner, George Will, William Buckley, and the dreaded Gerald Posner all noted this momentous event by playing the theme that it was now over and still nothing had changed. Max Holland, *The Nation* magazine's answer to Posner, did the same in the pages of that supposedly progressive publication and also over the airwaves of Pacifica radio. Did all these men digest over four million pages of newly declassified documents overnight in order to certify their pronouncements? Let's put it this way: I would love to cross-examine them under oath on that point. But even though they did no such thing, the relentless desire to misinform the American public on this issue still holds paramount importance. And as the *New York Times*, *Newsweek*, and *The Nation* have done since 1963, the litany of fabrication and denial continues unabated.

But if the pundits doth protest too much today, it is because the necessity for deception is stronger now than it ever has been. Whatever the shortcomings of the ARRB, (and there were several), no serious person—of which the above-mentioned personages are not—can examine this new record and not come to the conclusion that both of the official verdicts in the JFK case are flat wrong. That is, both the Warren Commission verdict and the conclusion of the House Select Committee in 1979 are now negated. And negated resoundingly in every aspect of both of those bodies' official reports regarding the real identity and function of Lee Harvey Oswald, his journey to Mexico City, the medical examination of John Kennedy's body, the strange maneuverings of Ruth and Michael Paine, the actions of the FBI after the assassination, the monitoring of Oswald by both the Bureau and the Central Intelligence Agency before the crime, etc. The most serious questions can now be mounted in all of these areas of this most heinous murder. And in all them, it can now be demonstrated that the critics were correct.

This is the real reason the mainstream media wants no one to notice what is in these newly open files. And, of course, one area of inquiry they certainly want to conceal is what was going on in New Orleans in the summer and fall of 1963. For to honestly study this new record is to see that Jim Garrison was anything but the caricature the media made him back in 1967. Any curious prosecutor would have been interested in the odd associations and meanderings of the alleged communist assassin Oswald during that strange summer. The communist Oswald who had no communist friends. The Fair Play for Cuba advocate who stored his flyers in the office of rightwing zealot Guy Banister. The supposed loner who had so many acquaintances who just happened to have intelligence connections. Yes, New Orleans was an area that was much worth investigating and in which many, many tantalizing leads should have been followed. The media needs to let those sleeping dogs stay dormant. If fully awakened, their barking would be deafening.

Since the media wants to keep us asleep, what the curious reader can do is read Bill Davy's book. Bill Davy is someone who actually did read a lot of the newly declassified record. Bill then went down to New Orleans and talked to some of the people he read about it in the documents. Further, he really read and he really listened. Unlike people like Posner and his acolyte Gus Russo, there were no blinkers around his eyes, or plugs in his ears. Bill gives you the best of that new record and he renders it whole and complete. There is no fitting of square pegs into round holes, the hallmark of both Posner and Russo.

The reason for that of course, is that Bill has no political agenda. And he's not in this to make money. As many can tell you, for the people who tell the truth, there is no money in the Kennedy assassination. Quite the contrary. In fact, I don't think Bill could mold an agenda if he tried. He's just not that political, or mercenary. In fact, even though I have known him for over five years, I don't even know what political party he belongs to or who he voted for in the last two presidential elections. Bill Davy is just another citizen-investigator who was interested in finding out what really happened in November of 1963. And he also wanted to try and fathom the truth about what happened to Jim Garrison in 1963 and afterwards.

There were a lot of difficulties surrounding Bill's quest. First, with the Garrison investigation, it was tough to locate much of the primary data, that is the firsthand investigative records of the probe. But both the ARRB and Garrison's son Lyon helped in that regard. So Bill has had access to many of these new records-- as the reader can see by scanning his footnotes. There was also a resistance to this new work inside the research community.

Surprisingly, many in this segmented community showed little or no interest in what Garrison had actually dug up during his probe. They were too interested in spouting the negative cliches spun out in dubious and biased books authored by questionable writers like Edward Epstein and John Davis (who Bill takes apart late in this book). And of course, there was no honest publisher to give this book the promotion and care it needs and deserves. The big houses are too busy with the likes of Seymour Hersh, Posner and their ilk.

But Bill has overcome all these obstacles and written a compelling, objective, and, most of all, a highly informative volume. It is brimming with new information while it sheds light on and expands things that we knew before. It is the kind of book that you can mark a milestone with. And the reason of course is that the author actually read the new record. And that record was well worth reading.

Back in 1963 and 1964 Warren Commission assistant counsel Wesley Liebeler was the man most responsible for tracing Oswald's trail in New Orleans. According to Liebeler, he read all the relevant FBI reports compiled on this matter. Yet as Bill shows, he must have missed the ones in which the Bureau revealed that it knew that Clay Shaw used the alias of Clay Bertrand and that Shaw was acquainted with David Ferrie. He also missed the fact that some of the New Orleans FBI agents, like Regis Kennedy, were busy falsifying the record in regards to Dean Andrews, the man who first drew attention to the importance of Clay Bertrand. And, of course, the fact that Regis Kennedy did what he did shows that (a) this was OK with his superiors at the top of the FBI, and (b) he knew that something important was there to cover up, something that could not be allowed to survive unobfuscated. So with the help of the Warren Commission, specifically with Liebeler, the FBI did its bit in burying the truth about Oswald in New Orleans.

When Jim Garrison resurfaced the subject in 1967 he was cross-whipped by two hurricane blasts, one from Washington and one from New York. The first, of course, was from the government, specifically the Central Intelligence Agency, the FBI, and to a lesser extent, the White House. The blast from New York was from the major mainstream media e.g. Time-Life and NBC. Those two communications giants were instrumental in making Garrison into a lightning rod for ridicule and criticism. This orchestrated campaign—and Bill Davy proves it was just that—was successful in diverting attention from what Garrison was uncovering by creating controversy about the DA himself. As Bill shows, this is a common tactic by the Establishment press in negating those who uncover unpleasant truths about America. To illustrate his point, Bill uses the parallel example of Congressman Cornelius Gallagher. But we can also add the more recent paradigm of what happened to newspaper reporter Gary Webb when he uncovered the truth about the CIA and drugs in Los Angeles. But the example of Garrison, if anything, is much more extreme. I can think of no other public figure who was attacked so viciously, so constantly, by so many different media outlets and so unfairly. It was so excessive that, for the first time I can recall, the Establishment was actually willing to reveal part of the covert apparatus surrounding its orchestration; a fascinating phenomenon which Bill does a good job of detailing. In my view, the fact that they were willing to risk exposure shows how desperate they were to destroy Garrison. Which, one could logically conclude, indicates what was really at stake.

Once Garrison was stopped in the courts, it looked like the Kennedy case was also finished. But surprisingly, it resurfaced in the mid-seventies. The House Select Committee was formed in 1976 and got off to a surprisingly auspicious start. Illustrious Philadelphia lawyer Richard Sprague was finally going to give the Kennedy case the extensive professional examination that it deserved. And do it with what Garrison did not have, i.e. a multi-million dollar budget and over 100 employees. It appeared as if there was finally going to be a reckoning on this case. Sprague's deputy on the Kennedy side, Robert Tanenbaum, was just as uncompromising as he was. Both men seemed truly interested in what had happened in New Orleans.

It was not to be. The Sprague-Tanenbaum team never got to complete any New Orleans investigation, or any JFK investigation for that matter. In another striking parallel, Dick Sprague was deposed as a result of a vicious attack by both the media and certain congressmen who were determined not to see any serious inquiry into the murders of either Kennedy or Martin Luther King. (As Bill notes here, some of the tactics used on the floor of the House during the debate are pure echoes of the smears used against Garrison.) But some of the investigators for the House Select Committee—Jonathan Blackmer, L. J. Delsa, Al Gonzalez, and Bob Buras—kept probing into New Orleans. And they kept on coming up with leads and discoveries that bolstered many of the things that Garrison had been saying. But the HSCA went further. They found people who were willing to talk to them who Garrison never talked to; for example, William Gaudet. They also extended the New Orleans investigation outward until they were able to link it with the giant CIA station in Miami, JM/WAVE. As Bill notes, one of the interesting links was through Bernardo De Torres, a Bay of Pigs veteran who infiltrated Garrison's investigation at an early stage.

But the most potent HSCA discoveries about New Orleans, and nearly all of the substantive details, were not to be seen in the Final Report written by Chief Counsel Robert Blakey and Richard Billings. In fact, much of that material is not even in the accompanying HSCA volumes. Some of it leaked out --in very small bits and pieces-- after the HSCA closed down in 1979. Garrison had worked with some of the HSCA investigators and talked to some researchers at the time. So writers like Robert Morrow and commentators like Ted Gandolfo managed to get some unverified hints out of what had actually been dug up by the HSCA. But it was not until over a decade later that we finally began to get a real view of the gold that the HSCA had mined in the Crescent City. That, of course, was done by the ARRB. Which was caused by the furor over Stone's film. Which was based on Jim Garrison's book. So, through three decades, we have come full circle.

Foreword

It was left to Bill Davy to collate and arrange the evidence in these new files. He had a little help from me, and more important help from ace archive researcher Peter Vea. But it was Bill who spent all the time collecting and putting the documents together into a striking mosaic. He then wrote, in clear and serviceable prose, a tale that no one has been able to assemble and detail before. Not me, not Paris Flammonde, not Bill Turner, not even Jim Garrison. Not one of us had access to the documents that the government had been concealing about what is probably the most significant murder of the so-called American century. Bill Davy did. That's why his book stands as a milestone in that library of the 700 or so books dealing with the Kennedy assassination. It is, to turn a phrase, New Orleans declassified. And with these new documents, Bill draws not a precis, not a sketch, but an in-depth portrait of the beehive that was New Orleans in the 1960's. People's histories are now drawn in at length and in detail e.g. Guy Banister, David Ferrie, and especially Clay Shaw. Events and associations are now much more clear and distinct. What Bill does with the incident in the Clinton-Jackson area is worth the price of the book. Shaw's dealings with the Swiss-Italian front organization called Permindex is given its own special chapter. The sections dealing with the trial of Clay Shaw and the media coverage of it are simply splendid. And this could only have been written with the new files. There was no way that the government was going to reveal that (a) it was interfering with the judicial process in a large, unprecedented way, and (b) some prominent journalists were, to say the least, not as independent as they seemed. *Newsweek* reporter Hugh Aynesworth was working for Shaw's lawyers. James Phelan of the *Saturday Evening Post* was an informant for the FBI. Neither one of those publications told its readers about those facts. And neither Phelan nor Aynesworth ever admitted that they were compromised. In fact, they both denied it. What Bill is able to do here is to show the mighty combination that emerged to block Jim Garrison, and the people of his parish and state, from getting a real opportunity to do their best at the trial of Clay Shaw. That massive interference shortchanged not just them, but all of us.

Shaw's trial was the first and last criminal case brought against the conspiracy to murder President Kennedy.

One last achievement should be noted about Bill Davy's book. As the reader will note, Bill does very little in the way of drawing conclusions. And the book has almost no theorizing in it at all. Bill didn't have to resort to that. His book is just too full of verifiable and/or corroborative facts and information. One of the deplorable hallmarks of all too many books in this field prior to the declassification process was that they drew conclusions based on very little evidence. And the evidence produced was sometimes little more than past associations. That is, if Person A met with Person B six months before the assassination, or if they even called each other, that was enough to set up a nexus point that could be used to show responsibility for the assassination. The Mob-did-it enthusiasts were especially prone to this. Anyone who practices this kind of thing in the future should be looked upon with suspicion. These new files provide an abundance of *real* evidence, the kind that could be used as a working background on a genuine criminal investigation. And some of it could be used as direct evidence in a court of law. It is this kind of research and documentation that we all should be looking at now. There should be no more books that are strong on speculation and weak on documentation.

I was fortunate enough to know Bill at the beginning of the journey that led to this book. He, Peter Vea, and myself met on more than one occasion in both Washington D.C. and New Orleans. He has always struck me as being an honest, bright, straightforward type of guy. He wasn't out to make a buck. He wasn't out to solve the Kennedy assassination. He had no plans to make a career out of this. He just wanted to find out the truth about what happened in New Orleans in relation to the events surrounding November 22, 1963. We need more people like him, and books like his, in this endeavor.

James DiEugenio

Preface

By now the story is all too familiar. November 22, 1963. Dallas, Texas. President Kennedy is assassinated while riding in an open limousine. Within a few hours, Lee Harvey Oswald is arrested after sneaking into a local movie theater. Oswald is first booked for the murder of a local police officer, J.D. Tippitt and is later charged with the murder of the President. On November 24th as Oswald is being transferred from the local jail Jack Ruby, "patriotic night club owner" and fellow lone nut, shoots him. The following day, President Kennedy's funeral is held with all of the requisite ornaments.

Within days, a Presidential commission is formed to investigate the circumstances surrounding the murder of the President. Headed by widely respected Chief Justice Earl Warren it comes to be known as the Warren Commission. In 1964, the Commission issues their report and 26 volumes of supporting "evidence." Its conclusion, that Oswald a lonely, disgruntled ex-Marine whose obsession with communism caused him to defect to the Soviet Union, and later kill the President with three shots from a war surplus rifle, was widely accepted at face value by the American people and trumpeted loudly by the mainstream media. Likewise, the Commission's conclusion that Ruby was yet another "loner" who killed Oswald during a fit of patriotism found its way into mainstream consciousness as well.

Then something happened. People began to analyze the 26 volumes that purportedly was the evidentiary basis of the Report and discovered that much of the evidence either didn't support the Commission's conclusions or was just completely irrelevant. In the mid-1960's several scholarly books were released challenging the central tenets of the Warren doctrine. Mark Lane's *Rush to Judgment*, Harold Weisberg's *Whitewash*, Sylvia Meagher's *Accessories After the Fact*, and Josiah Thompson's *Six Seconds in Dallas* all raised reasonable doubts and started a groundswell of criticism of the Warren Report. Even mainstream magazines such as *Life*, *Look*, and *The Saturday Evening Post* were all taking a new look at the assassination.

Then something happened - again. A District Attorney from New Orleans had the temerity to launch his own probe into the assassination. In 1966 Jim Garrison, the wildly popular New Orleans D.A., began investigating Oswald's stay in the Crescent City during the summer of 1963. As his office began questioning various witnesses Garrison began to focus his probe on a suspect he believed may have conspired to have the President killed. David Ferrie was an ex-airline pilot and anti-Castro adventurer who Garrison believed had a long history with the CIA as well as with the accused assassin. Soon however, the story broke in the newspapers and Garrison's probe became worldwide news. Unfortunately for Ferrie, so did he. Less than a week after the story broke, Ferrie was found dead in his apartment, apparently of natural causes. With his main suspect now dead many felt Garrison would wind up his investigation. They were wrong. On March 1, 1967 Garrison arrested a local businessman named Clay Shaw and charged him with conspiracy to murder President Kennedy. Shaw, a respected figure among the New Orleans elite, expressed shock and outrage at the charge. For the next two years as Garrison sought to get Shaw to trial both Garrison and his office came under intense attack from the local and national media. Allegations of bribery, mob influence and other unsavory charges haunted the investigation. In 1969 Shaw was tried and acquitted on the conspiracy charge. The prevailing orthodoxy was that the Garrison probe seriously discredited and set back the Warren critics' "movement."

However, in the mid-1970's as a result of several congressional investigations, details of CIA abuses emerged. Amid the revelations of CIA operations to dose unsuspecting citizens with LSD, infiltrate the media with CIA agents and assets, spy on American citizens opposed to the Vietnam War, and assassinate foreign leaders, it was revealed that some of the more heinous projects were reserved for Cuban president, Fidel Castro. These included:

- Working in concert with the Mafia to assassinate Castro.

- Having a double-agent (Rolando Cubela, code-named AMLASH) kill Castro with a poison pen armed with a deadly poison known as Black-Leaf 40.

- Planting an exotic looking seashell, rigged with an explosive, in an area where Castro was known to skin dive.

- Treating Castro's skin diving suit and breathing apparatus with tubercle bacilli.

- Spraying an LSD aerosol at a radio station where Castro broadcasted his speeches.

Most of these operations were directed from New Orleans

and Miami. The Miami CIA station was located on a sprawling, heavily wooded tract on the University of Miami's South Campus. Code named JM/WAVE, the Agency disguised the operation with the front corporation, Zenith Technical Enterprises, Inc. It soon became the largest CIA installation in the world outside of the Langley headquarters. At its height JM/WAVE had a staff of over 300 Americans mostly case officers each employing scores of anti-Castro Cubans and renegade contract agents.

Along with the Watergate scandal - a domestic conspiracy that went to the highest levels of government - the involvement of intelligence agencies in our own domestic assassinations no longer seemed like fevered, paranoid fantasies to the general public. Amid an outpouring of popular support as well as efforts by Mark Lane, Virginia Congressman Thomas Downing and pressure from the Black Caucus, Congress established the House Select Committee on Assassinations to investigate the assassinations of President Kennedy and Dr. Martin Luther King. In 1979 the HSCA issued its report which concluded a high probability of conspiracy in both the King and Kennedy murders and recommended further investigation by the Justice Department. However, the Select Committee's recommendations were virtually ignored. There the matter lay until Hollywood stepped in.

In 1988 Garrison penned a second book on the investigation entitled, *On The Trail of the Assassins* (His first book, *A Heritage of Stone*, was published in 1970). Film director Oliver Stone optioned the book and in 1991 released his groundbreaking film *JFK*. Despite attacks similar to those incurred by Garrison, the film did remarkably well and led to the creation of the JFK Records Act which was signed into law by President Bush in 1992. The act provided for the creation of the Assassination Records and Review Board, whose task it was to declassify and release as many of the remaining documents and collections relative to the Kennedy assassination before their mandate ran out in October of 1998.

In 1995 I published a modest monograph entitled, *Through The Looking Glass: The Mysterious World of Clay Shaw*. Using many newly declassified documents and interviews of several witnesses (some of who spoke on record for the first time), the work was well received and sold briskly for a self-published volume. However, some felt I should have expanded the work to encompass more of the Garrison probe and the other individuals involved. I took those suggestions to heart - the result being this book.

Having utilized thousands of documents released before and subsequent to *Through The Looking Glass* as well as having supplemented this archival work with scores of interviews of various witnesses, including Senators, Congressional investigators, former CIA and FBI agents and officers, military intelligence officials, soldiers-of-fortune, lawyers and many others, I now feel it is possible to see the Garrison investigation unfold at a far finer grain of resolution.

Part One of this work looks at the beginnings of Garrison's New Orleans investigation and some of the principals involved. I have tried to use as much new information as possible and have only fallen back on previous research where necessary in order to provide context. Therefore many facts that have been oft repeated in other works have not found their way in here. Nor have any of the more salacious allegations leveled against Shaw or Garrison made their way into this volume. I will leave it to other authors to wade in that muck. Part Two is a complete revision and expansion of my earlier publication.

With the release of this new information, previous speculative possibilities now look more like historical truths. It is a sad commentary that the establishment news media have not taken the time to assimilate this information and present it to the nation. Instead it is left up to freelancers and researchers to bring this information out, mostly to an apathetic and somnambulistic public. As journalist Robert Parry recently wrote, "It is as if the final price for winning the Cold War is our confinement to a permanent childhood where reassuring fantasies and endless diversions protect us from the hard truth of our own recent history."

In closing, we would do well to remember the words of two

of the greatest thinkers of our time - one a philosopher, the other a poet. In *Life of Reason*, George Santayana wrote, "Those who cannot remember the past are condemned to repeat it." To ensure we have the truth about our past, we should heed the words of the great Welsh poet, Dylan Thomas:

> Do not go gentle into that good night...,
> Rage, rage against the dying of the light.

William Davy
January, 1999

Acknowledgments

Rarely is a book of this scope completed without it being a collaborative effort, and this volume is no exception. Friends, peers, and editors all make valuable contributions and I have been abundantly blessed in this regard.

In 1994, the author, along with Jim DiEugenio, Peter Vea, and a few others, made an investigative trip to New Orleans. We broke off into teams and "fanned-out," interviewing numerous witnesses, performing fieldwork and then sharing the fruits of our labors. This was followed up by another trip to New Orleans and many long hours logged at the National Archives, mostly by my colleague, Peter Vea. Both Peter and Jim were crucial to the completion of this project. This book is as much theirs as it is mine and I extend my greatest gratitude to both.

Additionally, a most heartfelt thanks must go to Mike Willman whose hospitality and generosity with his investigative materials contributed greatly. I am also grateful to Drs. John Newman and Donald Gibson who made several Clay Shaw/CIA documents available to the author.

Appreciation also goes to New Orleans filmmaker, Steve Tyler, for sharing the fruits of his labors. I also owe a debt of gratitude to Louisiana historian, Claude Slaton, for his help in the Clinton/Jackson areas of research. Thanks also to Dr. Jeff Caufield. A special thanks to Evelyn Cochran who provided much needed editorial assistance in the preparation of the original manuscript.

PROBE magazine editor, Lisa Pease's research and analysis of the New Orleans evidence was, as always, illuminating and provided a fresh perspective to the author. Dennis Lee Effle also provided early assistance and encouragement.

Veteran researcher and Warren Commission critic, Harold Weisberg, deserves a special thanks for allowing the author access to his voluminous collection of declassified materials.

Bob Spiegelman, who wrote the splendid afterword to this book, helped greatly with the New Orleans research, as well as providing a "big picture" analysis.

A very special thanks must go to Daniel Tsang at the University of California, who did such an exceptional job indexing this work. Joan Mellen's kind words and encouragement were also much appreciated.

I would be remiss if I didn't mention the Assassination Archives and Research Center in Washington, D.C. The AARC is one of the largest repositories of assassination related documents in the world and was an invaluable resource in the preparation of this work. I urge all serious researchers to support this organization. The AARC is located at 918 F Street, NW, 6th Floor, Washington, D.C., 20004 and is headed by Jim Lesar. They can be reached on (202) 393-1917.

Also of great assistance, was the Last Hurrah Bookshop. It is *the* premier bookshop in the country for the location of in and out-of-print volumes necessary for this kind of research. The proprietor, Andy Winiarczyk, is most helpful in locating those esoteric, hard-to-find books. Last Hurrah is located at 849 W. Third Street, #1, Williamsport, PA 17701. Their phone and fax number is (570) 321-1150.

A big thanks has to go to former FBI agent and author, Bill Turner. Bill's early writings for *Ramparts* magazine were an inspiration to this author. Our later exchanges enhanced this volume greatly. I feel fortunate to be able to consider Bill my friend.

Jim Garrison's sons, Lyon and Eberhard, are due a big debt of gratitude for allowing the author unprecedented access to their father's public *and* private papers.

I'm also thankful to all of the witnesses who were most generous with their time in allowing us to interview them, especially Bill Alford, the late Dr. Alfred Butterworth, Allen Campbell, Dan Campbell, Harry Connick, Sr., Warren deBrueys, L.J. Delsa, Jack Dempsey, Irvin Dymond, Hugh Exnicios, Eberhard Garrison, Lyon Garrison, Edward Joseph Girnus, Jr., Lou Ivon, Mary Morgan Jenkins, Buddy Johnson, Herman Kohlman, Art Kunkin, Senator Russell Long, Victor Marchetti, Ray Marcus, Lea McGehee, the late Reeves Morgan, Van Morgan, Joe Newbrough, Dr. Martin Palmer, Sal Panzeca, Niles Peterson, Colonel L. Fletcher Prouty, Jim Rose, the late Perry Russo, Bill Triplett, and Steve Tyler.

And last but not least, a very special debt of gratitude to my wife, Karen, who saw me through the home stretch.

Part One:

Masquerade

Introduction

It can be safely said that New Orleans District Attorney Jim Garrison's investigation into the assassination of President Kennedy began on the weekend of November 22, 1963. The catalyst was not the assassination itself, but rather the pistol-whipping of a lowly private eye named Jack Martin. Martin's beating came at the hands of his employer, a notorious political extremist known as Guy Banister. An ex-FBI man and former New Orleans police official, Banister operated a private detective agency on the corner of Camp and Lafayette streets. On November 22, Banister and Martin were drinking at a local watering hole called the Katz and Jammer Bar.[1] Later, they went to Banister's office where a quarrel erupted between the two men. In the heat of the argument, Martin blurted out to Banister, "What are you going to do - kill me like you all did Kennedy?"[2] In response, an enraged Banister drew his .357 magnum revolver and beat Martin in the head. Martin believed that had not Banister's secretary Delphine Roberts intervened, Banister would have killed him. Banister shoved some money in Martin's pocket and told him to get to a hospital or doctor.[3] As Martin left he ran back to the bar and remarked to the bartender, "The dirty Nazi bastards did it to him in Texas and tried to, to me here!"[4] Martin was treated at Charity Hospital where he filed a police report on the incident and was released.[5]

The next day Martin related his suspicions about the JFK murder to local officials. Curiously, Martin would not implicate Banister, but rather a mutual associate; an ex-airline pilot named David Ferrie. Martin contacted assistant District Attorney, Herman Kohlman and told him Ferrie and the accused presidential assassin, Lee Harvey Oswald were associates. Furthermore, Ferrie had taken a mysterious trip to Texas on the 22nd, ostensibly to go ice-skating. But Martin suggested Ferrie might have been some sort of getaway pilot. When Ferrie returned to New Orleans on the 24th, the police were waiting. Ferrie was questioned by Garrison's office and turned over to the FBI who promptly released him. There the matter rested for three years. Before we more closely examine Garrison's investigation, it might be instructive to look at the backgrounds of the principal players in this drama.

Chapter One

~

Swept Up in the Gales of History[1]

David William Ferrie, an Ohio native, was born March 18, 1918 in Cleveland.[2] He attended a series of Ohio Catholic schools including St. Patrick's Elementary and St. Ignatius High School. With hopes of becoming a priest Ferrie entered St. Mary's Seminary in 1938. Former classmate Monsignor Joseph Heruday considered Ferrie "erratic in behavior" and someone who had to "be the leader or [he] didn't want to do anything."[3] Reverend Francis B. Sullivan felt Ferrie was a "preconditioned psycho; impresses people by pretending to be an expert on everything; definitely has a talent for character assassination."[4] Reverend Edward Siegman, also a classmate of Ferrie's, recalled Ferrie as a disappointing student who was given to using psychological jargon but "had a good line with him."[5] According to Siegman, Ferrie "always had the younger seminarians in tow and had to be in charge of the work details."[6] Siegman concluded Ferrie was "unbalanced."[7] Apparently Ferrie's superiors concurred, as Ferrie was dismissed in 1940. Nevertheless Ferrie went on to complete studies in psychology at Baldwin-Wallace College, receiving a Bachelor of Arts degree on June 9, 1941, graduating 18th in a class of 93.

To take his mind off his failures at the seminary Ferrie took up flying. He took lessons at the Sky Tech Airway Service in Cleveland between 1942 and 1945. From 1945 through 1950 Ferrie held a series of jobs including piloting for the Jeda Oil and Drilling Company as well as an engineering position at Atwell Vogel Sterling and was an inspector trainee for Bankers Indemnity. He also briefly taught at Benedictine High School but was fired in 1948 for taking students on joy rides in his airplane. In 1950 Ferrie enlisted in the Army Reserve receiving an honorable discharge in 1953. In 1951 Ferrie applied for employment with Eastern Airlines. Ferrie's application was accepted and he was assigned a southern route. Ferrie moved to Miami for a brief time, eventually settling in the New Orleans area.

Ferrie also commanded a Civil Air Patrol (CAP) squadron, which allowed him to combine his two main passions: flying and the company of boys. Ferrie actually commanded his first CAP squadron while still in Cleveland. Colonel Harry A. Webb would later tell FAA investigators that when Ferrie first came to the CAP everyone thought he was an Air Force Lieutenant.[8] As a CAP instructor Webb recalled Ferrie "had the ability to get the affection of the cadets" adding "that they would do almost anything for him."[9]

In New Orleans Ferrie commanded the Eagle CAP Squadron and was just as memorable there. While regarded as a disciplinarian (Ferrie had a championship drill team) he nevertheless encouraged his cadets to drink, took them on illegal flights in his Stinson Voyager, and taught them "mouth-to-mouth resuscitation."[10] Ferrie gave people the impression that he was a

Colonel and that he was studying medicine at Tulane University. He also led overnight encampments with his cadets at Keesler Air Force Base in nearby Biloxi, Mississippi. In addition Ferrie told his cadets that he was going to control their outside activities completely.[11] This is borne out in some of the CAP veterans' recollections. Both Ted Abernathy and Robert E. Morrell recalled that Ferrie convinced at least four cadets to join the Marines.[12] Morrell also remembered an incident where one of the cadets injured his finger and "Dave hypnotized the boy into a state of painlessness."[13] Others would recall that Ferrie seemed to "hold the cadets in the palm of his hand" and that he "had a group of young boys whom he supports and controls completely."[14]

Enter Lee Harvey Oswald

In 1955 a 16-year-old fatherless boy from New Orleans joined the local CAP squadron. Lee Harvey Oswald was remembered by several of his fellow cadets. Frederick O'Sullivan, George Boesch, John Irion, Jerry Paradis, Collin Hamer, Anthony Atzenhoffer and Edward Voebel all recalled Oswald as a member of Captain Ferrie's squadron.[15] Paradis in particular was emphatic in his recollection. When congressional investigators interviewed him in 1978 Paradis, by then a corporate attorney stated, "Oswald and Ferrie were in the unit together. I know they were because I was there. I specifically remember Oswald. I can remember him clearly, and Ferrie was heading the unit then. I'm not saying that they may have been there together, I'm saying it is a certainty."[16] Likewise Anthony Atzenhoffer recalled the pair stating, "Ferrie was always around the unit during those days. I can't say I know anything about Ferrie and Oswald being together anywhere else, except at the meetings."[17] Atzenhoffer added that Ferrie was trying to recruit CAP cadets for "experiments" that were supposedly being conducted by the Medical School of Tulane University.[18] Although not a CAP cadet, Thomas Clark was one of Ferrie's young acolytes. He revealed to Garrison's office that Ferrie had once confided to him that he had "taught Oswald."[19]

Defenders of the Warren Commission's lone gunman thesis have attempted to discredit the cadet's recollections over the years. Chief among them is *Case Closed* author, Gerald Posner. Posner claims that he discovered CAP records that show that Ferrie was dismissed from the CAP in 1954 and was not reinstated until 1958.[20] He repeated this claim on the PBS show *Frontline*. Immediately following this statement *Frontline* cut to a photograph, recently discovered by former CAP member John B. Ciravolo, Jr., of several cadets and leaders at a CAP barbecue. Clearly depicted together in the photo is none other than David Ferrie and Lee Harvey Oswald.[21] In a matter of seconds, the schizophrenic *Frontline* program managed to impeach the credibility of its star witness Gerald Posner. Had Posner dug a little deeper he could have saved himself some embarrassment. An FAA report on Ferrie from December of 1963 contains the statements of several CAP leaders and cadets all of whom recalled that Ferrie had started his own *non-chartered* CAP squadron at Moisant Airport.[22] Also Ferrie's successor at CAP, Mrs. Gladys Durr, recalled that she did not take over the Moisant CAP squad from Ferrie until *late* 1955.[23] Oswald had served in the CAP during the summer of 1955. Of course, with the appearance of the Ferrie/Oswald photo, this is all a moot point.

During Oswald's tenure in the CAP his mother Marguerite recalled being visited by a man in uniform who she presumed was a Marine Corps recruiter. Her visitor encouraged her to allow her son Lee to quit school and join the Marines.[24] As this was a clear violation of the law (Oswald was only 16 at the time) it is doubtful Mrs. Oswald's visitor was a legitimate Marine recruiter. Could it have been Ferrie? Considering the statements that Ferrie often posed as a military officer, his domineering and controlling behavior towards his cadets, and his encouragement of others to join the Marines, Ferrie's appearance at the Oswald home cannot be ruled out.

It is also interesting to note that Oswald's mother and

brother have stated that Lee's favorite television show of the time was "I Led Three Lives."[25] The show was based on the true story of Herbert Philbrick, an FBI agent who had infiltrated the Communist Party for nine years. As we will see later, Oswald's life strangely parallels that of his early TV role model.

In the mid to late 1950's Ferrie was constantly in trouble with his employer, Eastern Airlines. In 1954 Ferrie was suspended for three days without pay for illegally transporting a "pass-rider" from New Orleans to Houston. In August of 1959 Eastern records show that Ferrie was under investigation by U.S. Customs for possible gun running activities. Later that same year Ferrie was involved in a "near miss" incident with another aircraft.[26]

During this time Ferrie's physical appearance grew increasingly bizarre. As the result of an affliction known as *alopecia totalis*, Ferrie lost all of his body hair. He compensated for his hair loss by creating a makeshift toupee out of reddish-brown monkey fur and drawing on his eyebrows with greasepaint.[27] Ferrie also began developing such eclectic interests as psychology, hypnotism, and medical research.[28]

Also during this time Ferrie's anticommunist fervor began to manifest itself. He once offered his services to the Air Force writing, "There is nothing that I would enjoy better than blowing the hell out of every damn Russian, Communist, Red or what-have-you. We can cook up a crew that will really bomb them to hell...I want to train killers, however bad that sounds. It is what we need."[29] This ardor reached a fever pitch after Fidel Castro took power in Cuba and revealed his communist sympathies. Reportedly as one of his many assignments into Cuba, Ferrie fire-bombed the Cuban sugar cane crop from his airplane while in the employ of a former Cuban Congressman named Eladio "Yito" del Valle.[30] A former CAP cadet and close Ferrie associate, Al Landry, revealed to Garrison's office that sometime in 1959 Ferrie disappeared for about seven to nine weeks before he finally showed up at a CAP meeting. Ferrie told Landry that he and several other Cubans had been to Cuba in an effort to help Cubans escape from Castro's prison. Ferrie explained that during one of these raids he was attacked by a Cuban soldier and was stabbed in the stomach. To prove his point Ferrie lifted his shirt and revealed a large scar across his stomach. Ferrie then further elaborated on his Cuban mission. He told Landry that he was working specifically for the CIA and that he was called to Miami and stayed there for approximately one week in a hotel before he made contact with a CIA officer. Ferrie said that shortly thereafter he and about nine Cubans flew down to a point close to Cuba and then got out on rubber rafts, went ashore in Cuba and rescued some prisoners. He said it was during this incident that he was stabbed.[31] It is important to note that Carl McNabb, a former CIA pilot, confirmed to the author that he met Ferrie while both were flying missions for the CIA.[32] Another of Ferrie's CAP cadets, Robert Boylston, revealed that in 1961 Ferrie talked a great deal about "a group who knew what was going on in this country and was going to take care of it."[33] Boylston strongly felt that Ferrie and some of his associates were "not playing when they talked about "taking care of something.""[34]

With this communist "menace" 90 miles from American shores Ferrie had obviously found kindred spirits among the CIA and the New Orleans anti-Castro Cuban community.

Ferrie and Arcacha

Ferrie's closest associate in this crusade was Cuban exile Sergio Arcacha Smith. Arcacha, who served as Cuban Consul in several embassies during the Batista regime, fled Cuba and settled in New Orleans in 1960. His family followed later, arriving in New Orleans in grand style. According to Jack Martin arrangements were made with the Office of Naval Intelligence to reunite Arcacha with his family. Martin stated he was present with Arcacha at the Alvin Callender Naval Air Base in Belle Chasse, Louisiana when the planes carrying Arcacha's family and personal belongings landed.[35]

8

Once he was settled in the Crescent City Arcacha assumed the role of New Orleans delegate to the Frente Revolucionario Democratico (Cuban Democratic Liberation Front or FRD). A CIA memorandum describes the organization thusly:

> The FRD was *created by the Central Intelligence Agency* in May of 1960 and consisted of several anti-Castro groups. The FRD was formed as a political action, propaganda and military unit. It not only helped recruit for Brigade 2506 but also carried on a massive program of social assistance for Brigade 2506 members and their families. The FRD headquarters was in Miami but delegates were assigned to New Orleans, Tampa and Mexico City. In late 1960 or early 1961 the Cuban Revolutionary Council (CRC) was formed to coordinate and direct FRD activities with Agency and White House support. The FRD continued to function until October 1961 when it was completely absorbed by the CRC.[36] [My emphasis]

Ferrie's importance to Arcacha's anti-Castro operations is underscored in a letter sent by Arcacha to Eddie Rickenbacker then Chairman of the Board of Eastern Airlines. Written shortly after the Bay of Pigs debacle, Arcacha is requesting a leave of absence for Ferrie. Arcacha writes:

> When the FRD was originally organized, under the demands of the U.S. government, the FRD was to "front" for the efforts of the CIA to reinstate democratic government in Cuba. The effort of April 17 failed, as you knew.
> Thereafter, the morale of the Cubans in exile and the underground in Cuba fell to zero.
> Then along came Captain Ferrie. He strongly prodded our whole organization until it was revitalized. Thereafter, dissident elements were removed. Fund collecting began. The underground was reorganized and the re-harassment of Castro has begun...
> The reinvigorating of our program was the result of the prodding of Captain Ferrie, and his associates, here in New Orleans.
> Through him we have been able to get the best advice in affairs political, economic and military. Further, he has helped us straighten other affairs.

As a result, our organization is running smoother every day and our operations have begun. In addition, Captain Ferrie has been assisting in the handling of the refugees. Since events are approaching a climax, we sorely need his advice on a day to day basis. Knowing your own often demonstrated patriotism, we are requesting that Captain Ferrie be given either a 60 or 90 day leave with pay so that the work at hand can be completed. At this time he holds in his hands so many threads which pertain to the security of the Caribbean area that no substitution could be made.[37]

Ferrie was never granted his leave, but his work was far from over. Ferrie and Arcacha would now join forces with New Orleans' foremost anticommunist, the virulently right wing, Guy Banister.

Chapter Two

~

A Most Frighteningly Violent Person

Reportedly born in a log cabin in Caldwell Parish on March 7, 1901, William Guy Banister began his law enforcement career in 1929 as an investigator with the Monroe Louisiana Police Department. On November 5, 1934 Banister was sworn in as a Special Agent for the Federal Bureau of Investigation (At that time known as the Division of Investigation of the Department of Justice). Banister's star rose quickly as he was promoted in May of 1938 to Assistant Special Agent in Charge of the Butte, Montana office. After stints as the SAC of the Oklahoma City and Minneapolis offices, he was transferred to the prestigious Chicago office in 1953.[1]

Banister's rapid ascendancy within the Bureau may have been as a result of his skills as a covert operator. According to an informant for George Eckert, one of Garrison's investigators, "Banister was considered one of the FBI's greatest room search and electronics men... Banister gained intra-bureau fame and J. Edgar Hoover's undying gratitude for a World War II operation which he commanded in Mexico City - a "bag job" on the safe of the German embassy, from which Banister is said to have obtained the code book of the German diplomatic service."[2]

Still, Banister proved to be something of a loose cannon. As a result of Banister openly defying Hoover's prime directive never to embarrass the Bureau (Banister is quoted at the time as saying, "The Bureau and the field have been living in adultery for years.")[3] he retired from the FBI in 1955. Banister relocated to New Orleans at the invitation of then mayor deLesseps "Shep" Morrison. Morrison, reeling from allegations of police corruption, brought Banister on as head of Internal Affairs of the New Orleans Police Department. Five months later Banister was promoted to the number three post in the department - Deputy Superintendent of Police. Banister joined forces with Aaron Kohn who, like Banister, was an ex-FBI man from Chicago. Kohn later headed up a citizen's watchdog group called the Metropolitan Crime Commission and together they launched a probe into the police scandals, but communism, not corruption, was Banister's obsession.[4]

The following year Banister was appointed by Morrison to conduct a study of communist subversion in New Orleans in conjunction with McCarthyite Senator James Eastland's Senate Internal Security Sub-Committee. The fact that the Big Easy wasn't exactly a hotbed of communist activity didn't deter Banister who obviously retained his old boss's anticommunist fervor. After meeting with Eastland at his Mississippi home, Banister returned to New Orleans and explained to waiting reporters that "New Orleans is a logical place for communist infiltration because of its importance as a port and its location in relationship to Russia. New Orleans is a lot closer to Siberia than Chicago. All they would have to do is drop an atom bomb in the river and you couldn't live in

New Orleans for 10 years."[5]

Banister cut quite a figure through the city that care forgot. A swaggering bigot given to drink, he was always nattily dressed and frequently sported a rosebud in his lapel. He also toted a gold monogrammed, pearl-handled .357 magnum. Banister was said to have a quick temper and would often fly into fits of rage.[6] One such incident resulted in his being sacked from the police department.

In March of 1957 Banister was drinking at a French Quarter bistro called the Old Absinthe House. When he got up to use the public telephone Banister shoved two men out of the way and yelled to the bartender to "get over here." When the bartender failed to respond, Banister reached across the bar, grabbed the bartender by the jacket and pointing his .357 magnum in the bartender's face boasted, "I have already killed two men and another wouldn't make any difference." One of the patrons alerted the police and a local patrolman disarmed Banister who was later escorted to police headquarters by Sgt. Hubie Badeaux and Captain Presley Trosclair. Banister, who denied the bartender's version of the incident was nevertheless suspended three days later. This scandal effectively ended Banister's police career and in less than a year Banister would start his own private investigative firm.[7]

Guy Banister Associates, Inc.

On January 21, 1958 the articles of incorporation for Guy Banister Associates, Inc. were filed in Orleans Parish by attorney William Wegmann.[8] Banister first hung his shingle out of a small office on Robert E. Lee Boulevard but shortly thereafter moved into the Balter Building.[9] Listed as treasurer of the firm was Joseph Oster one of Banister's investigators from the New Orleans Police days. Oster recalled that his tenure with the Banister firm was a short one. He would do the bulk of the investigative work and became dissatisfied when Banister would not take an interest in landing some of the more potentially lucrative investigations.[10]

Oster was not alone in taking note of this cavalier attitude on the part of Banister. An informant of Garrison's investigator, George Eckert, recalled that "[Banister's] friends say they never believed he had actually separated himself from government service. They say he accepted private investigation "cases" for fees considerably under the going market price for similar services by other agencies, and that he maintained mysterious "connections with sources which provided him technical assistance."[11]

One of the key things Oster remembered was that Banister used to call Washington and speak directly to J. Edgar Hoover.[12] Oster also recalled the steady stream of investigators, operatives, and hangers-on that paraded through Banister's office. Early on Banister seemed to employ legitimate investigators - ex-FBI men who, like Oster, would handle the majority of the case work - while Banister would preoccupy himself by clipping newspapers and building his collection of anticommunist intelligence.[13] Later, as we shall see, Banister became less discerning in his choice of employees.

Oster soon left and was replaced by Vernon Gerdes whose brief stay with Banister was memorable to him because he had seen American Nazi Party President, George Lincoln Rockwell, in Banister's office.[14] Gerdes left Banister's employ around the same time Banister relocated his offices to the weather-beaten Newman Building at 531 Lafayette Street. Curiously, Arcacha's anti-Castro organizations moved with Banister from the Balter Building to 531 Lafayette at the same time.

Replacing Gerdes in Banister's operation was another ex-FBI man, Ivan "Bill" Nitschke. He recalled a steady parade of Cuban guerrillas passing through Banister's offices, many clad in green army fatigues. Nitschke would have conversations with Banister and the Cuban exiles on how to obtain firearms and the manufacture of rifle silencers. Nitschke specifically remembered having recommended Klein's of Chicago as a source for weapons.[15] Ironically Klein's is the same firm from which Oswald's alleged assassination weapon, a Manlicher-Carcano rifle, was purchased under the name of A. Hidell.

Around this time the CIA was keenly aware of Banister and his operation. CIA memoranda notes that "Banister was of interest to OO/C [Note: OO is a designation for the CIA's Domestic Contacts Service] in 1960 [remainder of line redacted] and that interest in the use of Guy Banister Associates, Inc. as a cover mechanism in August 1960 was dropped upon receipt of an unfavorable report from the Field."[16] Although Domestic Contacts may have dropped Banister, when one considers that the CIA was actively using the Mafia in their assassination plots against Fidel Castro it seems unlikely that this branch of the Agency that was running these anti-Castro operations would consider Banister too unsavory. It may also be significant that the CIA's Office of Security designated numbers for both Banister (EE-28810) and Guy Banister Associates (222918).[17] Also an FBI memo states that on March 30, 1961 the CIA's Deputy Director of Plans sent J. Edgar Hoover a letter informing him that Banister had opened a detective agency at 531 Lafayette Street.[18] Further, a former Banister investigator and close associate, Joe Newbrough revealed to the author that he believed Banister worked for the CIA. "Guy was a conduit of "Company" money...he passed out money for the training camps."[19]

With the election of JFK, the level of Cuban operations within the Banister apparatus heated up and boiled to the surface with an incident that to this day still confounds and intrigues researchers.

The Bolton Ford Incident

On the same day that John F. Kennedy took the oath of office as the 35th President of the United States two men entered the Bolton Ford Truck Center on North Claiborne Avenue in New Orleans and approached assistant manager Oscar Deslatte. They identified themselves as representatives of an anti-Castro fundraising group called the Friends of Democratic Cuba.[20] The older of the pair described by Deslatte as "olive-complexioned with an athletic build and a scar over his left eye" spoke with a Cuban accent. He told Deslatte that the Friends wished to procure ten Ford Econoline vans presumably for support in the upcoming Bay of Pigs invasion. Deslatte conferred with his manager, Fred Sewell, and prepared a bid form at a price of fifty dollars over cost for each truck. The Cuban gave his name as Joseph Moore, which Deslatte noted on the bid. However, Moore requested that his companion's name actually appear on the form. Above Joseph Moore's name Deslatte wrote the name "Oswald."[21]

The second man spoke up and said that he was in fact Oswald and confirmed that his name should be on the bid as he was "the man with the money" and would pay for the trucks if purchased. Sewell spoke with both men and would recall the incident in detail six years later when Garrison launched his probe into the Kennedy assassination. "Oswald," Sewell said, was a thin young man about five feet seven inches and weighed approximately 140-145 pounds. Although only the surname "Oswald" appears on the bid Sewell recalled that the young man also used the first name of "Lee." Which, of course, is curious because at the time of this incident the real Lee Oswald was spending his last months in a radio factory in Minsk having defected to Russia in September of 1959.

Three years later, as the accused assassin's picture was plastered over every TV screen in America, Deslatte was disturbed by the resemblance in both name and appearance to the young man who had earlier paid him a visit. On November 25th he called his boss at Bolton Ford, William Watson, who, in turn, notified the New Orleans office of the FBI. The Bureau wasted little time in dispatching Special Agents William F. McDonald and W.J. Danielson, Jr. Deslatte offered the original bid form to the agents, which they picked up with solenoid tongs and placed in between two sheets of plastic. Danielson and McDonald dutifully prepared a brief one-page report on the incident, which was promptly buried along with the bid form among the Warren Commission documents.[22]

The Friends of Democratic Cuba

But what of this organization, the Friends of Democratic Cuba? Ostensibly, it was a group of New Orleans civic personalities incorporated for the purpose of collecting funds to aid the anti-Castro cause. The funds were to be channeled through the FRD whose New Orleans delegate, Sergio Arcacha Smith, would receive the collections less a twenty-percent discount to be retained by the Friends of Democratic Cuba. However, no public collection of money ever took place. The Friends of Democratic Cuba was strictly a dummy front.

In fact a Garrison informant revealed that the group was "an undercover operation in conjunction with the CIA and FBI which involved the shipment and transportation of individuals and supplies in and out of Cuba."[23] As for the altruistic citizens who made up the board of the FDC, the list is a mixed bag indeed.

Martin McAuliffe, owner of a publicity agency that handled propaganda for Arcacha's exile groups, was listed as president. McAuliffe would later state that an FDC member asked him if the Friends could use his name on their letterhead. "Next thing I knew I was down as president of the organization," he recalled.[24]

Alfred Chittenden, chief of the New Orleans Stevedores Union, was included, presumably, because of his ability to obtain salary donations from his fellow union members.

The vice-president of the organization was Gerard F. Tujague, owner of Tujague Inc. Forwarding Company, an import/export firm.[25] In the months between November 1955 and January 1956 Tujague employed a 16-year-old messenger by the name of Lee Harvey Oswald. (Could Tujague have been the source of the Oswald name to the FDC?).

Grady Durham, one of many in the Banister menagerie of investigators, was also listed as an incorporator. Durham an attorney who was first cousin to former Louisiana Governor Jimmy Davis was reportedly a frequent chess partner of the CIA liaison to the FDC.[26]

Another incorporator was William Dalzell. Dalzell was a private investigator closely associated with Guy Banister Associates. A Navy veteran, Dalzell also worked as a cryptographer for the Department of Defense. He later shows up in Ethiopia and Yemen as a petroleum advisor with the Agency for International Development, whose links to the CIA have been amply documented.[27] According to HSCA files Dalzell also operated out of the American Embassy in Rome for a time and spoke about a half dozen languages, including Swahili.[28] An FBI memorandum characterizes Dalzell as "a friend of Clay Shaw."[29] (Shaw's own activities in Rome will be discussed in a later chapter). In the early 1960's Dalzell helped form an anti-Castro group called the Free Voice of Latin America and spent his time attempting to obtain weapons for Honduran revolutionaries as well as a PT boat and submarine for Arcacha and the Cuban exiles.[30] Dalzell also admitted that the Friends of Democratic Cuba was set up at the implicit direction of the CIA.[31] A CIA memorandum, released in 1983, indicates that Dalzell had at least three separate contacts with the New Orleans CIA office. Coincidentally, one of these contacts was on January 20, 1961, the date of the Bolton Ford incident.[32]

And finally, listed on the board of directors was the principal founder and guiding light of the organization, Guy Banister.

An informant who had briefly joined the Friends of Democratic Cuba in 1961 later reported to Garrison that at least three separate Cuban invasion plans were discussed in his presence.[33] (The aforementioned Bolton Ford incident was undoubtedly an adjunct to one of these operations). Author Bill Turner writes in *Deadly Secrets* that one of Banister's plans called for the introduction of poison gas into the air conditioning ducts of the Cuban Presidential Palace in Havana.[34] Banister discussed this operation with Colonel Orlando Piedra. A man with a fearsome reputation, Piedra was ex-chief of former Cuban President Batista's secret police and a frequent visitor to Banister's office.[35] Indeed, Banister stated he expected to be rewarded a high office in Cuba after the successful overthrow of Castro.[36] After the failure of any of these plans to materialize Banister suggested organizing a group of mercenary anticommunist "banditos" to be named "Banister's Bastards" that would bring the fight to Central and South American Communist guerrillas in return for money from the governments involved.[37]

Further evidence of Banister's preoccupation with Latin politics is his membership in the Anti-Communist League of the Caribbean. Part of the global family of "professional" anticommunist organizations, this offshoot was funded by Latin American dictators Rafael Trujillo and Anastosio Somoza as well as the aforementioned Colonel Piedra.[38] Banister associate Maurice B. Gatlin, Sr. served as its general counsel. Gatlin once bragged to former Minuteman, Jerry Milton Brooks, "I have pretty good connections. Stick with me - I'll give you a license to kill."[39] Turner claims that Gatlin, in his role as a reported CIA courier, supposedly delivered $100,000 to the radical French OAS generals in 1961 to fund an assassination attempt on French President Charles deGaulle.[40] Brooks added that Gatlin was in Cuba at the same time as Jack Ruby in 1959 and that he knew Colonel Robert Castorr. Colonel Castorr was closely associated with the Cuban exile community in Dallas and is believed to have been involved with Ruby in running guns to the exiles.[41] As with Banister the CIA records reveal an interest in Gatlin as well. On January 13, 1954, Gatlin was approved for "Limited Contact" with the CIA.[42] The record shows that in 1953 Gatlin attempted to procure military supplies for use in a possible anticommunist revolution in Guatemala.[43] As history shows, the following year a CIA sponsored coup overthrew the Arbenz regime in Guatemala. Also, like Banister, Gatlin was "dropped" as a Domestic Contact source in 1954 due to the receipt of adverse information.[44] But as I posited with Banister it is quite likely that other factions of the CIA utilized Gatlin. In fact the record seems to prove this to be the case.

Gatlin was a leading figure in the Inter-American Confederation for the Defense of the Continent, a CIA supported front, organized with the assistance of E. Howard Hunt which played a major role in overthrowing Arbenz.[45] After the coup Gatlin remained well connected. In 1957 while in Washington, D.C. Gatlin was put up in the exclusive Willard Hotel at the expense of the Fairchild Airplane Corporation.[46] Unfortunately Garrison would not have the opportunity to question Gatlin about his illustrious career. In 1964, the unfortunate Mr. Gatlin either fell or was pushed from the sixth floor of a hotel in San Juan, Puerto Rico, apparently suffering a heart attack on the way down.

Gordon Novel, a one-time Banister operative who we will examine more closely in the next chapter, accurately described the Banister organization as a deep cover operation. According to Novel, "Something was going on, obviously they were trying to put a cover on it. The idea behind it was cover, cover, cover because if you look at the thing...you are going to have a real difficult time of alleging anything."[47]

Banister's association with Arcacha and the Cuban exiles naturally brought David Ferrie into his orbit. Ferrie and Banister would maintain a close professional and personal relationship over the next few years. With the Bay of Pigs invasion rapidly approaching, the CIA and the Banister/Ferrie/Arcacha nexus would ratchet up the level of preparation.

Chapter Three

~

Cold War in the Big Easy

Sometime in late 1960 a new face was added to the Banister crowd. Gordon Novel, a local electronics specialist, was recommended to Banister and Arcacha by one of Banister's close associates Ed Butler.[1] (Butler, a former member of the Free Voice of Latin America, was about to launch his own anticommunist propaganda mill called the Information Council of the Americas or INCA. As we will see later, Butler was a CIA informant and asset). Novel first met with Arcacha in a local coffee shop where Arcacha apparently sounded out Novel regarding his views on Castro and communism. Satisfied he had found a like-minded individual Arcacha invited Novel to attend a meeting about four days later in Banister's office. Later in a sworn deposition Novel recalled the meeting, the implications of which are chilling:

Q: Did you go alone to that meeting?
A (Novel): As I recall I did, yes.
Q: Who was there?
A: Mr. Banister, Mr. Arcacha Smith and Mr. Phillips.
Q: Do you know his first name?
A: No.
Q: Had you ever seen him before?
A: No.
Q: Was he a Latin?
A: No.
Q: What was his interest in the meeting?
A: He seemed to be running the show.
Q: Telling Banister and Arcacha Smith what to do?
A: His presence was commanding. It wasn't in an orderly military situation, you know. It was just they seemed to introduce Mr. Phillips.
Q: How old a man was he?
A: I would say he was around 51, 52.
Q: American?
A: American.
Q: Was he identified as to his background?
A: No.
Q: Were any hints dropped as to his background?
A: Just that he was from Washington, that's all.
Q: Did you assume from that he was with the CIA?
A: I didn't assume anything. I never assume anything.
Q: Did you speculate about it?
A: If I did, I didn't say it at the time.
Q: Well, I am not asking you whether you said it at the time. I am asking you did it give you cause for speculation?
A: He seemed to have a very commanding presence at the meeting and that - I just took it that he was - whoever he was, he was the commanding presence.
Q: What was said at the meeting?

A: They wanted to organize a telethon, period. That they would give me a complete breakdown on how they wanted the thing presented.

Q: By they, do you mean Banister and Smith or Banister and Phillips?

A: Banister and Phillips.

Q: Was there any political discussion of any kind?

A: Nothing other than the idea was to raise money and to show what Castro's Cuba was like at the time, especially the Isle of Pines.

Q: Did anyone of them tell you that you were not to discuss this with anyone else when you left there?

A: I think somebody mentioned something about this conversation isn't taking place.

Q: Was there any discussion of United States government involvement?

A: That was taken for granted. It was not discussed.

Q: You have no notes of this meeting?

A: I don't think that would have been quite proper under the circumstances at the time. The only person that had notes was Mr. Phillips.

Q: Was he making notes?

A: He seemed to be reading from a typewritten sheet covering topics.

Q: Did you ever see Mr. Phillips again?

A: Once or twice, yes.[2]

Later Novel is asked:

Q: After the first meeting you had in Guy Banister's office, you testified that you did see Phillips again once or twice. Where and when did you see Mr. Phillips?

A: He kept coming out of the federal building right across the street from the Balter Building.[3]

The only Mr. Phillips familiar to this milieu is the late CIA officer David Atlee Phillips. Phillips, a propaganda specialist, was a key player in the 1954 overthrow of the Jacobo Arbenz government in Guatemala. It was during this coup that Phillips became close to CIA spook and future Watergate figure E. Howard Hunt.[4] Gaeton Fonzi, an investigator for the House Select Committee on Assassinations would write that "Phillips would later work very closely with Hunt during the planning of the Bay of Pigs invasion and in other, less visible, operations."[5] Hunt was instrumental in organizing the Cuban Revolutionary Council whose New Orleans office was co-located with Guy Banister's.[6] As we have seen Sergio Arcacha Smith was the New Orleans delegate to the CRC. After Hunt's notoriety from the Watergate scandal, Banister operative Jack Martin recalled seeing Hunt at 544 Camp Street.[7] As for Phillips, during the time of the Banister meeting Phillips was indeed headquartered in Washington as propaganda chief of the Bay of Pigs operations.[8] But as Fonzi notes Phillips had a certain freedom and flexibility of movement that most desk-bound Washington officers did not have. Phillips would frequently make trips into the field to check on the activities of the various anti-Castro organizations.[9] It was the conclusion of Fonzi and many other HSCA staff members that Phillips used the cover name of Maurice Bishop. It was a Maurice Bishop who was the case officer of Cuban exile and Alpha 66 leader Antonio Veciana.[10] Veciana gave testimony to the HSCA that Bishop met with Lee Harvey Oswald in Dallas just months before the assassination.[11] Novel offered another clue as to the background of his Mr. Phillips. Novel stated in his deposition that Phillips said he was with the Double-Chek Corporation.[12] In the book *The Invisible Government* authors David Wise and Thomas Ross reveal that the Miami based Double-Chek was one of the CIA's many corporate fronts. Among other things Double-Chek hired American pilots who flew at the Bay of Pigs.[13] Overseeing the organization of an anti-Castro telethon would certainly fall within Phillips' area of specialty. The plans for the telethon eventually fell through but this group's next operation was brought off successfully.

The Houma Raid

Shortly after the Phillips meeting Novel received a call from Banister notifying him that he would soon receive a key in the mail and that a follow-up meeting would be scheduled.[14] A few days later Novel received a key and one-half of a five hundred bill. He then met in a restaurant with Banister, Arcacha, Ferrie, an ex-Marine, Jerome Blackmon and two unidentified Cubans. At the meeting Arcacha asked Novel if he could procure a fleet of trucks for an upcoming operation. (Shades of Bolton Ford!) Before Novel could produce any trucks Arcacha notified Novel that he had found a truck and to meet him at Ferrie's house. On a following night in late February of 1961, Novel arrived at Ferrie's home clad, as requested, entirely in black. Once inside Ferrie's place Novel glimpsed a scene others would also recall - a large map of Cuba occupying one wall, a homemade two-man sub, and, for use in his cancer research, several cages filled with white mice. Joining Novel at Ferrie's were Arcacha, Blackmon and Layton Martens, a mutual young friend of Clay Shaw and David Ferrie. Novel brought a friend of his, Rancier Ehlinger, as well as a date(!), the future Mrs. Novel, Marlene Mancuso.

With Ferrie, Martens and Blackmon leading in the truck, Novel and the others followed in Novel's '56 Lincoln. The convoy crossed the Mississippi River into Houma, Louisiana eventually arriving at an abandoned Navy blimp base then owned by the CIA connected Schlumberger Well Services Company.[15] Located on the site was a padlocked bunker that Novel's key unlocked. Once inside the bunker the team unloaded crate after crate of hand grenades, small arms ammunition and bazooka shells, all marked *InterArmco, Alexandria, Virginia.* (InterArmco was another of the CIA's dummy fronts. Set up through former CIA employee, Samuel Cummings, InterArmco was given $100,000 in start-up capital directly from the CIA in the 1950's. The money went towards procuring rifles, submachine guns and 50-mm. mortars for use in the CIA sponsored coup in Guatemala. The surplus apparently ended up in the Houma bunker).[16] Once the truck was loaded, the war materiel was temporarily dropped off at Ferrie's house and Banister's office. Sometime later Novel spoke with Arcacha, who told Novel the weapons were "half way down the Mississippi on a boat." Indeed the cache found its way into the hold of the *Santa Ana*, an old banana boat flying a Costa Rican flag.[17] A week before the Bay of Pigs invasion the *Santa Ana* shoved off from the Algiers naval base on the Mississippi River near New Orleans. On board were 168 Cuban exile troops on their way to Baracoa, a town located near the Guantanomo U.S. Naval Base. The *Santa Ana* had in fact been leased by the CIA for $7,000 a month.[18] Also on board were a CIA adviser named Curly Sanchez and Nino Diaz who was associated with the exile group, MRR, that had trained in a camp north of Lake Pontchartrain. Although their mission was to launch a diversionary strike in Baracoa to steer Cuban troops away from the Bay of Pigs, Diaz's men were in fact outfitted with the uniforms of Castro's army. Their real mission was a dangerous attack on U.S. forces at Guantanomo which would force the hand of President Kennedy into launching a full-scale military invasion of Cuba. The night before the Bay of Pigs invasion a landing by the *Santa Ana* had been aborted. On the night of the invasion the ship made another attempt at a landing. Author Bill Turner describes what happened next:

> The scouting party returned to the ship with reports of jeeps on the roadways, undoubtedly the soldiers Castro had rushed to the area after hearing of ship sightings on Friday night. Diaz radioed Base Tide that it would be suicidal to land. He was ordered to proceed. He refused. The orders were changed for the *Santa Ana* to head for the Bay of Pigs and wait offshore for landing instructions.
> The CIA had lost its planned excuse to send in the Marines, who were aboard ship nearby.[19]

The Bay of Pigs invasion failed and the rest, as they say, is history. As for Novel, he received the other half of the five hundred bill and a letter from the chairman of the CIA funded Cuban Revolutionary Council, Jose Miro Cardona, thanking him on behalf of the CRC.[20]

War Games

After the Bay of Pigs there was a brief decline in the kinetic activity swirling around the Banister apparatus. Amid allegations of skimming off the donations he received, Arcacha stepped down as the New Orleans CRC delegate.[21] His adjunct group, the Crusade to Free Cuba, closed up shop and Arcacha moved to Miami and then to Texas, settling first in Houston and later in Dallas.[22]

Ferrie was once again in trouble with his employer, Eastern Airlines. In the summer of 1961, Ferrie was arrested for a crime against nature on a 15-year old boy and indecent behavior with three others. Shortly thereafter Eastern removed Ferrie from the payroll indefinitely. Ferrie filed a grievance through the Airline Pilots Association and the FAA opened their own investigation. Banister not only assisted Ferrie with his grievance but also testified as a character witness at Ferrie's hearing. Some of Banister's testimony is illuminating especially when describing one of his specialties: "I have had high-ranking Cuban refugees in my office asking me how to go underground, and I gave them diagrams for that. I have talked to military and leaders from the various provinces of Cuba that have slipped out and slipped back."[23] Although during this time Ferrie was out of work, he still managed to make payments on his car and meet living expenses.[24] To friends, Ferrie would also obsess on the failed Bay of Pigs invasion revealing apparent inside information on the operation. As Ferrie would hold forth in his apartment he would illustrate on a blackboard the actual plans for the invasion of Cuba, explaining what the Cubans were supposed to do and at what point the CIA was supposed to send in air support.[25] In addition Ferrie associate Al Landry recalled visiting Arcacha Smith's house with Ferrie and watching films of the Bay of Pigs invasion.[26] Ferrie's own godson, Morris Brownlee, recalled that Ferrie encouraged him to join the CIA; an organization, Brownlee remarked, Ferrie had a long association with.[27] Once, while applying for a loan, Ferrie let it slip that he was working for a CIA operation. The loan officer thought that Ferrie had mentioned "Operation Mosquito," a mistaken recollection, but no doubt an obvious reference to the CIA's Operation MONGOOSE.[28]

In October of 1962, President Kennedy faced the greatest challenge of his presidency: the Cuban missile crisis. Kennedy struck a deal with Russian Premier Nikita Kruschev to remove the Soviet missiles from Cuba and gave a "no invasion" pledge. The Kennedy sanctioned Cuban destabilization project, Operation MONGOOSE, was abruptly canceled. Although Kennedy averted a crisis of a massive scale, the perception among many Cuban exiles and their CIA handlers was that JFK had caved in and was soft on communism. Coupled with the failure at the Bay of Pigs anti-Kennedy sentiment ran high. Kennedy had already added to the CIA's pique by issuing National Security Action Memorandum #55 in June of 1961. NSAM #55 directed the Joint Chiefs of Staff to be responsible for Cold War operations thereby removing the CIA from this responsibility.[29] Covert operations were the lifeblood of the CIA cowboys and Kennedy had cut them off. Kennedy made no secret about his anger with the CIA. He vowed to splinter the Agency into a thousand pieces and indeed fired its longtime Director, Allen Dulles as well as his deputies, Richard Bissell and Charles Cabell. Although Kennedy had decapitated the CIA leadership, recalcitrant factions in the CIA - especially in New Orleans and Miami - continued to operate independently. In October of 1963, the *New York Times* carried an article by Arthur Krock that noted the CIA had refused to carry out certain Kennedy administration policies in Vietnam. The article further quoted "a high level administration official" as saying that the CIA was a malignancy on the White House and if the U.S. ever experienced a coup attempt, "it will come from the CIA and not the Pentagon...The Agency represents a tremendous power and total unaccountability to anyone."[30] A month later, the President was dead.

In New Orleans Ferrie, in a speech before the New Orleans chapter of the Military Order of World Wars, was asked to step down from the podium after his anti-Kennedy rhetoric became offensive.[31] Banister was asked about this incident during Ferrie's Eastern Airlines grievance hearing. Note how he tries to obfuscate Ferrie's criticism of Kennedy.

Q: As I recall your testimony, you spoke of Mr. Soule telling you that Captain Ferrie was criticizing President Eisenhower, is that correct?
A: Yes, there was criticism of President Eisenhower's administration. I do not know if there was any criticism of President Eisenhower.
Q: Sir, this bears the date of July 1961. Are you acquainted with that fact?
A: Well, this was the date of the meeting, July, 1961.
Q: The Commander in Chief on that date was whom?
A: It was President Kennedy, wasn't it?[32]

To others, Ferrie would confide that JFK "ought to be shot."[33] Banister also shared Ferrie's enmity towards JFK. In 1963, Banister remarked to an associate that "someone should do away with Kennedy."[34]

Soon previously dormant training camps were once again activated as covert funds began to pour in. As we saw earlier longtime Banister associate, Joe Newbrough revealed in an interview with the author that Banister was a conduit of CIA funds to the Cuban training camps.[35] One of the camps was located across Lake Pontchartrain on land owned by Bill McLaney, a mob-related gambler who, along with his brother Mike (an acquaintance of Jack Ruby), had once operated casinos in Cuba. On President Kennedy's orders, the FBI raided a house near this camp on July 31, 1963. Several people were arrested, a cache of munitions and explosives was confiscated and the nearby camp was shut down. Needless to say this did not further endear Kennedy to the anti-Castro movement. Ferrie was a frequent presence at this camp often drilling the Cubans and mercenaries in guerrilla warfare.[36]

It is possible that a film once existed of this training camp. The former Deputy Chief Counsel of the House Select Committee on Assassinations, Robert Tannenbaum, recalled that the committee viewed the film and to Tannenbaum it was a shock to the system. "The movie was shocking to me because it demonstrated the notion that the CIA was training, in America, a separate army," he said. "It was shocking to me because I'm a true believer in the system and yet there are notorious characters in the system, who are funded by the system, who are absolutely un-American! And who knows what they would do, eventually. What if we send people to Washington who they can't deal with? Out comes their secret army? So, I find that to be as contrary to the Constitution as you can get."[37] What is even more shocking is what the film reveals. According to Tannenbaum depicted in the film among the Cuban exiles was Guy Banister, David Atlee Phillips and Lee Harvey Oswald.[38] Inexplicably, the film would later disappear from the Committee's files.

As for Ferrie it appears he actually had previous experience at anti-Castro training grounds. According to former CAP member John Irion, prior to the Bay of Pigs Ferrie had trained Cubans at a camp at the Belle Chasse Naval Station just south of New Orleans.[39] Ferrie told Irion that equipment for the camp was coming in from the State Department and the CIA through Sergio Arcacha Smith.[40] The presence of this camp is corroborated for us by a recently declassified CIA memo. Titled, "Garrison Investigation: Belle Chasse Training Camp." the document describes the camp as having been activated on February 12, 1961 with the first group of trainees arriving on February 18. The site was located 8 miles from New Orleans at the Belle Chasse U.S. Naval Ammunition Depot which had been inactive for five years. The memo advises that:

Approximately 300 Cubans were trained at the site over a six-week period. The only known list of trainees which was available at Headquarters has not been located to date...The training consisted of weapons firing, demolition, guerrilla warfare, communications, UDT, etc. One group was trained as a strike force assault battalion and was sent to Guatemala on 22 March 1961 to join the Bay of Pigs invasion strike force.[41]

Finally, the author of the memo adds that *"the training camp was entirely Agency controlled and the training was conducted by Agency personnel"* [42](My emphasis). It is interesting to note that the memorandum's author is one David Atlee Phillips.

Recently released FBI files appear to indicate that the Belle Chasse camp was part of a classified project known as "CLIP." An FBI memo dated March 8, 1967, from the New Orleans SAC to the Director reads:

The only information contained in the files of the New Orleans Office regarding a training camp for Cuban exiles in the New Orleans area is contained in New Orleans letter to Bureau, dated 3/23/61, in the case captioned "CLIP," Bufile 105-89923, New Orleans file 105-1445, which sets forth information that **[name redacted]** appeared at the New Orleans Office on 3/13/61, and identified himself as the security officer in charge of an operation under the caption "CLIP" **[next 1 1/2 lines redacted]** located at the Belle Chasse Ammunition Depot. He advised that there were approximately one hundred forty to two hundred Cubans located at that base undergoing expert training in underwater demolition, use of sabotage techniques and combat techniques.
[Approximately the next half page is redacted in its entirety]
Information was also set forth in this communication that on 3/13/61, **[names redacted]** who identified themselves as investigators for CIA contacted **[next one and 1/2 lines redacted]** and furnished data relative to the nature of their operation.[43]

The rest of the pertinent information in the document is also redacted. An earlier FBI memo also makes reference to CLIP. Dated February 21, 1967 the memo's author makes reference to an attached Bureau letter entitled CLIP and expresses a desire to "inquire of CIA through liaison at SOG level whether or not CIA has an operational interest in Sergio Arcacha Smith, David William Ferrie and PCI (Potential Criminal Informant) Gordon Dwane Novel."[44] The earliest reference to CLIP this author located was a memo from the Miami SAC to the Director dated July 23, 1960 and marked "Urgent." The memo describes how an unnamed female informant overheard a conversation between a man with a Germanic accent, referred to as "Bender," and three young Cubans regarding a proposed enterprise against Castro. A fifth person named "Jimmy" joined the discussion during which several names were mentioned such as Tony Varona, Artime, Rasco, Carrillo, as well as other names.[45] The Miami SAC writes that "Due to the obvious relationship of this incident to CLIP operation Miami immediately notified Bernard Reichhardt, CIA, who indicated this constituted serious matter." The rest of the memo details the FBI's efforts to keep the informant from talking further about the matter.[46] One can understand the intelligence agencies' concern, given that CLIP was obviously the FBI codename for the Bay of Pigs invasion. In fact, CIA agent E. Howard Hunt wrote about this incident in his book, *Give Us This Day*. Hunt writes, "Unknown to me, [Bender] held a conference with a Cuban in a motel room near the Miami airport...The occupant of the adjoining room was a vacationing stenographer whose brother worked for the FBI. Hearing a discussion next door between two accented voices she took down the conversation in shorthand and turned over a transcript to the FBI, convinced she had overheard two foreign conspirators."[47] The Cubans mentioned in the conversation were all members of the CIA sponsored Cuban Revolutionary Council and "Bender" was an operational alias of CIA spook Gerry Droller, then Headquarters Chief of Political Action on the Cuba Project. It is intriguing that Ferrie, Novel and Arcacha are all mentioned in relation to Project CLIP.

Chapter Four

~

The Return of Lee Harvey Oswald

The Bolton Ford episode was not the only event to indelibly link Guy Banister with the accused assassin. In April of 1963, Oswald returned to the city of his birth. By May 9th he had found work at the Reily Coffee Company, conveniently located two blocks from Banister's offices. Its owner, William B. Reily, was yet another right-wing reactionary. Reily provided financial support to such groups as Arcacha's Crusade to Free Cuba and Ed Butler's propaganda outfit, INCA.[1]

Oswald's employment at Reily's lasted until July 19th, when he was let go, supposedly for spending too much work time next door at Adrian Alba's garage. The Crescent City Garage was home to the local government agencies' motor pools. One day Alba recalled observing an FBI agent handing a white envelope to Oswald, who was standing in front of Reily's. Alba watched as Oswald clutched the envelope close to his chest and walked back into Reily's.[2]

One of the things about Reily's that later aroused Garrison's suspicions was the number of employees that left shortly after Oswald's departure to begin careers in the aerospace industry. For example, Oswald's superiors, Alfred Claude and Emmett Barbee both left Reily's in July and went to work for NASA in eastern New Orleans.[3] Two of Oswald's co-workers, John D. Branyon and Dante Marachini, were also later hired by NASA.[4] Marachini is of particular interest since he was a self-described friend of David Ferrie's as well as Clay Shaw's next door neighbor.[5] A vice-president of Reily's who testified before the Warren Commission, William Monaghan, was a former career FBI man who left the bureau to become an executive with Standard Fruit.[6] After his stint at Reily's he, along with William Reily's brother, Eustis, show up on the board of directors of Aaron Kohn's Metropolitan Crime Commission.[7] According to an INCA bulletin from 1962, Monaghan is listed as a charter member of that organization as well.

All of this peculiar activity led Garrison to surmise that Reily's was part of an intelligence apparatus. Recent file releases seem to bear out Garrison's suspicions. A CIA memo dated January 31, 1964 reads, "this firm [Reily's] was of interest as of April 1949."[8] Also according to this memo, Reily's was assigned Agency number EE-334.[9] In addition, career soldier-of-fortune and CIA contract employee, Gerry Patrick Hemming confirmed that William Reily had worked for the CIA for years.[10]

After his departure from Reily's, Oswald began what Bill Turner wittily describes as his "guerrilla theater" on the streets of New Orleans - touting his one-man Fair Play for Cuba Committee and distributing pro-Castro literature amid this hotbed of anti-Castro sentiment.[11] On August 9th, Oswald was attacked by Carlos Bringuier and other Cuban exiles as he was handing out his literature, complete with pro-Castro placards, on Canal Street.

noted, it seems more likely Quiroga was <u>delivering</u> the pamphlets rather than attempting to infiltrate the FPCC. In fact, Quiroga was given a polygraph exam by Garrison's office and sent the needle off the chart when he answered "No" to the question, "You have said you tried to infiltrate Oswald's "organization." Isn't it a fact that you knew that his "Fair Play for Cuba" activities were merely a cover?"[20]

So what was Oswald's purpose in using the 544 Camp address? Was he trying to embarrass the notoriously right-wing Banister? Or was he in fact an operative in the Banister cell? There is compelling evidence that strongly indicates the latter.

Oswald and 544 Camp Street

Delphine Roberts, Banister's longtime secretary, mistress and confidante, revealed to the House Select Committee on Assassinations, and later to British journalist, Anthony Summers, that Oswald walked into Banister's office sometime in 1963. He was given a form to fill out as one of Banister's "agents."[21] After Oswald filled out the form, he met with Banister behind closed doors. According to Roberts, "Oswald came back a number of times. He seemed to be on familiar terms with Banister and with the office. As I understood it he had use of an office on the second floor, above the main office where we worked...Mr. Banister brought me upstairs, and in the office above I saw various writings stuck up on the wall pertaining to Cuba. There were various leaflets up there pertaining to Fair Play for Cuba."[22] Roberts' daughter, also named Delphine, told Summers that she and a photographer friend also saw Oswald at Banister's on occasion.[23] Further corroboration of Oswald's second floor offices comes from former Banister associate Bill Nitschke. In a 1967 interview with a *New Orleans States Item* reporter, Nitschke revealed that sometime before the Kennedy assassination, he visited Banister's office and the second floor anterooms. Nitschke recalled seeing crudely lettered placards that he believed had something to do with Castro. He told the *States Item* that "it didn't make any sense to me how Guy got tied up to those signs."[24] As a side note, Nitschke also recalled Delphine Roberts telling him that Banister, Ferrie, and sometime Banister operative and pilot, Hugh Ward, were all involved in running guns to Miami and other places.[25]

Dan Campbell, an ex-Marine that worked for Banister infiltrating left-wing groups on college campuses confirmed the gunrunning, recalling that "Banister was a bagman for the CIA and was running guns to Alpha 66 in Miami."[26] Campbell also assisted Banister in small arms training for the Cubans and received $50 per week for his services.[27] Campbell's recollection of Banister is telling. He describes Banister as "one of the most frighteningly violent persons I have ever known."[28] The Banister menagerie he added "were the worst kind of fanatics."[29] Campbell also remembered one day when he was in Banister's office and a young man came in and used the phone. "I knew he was a Marine from his bearing and speech pattern the minute he walked into 544 Camp Street," he recalled.[30] The next time he saw this young man was when his picture was on television as the accused assassin of President Kennedy. Interestingly, Campbell also recalled seeing Oswald's buddy from his Marine Corps days, Kerry Thornley, pop in and out of Banister's office.[31] Strangely enough on the day Kennedy was shot Thornley was with Allen Campbell, Dan's brother.[32] Allen, like his brother, also worked for Banister. On one of the days Oswald was handing out his leaflets, Allen remembered Delphine Roberts returning to the office and complaining to Banister that "that young man is passing out pro-Castro leaflets in the street."[33] Allen recalled Banister's reaction was calm, "Don't worry about him. He's a nervous fellow, he's confused. He's with us, he's associated with the office."[34] This cavalier attitude on the part of Banister was confirmed by George Higginbotham. Like the Campbells,

Higginbotham was also assigned to infiltrate supposed communist groups. Banister even went as far as providing him with false credentials. Higginbotham remembered bringing the Oswald leafleting incident to Banister's attention. Banister's response was, "Cool it. One of them is one of mine."[35]

Former Banister investigator Vernon Gerdes, who later went to work for New Orleans attorney Stephen Plotkin, told Plotkin that he had seen Oswald and Ferrie together with Banister.[36] Plotkin would later tell an attorney for Clay Shaw that he considered Gerdes "reliable."[37]

William Gaudet, a twenty-year CIA veteran who worked out of the International Trade Mart, told Anthony Summers that, "I did see Oswald discussing various things with Banister at the time," and added, "I suppose you are looking into Ferrie. He was with Oswald."[38] Finally Gaudet said, "Another vital person is Sergio Arcacha Smith. I know he knew Oswald and knows more about the Kennedy affair than he ever admitted."[39]

Jack Martin, who we saw earlier suffered at the hands of Banister, provided a statement to the New Orleans DA's office that he had seen Oswald with Ferrie in Banister's office in the summer of 1963.[40] Additionally, Banister's wife recalled seeing Fair Play for Cuba sheets in Banister's office.[41]

Infiltrating left-wing groups with his *agents provocateur* was a particular specialty of Banister's. Tommy Baumler, a New Orleans attorney, revealed in a 1981 interview that he too worked for Guy Banister, joining left-wing college groups and reporting back to Banister. Baumler also recalled that "Clay Shaw, Banister, and Guy Johnson made up the intelligence apparatus in New Orleans."[42] Johnson was a former Lieutenant Commander in the Navy in World War II and a former assistant D.A. in New Orleans from 1938-1942. In 1950, he was granted a Top Secret clearance by the Office of Naval Intelligence, while working out of the office of the Chief of Naval Operations.[43] Johnson later went into private practice as an attorney, but it is not known when his intelligence career ended.[44] In a letter from Banister to Johnson, dated January 5, 1959, Banister discusses the possibility of hiring a candidate for his infiltration squad. Banister writes:

> We have discussed the advisability as well as the feasibility of establishing certain channels of information and it is possible that the above named individual will qualify...
> Mr. Bergeron, in the course of conversation, advised that he served in the Air Force and had just gotten out and entered school. He said he served in the security section and has atomic clearance.
> I mentioned, during the conversation, the United States National Students Association and he said that he heard someone mention this organization on Channel 12 (WJMR-TV, the Citizen's Council Program) and said that he had checked and found that there is a small organization on the campus.
> If it is satisfactory and you can determine this individual's reliability, I will set him up to begin work with me and pass on to you any information he produces.[45]

Finally, evidence of Oswald's association with the Banister clique, may have come from the CIA itself. In an intriguing, but incomplete, memo from April 9, 1968, someone at the CIA wrote:

> Moreover, until then, there had been no secret as far as anyone was concerned in regard to the fact that Banister, David William Ferrie and Subj. [Oswald] may have known or been acquainted with one another.[46]

It should be noted however, that this is the exact same wording from an affidavit from Jack Martin. So it seems the CIA was quoting from Martin's affidavit in this memo rather than stating their own conclusion.[47]

At the end of August Oswald made a memorable appearance in Clinton, Louisiana, which we will examine in detail in Chapter 11. In September Oswald left from New Orleans for Texas, by way of Mexico City. He eventually found work at the Texas School Book Depository and settled in Dallas to await the denouement to this strange play, whose opening act may have begun that summer in New Orleans.

Chapter Five

~

The Ides of November

As doctors at Dallas' Parkland Hospital struggled to save the President's life,[1] David Ferrie was in a New Orleans courtroom assisting attorney G. Wray Gill who was fighting deportation charges brought against reputed underworld figure Carlos Marcello.[2] Marcello beat those charges and after his victory in court, Ferrie and two companions, Melvin Coffee and Alvin Beauboeuf, took off for Houston, Texas to take care of some business for Gill, relax, hunt geese, and/or ice skate, depending on whose statement you believe. One thing is certain, neither of these midnight ramblers told the same story to authorities.

For example, Coffee claims the reason for the trip was

for relaxation and that Ferrie had proposed the trip and made arrangements a day or two ahead of time. The trio left about 7:00 PM (Coffee remembered it was dark) and brought no guns with them.[3] Beauboeuf said the purpose of the trip was to go ice skating and that they had left about 4:00 PM. He concurred with Coffee that there were no weapons in the car. He also said the trip was planned in precision about a week before and that he had proposed the trip.[4] From Ferrie we have yet a third version of these events. Ferrie stated that "we left after supper time for Houston. We were going to go ice skating and then hunting."[5] Also, according to Ferrie, he was combining work with pleasure, as he was also doing some investigative work for Gill. Ferrie also told authorities that he and his companions had each taken a shotgun.[6]

Apparently the only point all three could agree on was that on November 23rd they eventually found their way to an ice skating rink in Houston. Once there, Ferrie proceeded to make a memorable impression on the rink's manager, Chuck Rolland. According to Rolland, Ferrie had actually called a week or so in advance and had inquired about their services.[7] As his two companions skated, Ferrie placed and received phone calls at the public phone. In between calls, Ferrie would introduce himself several times to Rolland. After about three hours, Ferrie told Rolland that they were leaving and would come back later that evening.[8] The trio never returned. Instead they drove on to Galveston where they checked into a motel. Meanwhile, an associate of Jack Ruby's, Breck Wall, drove from Dallas through Houston to Galveston.[9] Ruby's last long distance phone call during a weekend of frenzied phone activity was to Breck Wall in Galveston.[10] Two months earlier, Ferrie had made a long distance call to the apartment complex of a Jean West in Chicago.[11] Jean West, a.k.a. Jean Aase, would accompany Ruby associate, Lawrence Meyers, to Dallas the day before the assassination. West and Meyers spent several hours with Ruby at the Carousel Club on November 21st. Garrison would later suspect that this peculiar phone activity was part of a clandestine communications network.[12]

On Sunday the 24th, Ferrie and his two friends left Galveston for New Orleans. While gassing up at a filling station, they heard the news that Oswald had been killed in the basement of the Dallas jail. Ferrie placed a call to Gill who told him the local authorities wanted to question him. (Jack Martin had made contact with assistant district attorney Herman Kohlman by this time. See the introduction to this book for a recap of the Martin incident). Ferrie dropped off Beauboeuf and Coffee in New Orleans while he headed to the campus of Southeastern University in Hammond, Louisiana. Once there, Ferrie arrived at the dorm room of Thomas Compton, a former CAP cadet. Compton recalled Ferrie arriving in near hysterics stating, "The police are at my home and have taken some of my things."[13] Indeed in their attempt to locate Ferrie for questioning, the police arrested Beauboeuf and Layton Martens at Ferrie's apartment and charged them with vagrancy. While in custody, Martens said Gill had come by Ferrie's residence and relayed a message that Ferrie's library card was found among Oswald's effects.[14]

After making several calls to Gill, Ferrie returned to New Orleans on the afternoon of November 25. He and Gill appeared for questioning at the district attorney's office around 4:30 p.m. After questioning by Garrison's men, Ferrie was turned over to the FBI and Secret Service. He denied knowing Oswald and told the federal authorities that Jack Martin was a crackpot who was trying to implicate him in the assassination.[15] By November 25th the federal government was trying to close the book on the JFK case and Ferrie was promptly released with an apology.

At least two mysteries remain from Ferrie's post-assassination activity. If Ferrie was not guilty of something, why flee to Hammond once he found out he was under suspicion? Also, Ferrie took the allegation of Oswald possessing his library card seriously. Sometime shortly after he returned from Texas, Ferrie visited the home of Mr. & Mrs.

Eames, Oswald's neighbors in New Orleans. Ferrie asked Mr. Eames if he had any information regarding Oswald's library card. Eames told Ferrie he had seen Oswald in the public library but could offer him no information about the library card that Oswald used.[16]

Oswald's former landlady, Mrs. Jesse Garner, would tell congressional investigators that Ferrie visited her home and inquired about the Oswald library card as well. What is shocking about Garner's statement is that Ferrie arrived at her home on the evening of the assassination, *before* he left for Texas.[17]

After the FBI released Ferrie, they turned their attention to the source of the Ferrie information - Jack Martin. Noting the speed with which the FBI released Ferrie and how the official story was taking shape, Martin "recanted" his original statement. According to FBI reports, Martin said that he was drinking at the time he called assistant district attorney Kohlman and contracted a case of "telephonitis." Martin later described the FBI's lack of interest in Ferrie, as well as their pre-ordained conclusion, "They [the FBI] took a few notes [about Ferrie], they were more interested in punching at me...They were pretty well fixed in their opinion so I never questioned the FBI to their motives. The minute my wife and I saw those things, we snapped."[18] However, at the same time he was acquiescing to the FBI (and presumably while he was sober), Martin was further implicating Ferrie with the FAA. On November 25th, Martin wrote to FAA investigator, Richard Robey:

> Don't your case records on Ferrie show that this guy Oswald was a member of Ferrie's so-called phony CAP squadron?
> Remember, all of those large group pictures...Wasn't his picture in these? Perhaps you will also remember Ferrie had a bunch of these foreign rifles that he used to train his cadets with.
> Furthermore, I understand that Ferrie had been getting mail from those Cuban people he was connected with...Gill raised hell with Ferrie over having this type of propaganda at his office.[19]

The FBI certainly had plenty of leads to work with in New Orleans. Had one in particular been properly investigated, it could have been the key to cracking this case.

Dean Andrews

The flurry of phone activity that weekend continued on November 23rd with a call to colorful New Orleans attorney, Dean Andrews. Sometimes described as a Damon Runyonesque character, the obese Andrews often spoke in outdated "beatnik" jargon, which lent to his flamboyant reputation. While recovering from a bout of pneumonia at the Hotel Dieu Hospital, Andrews was contacted by a Clay Bertrand, who requested Andrews go to Dallas and provide representation for Oswald. This seemingly bizarre request is not so strange when one considers that Andrews knew both Oswald and Bertrand.

In July of 1964, Andrews described his first encounter with Oswald to Warren Commission counsel, Wesley Liebler:

> **Andrews:** I don't recall the dates, but briefly it is this: Oswald came in the office accompanied by some gay kids. They were Mexicanos. He wanted to find out what could be done in connection with a discharge, a yellow paper discharge, so I explained to him we would have to advance the funds to transcribe whatever records they had up in the Adjutant General's office. When he brought the money, I would do the work, and we saw him three or four times subsequent to that, not in the company of the gay kids. He had this Mexicano with him.[20]

Later, Andrews recalled how the "gay kids" were picked up in a police sweep of the French Quarter and how he was called by Clay Bertrand to defend them. Andrews also told the Warren Commission that on one of Oswald's subsequent visits, Oswald had asked about instituting citizenship proceedings for his Russian born wife, Marina. Andrews also ran into Oswald on Canal Street as he was handing out his Fair Play for Cuba literature. Andrews asked Oswald what he was doing "handing out that junk." According to Andrews, Oswald replied that it was a job and he was getting paid to do it.[21] As for his call from Bertrand, Andrews testified:

> **Andrews:** I was in Hotel Dieu and the phone rang and a voice I recognized as Clay Bertrand asked me if I would go to Dallas and Houston - I think -Dallas, I guess, wherever it was this boy was being held - and defend him. I told him I was sick in the hospital. If I couldn't go, I would find somebody that could go...He [Bertrand] is the one who calls in behalf of the gay kids normally, either to obtain bond or parole for them. I would assume that he was the one that originally sent Oswald and the gay kids...[22]

An obviously frightened Andrews would later offer authorities varying descriptions of Bertrand, but what is important for now is the intimidation of Andrews by the FBI to retract his statement. Liebler later asked Andrews about his claims to the FBI that the whole thing was "a figment of his imagination:"

> **Andrews:** That's what the Feebees [the FBI] put on...I told them, "Write what you want, that I am nuts. I don't care"... You can tell when the steam is on. They are on you like the plague. They never leave. They are like cancer. Eternal.[23]

The "figment of his imagination" defense has been promulgated through the years by defenders of the Warren Report who cling to the Report's conclusion that Andrews was heavily medicated at the time he supposedly spoke with Bertrand. However, a careful look at the evidence proves the opposite to be true. In fact, the FBI's own reports disprove the Warren position.

On December 3, 1963, Agents Regis Kennedy and Reed Jensen interviewed Andrews. Their subsequent report states:

> ANDREWS stated the principal reasons why he feels that the telephone call was not a dream was because of the action he took in contacting Mr. SAM "MONK" ZELDEN, President of the New Orleans Criminal Bar Association and a close personal friend on Sunday, November 24, 1963 by telephone, reaching him at the New Orleans Athletic Club and discussing with him the propriety of defending OSWALD and asking ZELDEN if he would be interested in assisting in the defense. ANDREWS recalls this call and further recalls that it was Attorney ZELDEN who told him that LEE HARVEY OSWALD had been shot and that this news had just come over the television station.
>
> ANDREWS advised that in addition to talking with ZELDEN, he had discussed receiving this call from CLAY BERTRAND with his investigator, Sergeant R.M. DAVIS, United States Army Retired, and his secretary, EVA SPRINGER, as well as his wife.[24]

Three days later on December 6th, Kennedy re-interviewed Andrews and wrote in his report that:

> ANDREWS advised that based on the discrepancy between his memory and facts as related to him by his employees and further the fact that he cannot identify CLAY BERTRAND, he can reach only one conclusion, that is, that the call received by him while in Hotel Dieu Hospital under sedation, was a figment of his imagination.[25]

But on this same day, Kennedy also interviewed Andrews' employees, R.M. Davis and Eva Springer. According to Davis, Andrews was "positive that a person named Clay Bertrand had called him on the telephone."[26] Further, Andrews mentioned Clay Bertrand to Davis on Sunday, November 24 and Davis was under the impression that Bertrand was well known to Andrews.[27] Davis also recalled Andrews mentioning to him on various occasions that an individual named Oswald had been in Andrews' office. In fact, Davis remembered discussing with Andrews the procedure for upgrading an undesirable discharge from the Marine Corps.[28] Although Eva Springer could not recall ever seeing Oswald in the office, she did recall Andrews speaking to her about amending a Marine Corps discharge.[29] Regarding the Bertrand call, Springer told Kennedy that Andrews called her at home on November 23rd and advised her that he was going to Dallas to represent Oswald at the request of a "Bertrand"[30] She was even able to fix the time of the call at 4:00 PM due to the fact that she had just returned home from her weekly routine trip to the grocery store.[31]

That still leaves open the question of whether Andrews was heavily sedated at the time of the call. A check of the hospital records would certainly resolve that issue and the FBI did just that. On December 5th, Special Agent Richard Bucaro reviewed Andrews' medical record. It clearly states that on November 23rd Andrews did not receive any sedation until 8:00 PM.[32] Recall that according to Eva Springer, Andrews informed her of the Bertrand call at 4:00 PM. Thus Special Agent Kennedy had corroborative statements from Andrews' employees regarding Oswald's visits and the Bertrand call, as well as medical records showing Andrews was not under sedation at the time of the phone call from Bertrand. Yet Kennedy falsified his report stating the opposite as fact. Even Andrews said as much to the Warren Commission. There can be no doubt at this point that a deliberate cover-up of this matter had commenced.

Before we leave this eventful weekend, it will be useful to examine one final episode.

Rose Cheramie

On the night of November 20th, a 34 year old woman was found lying on the road near Eunice, Louisiana, bruised and disoriented.[33] Rose Cheramie, a heroin addict and prostitute, was taken to a local private hospital and was treated for abrasions. She was released into the custody of Louisiana State Police Lieutenant, Francis Fruge, who put her in a jail cell to sober up. A short time later, Cheramie began to exhibit signs of severe heroin withdrawal and the local doctor was summoned. Cheramie admitted to the physician that she had been addicted to heroin for nine years and had last "shot up" at around 2:00 PM. The doctor, noting signs of mild shock and heroin withdrawal, administered a sedative and Fruge transported her to the State hospital in Jackson, Louisiana. (Known as the East Louisiana State Hospital, this hospital was in fact a mental asylum and will figure prominently later in the investigation).

During the trip to Jackson, Cheramie told Fruge that she was coming from Florida to Dallas with two men when they stopped at a lounge called the Silver Slipper. After a few drinks, she got into an argument with the two men and the bar owner threw her out. She attempted to catch a ride by hitchhiking when a car hit her. Fruge asked her what she was going to do in Dallas. Cheramie responded by saying she was going to, "number one, pick up some money, pick up her baby, and to kill Kennedy" Fruge had Cheramie admitted to the hospital late on November 20th.

Staff doctors at the hospital were able to corroborate aspects of the Cheramie allegations. Dr. Victor Weiss would later recall that on Monday, November 25, another physician, Dr. Bowers asked him, to see Cheramie. Dr. Bowers told Weiss that Cheramie had stated before the assassination that President Kennedy was going to be killed. When Weiss questioned Cheramie, she told him that she had worked for Jack Ruby and although she did not have any specific details about an assassination plot, "word in the underworld" was that Kennedy would be assassinated. Cheramie's role in this affair was as a drug runner, with the narcotics to be picked up in Houston. After the assassination, Fruge accompanied Cheramie to Houston where aspects of her drug story checked out. While en route to Houston, Cheramie noticed a newspaper story about Oswald's murder at the hands of Jack Ruby, who the papers claimed did not know Oswald. According to Fruge, Cheramie laughed and claimed Oswald and Ruby had been "shacking up for years." (While there may have been a Ruby/Oswald relationship, it is doubtful they sustained any kind of prolonged intimate contact as Cheramie suggests).

Four years later, while detailed to the New Orleans DA's office, Fruge questioned the owner of the Silver Slipper about Cheramie. Mac Manual told Fruge that Cheramie had arrived with two men he knew were engaged in the business of running prostitutes in from Florida. When Cheramie became drunk and out of control, one of the men "slapped her around" and threw her outside.

Fruge showed the bar owner a stack of photographs in an attempt to identify Cheramie's companions. Manual picked out photographs of Sergio Arcacha Smith and fellow Cuban exile, Emilio Santana.[34] As we have seen, Arcacha was closely associated with David Ferrie and Guy Banister. Santana, like Arcacha, was employed by the CIA in the anti-Castro efforts. A member of the CIA funded exile group, Alpha 66, Santana spent his time between New Orleans and Miami in the early 1960's.[35] Also like Arcacha, Santana was a familiar face among the Banister/Ferrie crowd.[36]

It is extremely interesting to note, that when Fruge was questioned about these matters by congressional investigators, he asked the committee if they had found diagrams of the sewer system in Dealey Plaza which were found in Arcacha's apartment in Texas.[37] Fruge believed Dallas Police Captain Will Fritz had originally told him about the diagrams. For his part, Arcacha has consistently denied any knowledge of these matters.

Neither Jim Garrison or Congress would be able to question Cheramie about her allegations. On September 4, 1965 Cheramie, apparently thrown from a car, was lying on a strip of road near Big Sandy, Texas, when a car, while attempting to avoid hitting her, ran over the top of her skull, causing fatal injuries.

In 1964, the President's Commission on the Assassination of President Kennedy, better known as the Warren Commission, issued its report. Their "no conspiracy/lone gunman" conclusions were no doubt comforting to the general populace. However, a foundation of lies is a weak one, as the early research of Mark Lane, Harold Weisberg, Joachim Joesten and others have proved. As they and other critics began to carefully scrutinize the evidence the Warren Report was supposedly based on, the cards began to fall. But it would be serendipity that would really start the first serious investigation into the Kennedy assassination.

Chapter Six

~

Origins of an Investigation

On September 14, 1966 Joseph M. Rault, president of the New Orleans based Rault Petroleum Corporation, sent a letter to Jim Garrison inviting him to attend the annual American Petroleum Institute meeting on November 13th in New York City.[1] Garrison accepted the invitation and on his flight home from New York, as he sat next to Rault and the United States Senator from Louisiana, Russell Long, the conversation turned to the subject of the Warren Report. Long expressed serious doubts about the Warren Commission's conclusions, stating he felt Oswald was a decoy for other assassins.[2] Hearing this skepticism from the Majority Whip of the U.S. Senate troubled Garrison. When he returned to New Orleans, Garrison began reading all of the current literature on the assassination. On December 6th, his office ordered the Warren Report and the 26 supporting volumes.[3] As he studied Oswald's activities during the time he was in the DA's jurisdiction, Garrison's mind kept drifting back to the aftermath of the assassination when his office questioned David Ferrie.[4] Feeling he may have dismissed Ferrie too lightly, he quietly reopened the investigation.

In addition to Ferrie, there were also other areas of concern to Garrison. Reading about Oswald's pamphleteering incidents, Garrison quickly discovered that the address Oswald used on some of his leaflets was the same address as the building, which housed Guy Banister's operation. Having known Banister and well aware of his extremism, Garrison naturally wanted to question him, but Banister had died of a heart attack in June of 1964.[5] However, Banister left behind a small testament to his political paranoia - his collection of "intelligence" data.

The Banister Files

Facing financial difficulties, Banister's widow, Mary, sold many of her husband's files to Aaron Kohn's Metropolitan Crime Commission.[6] Other files went to the State Sovereignty Commission and the State Police along with a complete index card catalogue.[7] Garrison's attempts to retrieve the files were unsuccessful. However, Garrison was able to obtain a list of the index cards from the State Police. Unfortunately the set was incomplete because the receptionist had used the backs of the cards to record phone messages for the police officers. However, the remaining cards did offer an inside peak into the Banister apparatus. Using an FBI-like classification system, some of Banister's files were as follows:[8]

Jose E. Aleman 10-209
American Central Intelligence Agency 20-10
Sergio Arcacha 23-5
Anti-Soviet Underground 25-1
Assassination of President Kennedy 15-16
Fidel Castro 23-3
Cuban Democratic Revolutionary Front 23-5
Civil Rights Program of JFK 8-41
Lloyd J. Cobb 23-14
Cuban Revolutionary Council 23-5
Dyna-Soar Space Warcraft 15-16
Fair Play For Cuba Committee 23-7
Inside CIA 11-9
International House 23-14
International Trade Mart 23-14
Italy - U.S. Missile Bases Dismantled In 15-16
Penkovsky, Oleg, Col. 11-9
Quiroga, Carlos 10-209
SAC - Strategic Air Command 15-16
Shaw, Clay 23-14
Walker, Edwin A. (Gen.) 15-16

For Garrison, this ended the myth of Guy Banister's "private detective agency." Although Garrison may have been unsuccessful in locating the contents of these files, apparently Clay Shaw's lawyers had better luck. In the papers of Edward and William Wegmann is a list entitled "Notes on Search Banister's Files Residue - Sovereignty Commission - 7/68." Included in the seven-page list is a handwritten summary of the remaining contents of each file. A partial example is listed below:[9]

10-42 – "GB note on a youth's (?) CIA affiliation in Allen Campbell memo to GB Re Richard C. Bell 8/17/59"

10-60 – "Students reading Red propaganda in library - Oct. 26, 1962"

10-41 – "Security name checks @ FBI - 9/25/62"

10-58 – "8/27/59 - Casing Rpt. for surrep. entry to Dr. James Dumbrowski's Perdido Bldg. from Allen Campbell to GB"

11-9 – "Central Intelligence Agency (14-7 out in red. File empty)"

Following the Oswald trail, Garrison soon contacted Cuban exile, Carlos Bringuier. Bringuier was the DRE delegate in New Orleans who participated in the August street scuffle with Oswald. Offering little of substance to Garrison, Bringuier duly reported on this meeting to the local office of the CIA.[10] This should be of little surprise since the DRE was conceived, created, and funded by the CIA, earning the cryptonym, AMSPELL.[11] The DRE was filled with rabid, anti-Kennedy extremists. Even the CIA speculated that the DRE may have gotten out of control and could somehow be involved in the Kennedy assassination. On March 3, 1967, a CIA official authored an internal memo entitled, "Possible DRE Animus Toward President Kennedy." Having been assigned to the Miami station from July 1962 to August 1963, the CIA officer considered the DRE "unpredictable and untrustworthy" and speculated that DRE elements could have been involved in the Kennedy assassination.[12] The author of the memo urged further investigation. Recently declassified reports show that a year later the CIA ran traces on 47 Cubans who were connected to the Garrison case, but it seems no serious investigation of a CIA/anti-Castro "blowback" operation ever took place.[13]

Returning to the source of the Ferrie accusations, the DA's office called in Jack Martin. On December 13th Martin provided information to Garrison that he had seen Oswald and Ferrie together in Banister's office.[14] The following day Ferrie was called into Garrison's office and questioned about Martin's accusations as well as his trip to Texas in November of 1963. Ferrie denied he had ever met Oswald and, as noted earlier, provided information about his Texas trip, which was at variance with his two companions' version of events.[15] Consequently, Garrison ordered round the clock surveillance on Ferrie and infiltrated an informant into his circle.[16]

In the meantime, Garrison's small staff was being augmented with an unusual number of volunteers. Unusual, because at least two of them volunteered their services before any publicity had emerged. Tom Bethell has written that he was introduced to Garrison in 1966. Bethell, an Englishman, was in New Orleans studying jazz and was introduced first to assistant DA John Volz through Volz' girlfriend. Volz then introduced Bethell to Garrison, who hired him on the spot.[17] What Bethell doesn't tell us (and presumably didn't tell Garrison) was that he was in New Orleans much earlier - in the summer of 1963. Bethell's friend, Warwick Reynolds, just happened to be the roommate of Oswald's friend, Kerry Thornley.[18] Several witnesses place Oswald's Marine buddy, Thornley, and Oswald together at a couple of the local French Quarter hangouts at this same time.[19] As we'll see, Bethell later ingratiated himself with the Shaw defense team in a big way.

William Gurvich, like Bethell, came to Garrison very early on and would later "defect" from the staff. Unlike Bethell, however, Gurvich was a little more high profile. Gurvich, along with his two brothers, had inherited his father's business, the Gurvich Detective Agency. The father, a former FBI agent, had grown the business from a small agency specializing in dockfront intrigue to a large firm employing some 340 men and women, offering a wide range of services including "undercover infiltration."[20] Garrison always maintained that Gurvich volunteered his services to the office, even donating a color TV to the cause. Gurvich, on the other hand, claimed that Garrison asked him to join the team and had appointed him Chief Investigator. Once again the written record bears out Garrison's version of events. In the numerous memos that Gurvich authored, he always used the title "Special Aide" or "Investigative Aide" never Chief Investigator. In fact, for the duration of the investigation, Lou Ivon was the only Chief Investigator on the staff. Furthermore, in Gordon Novel's deposition, he relates how local businessman Willard Robertson introduced him to Garrison early in the investigation. Novel states that when Garrison told him Gurvich was working on the case, he asked how long Gurvich had been with the office. Garrison said, "He [Gurvich] went to work for the DA's office about two weeks ago...He begged me to give him a job because he wanted to get in on the thing."[21] Since Garrison's comments to Novel were well before Gurvich's departure from the DA's office, Garrison would have no reason to be deceptive.

The FBI Steps In

At approximately the same time Gurvich "volunteered," the FBI launched their own discreet re-investigation into the assassination. Once again Gordon Novel provides the lead. In his deposition, Novel describes his first meeting with Garrison. The DA confided to Novel that he felt the FBI was bugging his telephone. He added that the FBI "have got investigators all over the place. They, the public, don't know it but they have reopened the investigation clandestinely."[22] However, it would be the CIA that would provide the confirmation, as well as an insight into how they regarded the Garrison investigation. In early February of 1967 the Chief of the New Orleans office, Lloyd Ray, authored a memo to the Director of the Domestic Contact Service. In it he wrote, "We believe that there is some truth in the allegation of the Garrison investigation and that the matter is under a discreet and sensitive investigation by the FBI."[23]

The Search for Clay Bertrand

After questioning jive-talking attorney Dean Andrews about his Warren Commission testimony concerning the mysterious Clay Bertrand, Garrison sent his assistants into the French Quarter clubs in an attempt to ascertain the true identity of Bertrand. At Cosimo's they hit pay dirt. The bartender told assistant DA Andrew Sciambra that Bertrand was a regular customer and that he was in fact Clay Shaw, the retired long-time director of the International Trade Mart. He remembered seeing Shaw on television newscasts from time to time, "usually with important people." He knew right away that Shaw was the Clay Bertrand that patronized his club.[24]

Two days before Christmas in 1966, Sciambra interviewed Shaw in the DA's office. Garrison found Shaw's answers evasive and in conflict with other information they had acquired. For example, when Shaw was asked where he was at the time of the assassination, he said he was traveling by train, on his way to San Francisco.[25] With the exception of E. Howard Hunt, just about every American who was alive at the time of the assassination can remember where they were on that fateful day. It was ascertained later that Shaw was already in San Francisco at the time of the assassination, in the company of San Francisco Trade Mart Director, J. Monroe Sullivan.[26] After his arrest, Shaw related yet another version to the *New Orleans Times-Picayune* that he was at the St. Francis Hotel at the time of the assassination.[27] Later, under oath at his own trial, Shaw said he was invited to make a speech at the request of Sullivan. Sullivan, to this day, disputes this. In an interview with author, Bill Turner, Sullivan recalled that Shaw had *called him* several weeks before the assassination and asked him to put together a lunch because he had a big program to obtain tenants for the New Orleans International Trade Mart.[28] Shaw indicated he would pay for everything and asked Sullivan to make reservations for him at the St. Francis Hotel. Sullivan stated that following the phone call there was an exchange of correspondence to confirm details of the meeting. Shaw arrived at the San Francisco Trade Mart about mid-morning on the 22nd. As Shaw and Sullivan were talking, news arrived that JFK had been shot. Sullivan was stunned but Shaw exhibited no reaction and remained silent. After news confirmed the President's death, Sullivan asked Shaw if he wanted to go ahead with the lunch meeting. Surprisingly, Shaw said he did. Again, this is at variance with Shaw's statements.[29]

On another matter, Shaw said that his assistant, J.B. Dauenhauer, had come to him in August of 1963 and said Oswald had asked permission to distribute his handbills in front of the Trade Mart. This was remarkably different than Dauenhauer's statement to the DA's office.[30] Finally, Shaw denied knowing Dean Andrews, even asking Sciambra what he (Andrews) did for a living - despite the fact that Andrews represented Gordon Novel to Shaw when Novel attempted to open a concession in the International Trade Mart just two years earlier.[31] At the same time Garrison was building his case against Ferrie, he was quietly beginning to build his case against Shaw. And as we'll see later, the FBI was also receiving information that Shaw and Bertrand were one and the same.

On the Trail of the Investigators

Jack Dempsey was a crime beat reporter from the old school. With a network of well placed sources in the courts, the DA's office and the police department, Dempsey wrote a column for the *New Orleans States Item* called "On the Police Beat." On January 23rd, 1967, Dempsey's column asked rhetorically:

DID YOU KNOW? At least five persons have been questioned by the District Attorney's office in connection with another investigation into events linked to the Kennedy assassination.

After further follow-up, Dempsey fleshed out his story and submitted it to his editor for approval. It was suggested to Dempsey that he attempt to elicit comments from Garrison before printing the story. Knowing of Dempsey's somewhat contentious relationship with Garrison, the paper instead sent Rosemary James, a young reporter whose specialty was maritime reports. Ms. James contends that when she met with Garrison and showed him the article, Garrison simply said, "No comment." James alleges that this was a winking approval from Garrison to go ahead and print the story.[32] But Dempsey emphatically remembers a very different series of events. According to him, when Ms. James returned from Garrison's office, she met with Dempsey and told him that an angry Garrison had asked, "Who wrote this garbage?" When she replied that Dempsey wrote it, an enraged Garrison said something to the effect that "I might have known it. Jack's flaky. There's not a word of truth to that article and if you use this story you're going to be in trouble."[33] Thus contradicting Ms. James' fabrication and the early image of Garrison as a publicity hound.

Nevertheless, on February 17, 1967, the *States Item* ran a page one story with a banner headline which read "**DA HERE LAUNCHES FULL JFK DEATH PLOT PROBE**." The article revealed that Garrison's office had spent some $8,000 on travel expenses to cities such as Dallas, San Francisco, and Miami while investigating a New Orleans-based plot to assassinate JFK. It was also soon revealed that Garrison had a suspect - David Ferrie.

Ferrie's Final Days

As the national media descended upon New Orleans, Ferrie made an attempt at damage control by calling the *States Item* and telling them the investigation was all "a big joke." But Ferrie was hardly doing much laughing. On Saturday, February 18, Sciambra and Chief Investigator Lou Ivon, questioned Ferrie again in his cluttered Louisiana Avenue Parkway apartment. Subsisting on a diet of black coffee, cigarettes, and nervous energy, Ferrie was showing definite signs of deterioration. The following day Ferrie contacted Ivon at his home and asked for help. Ivon told Ferrie to meet him downtown at the Fountainbleau Hotel where he would check him in under an assumed name. Ivon recalled to the author that Ferrie was "very scared - a wild man."[34] Ferrie confided to Ivon that he had done work for the CIA and had known Oswald. He admitted he knew Clay Shaw and that Shaw too worked for the CIA. He added that Shaw hated Kennedy. However, he did not yet admit any involvement in the assassination. Ivon stayed with Ferrie until about 2:00 A.M. Later that morning when Ivon went to check on Ferrie, he had vanished. Knowing he had not returned to his apartment, Ivon and his fellow officers unsuccessfully combed the Cuban community on Decatur Street where Ferrie often stayed.[35] Three days later, on February 22, police found Ferrie dead in his home.[36] Left behind in his clutter among the many volumes of esoteric literature was a book on firearms. Filled with underlining and marginal notations, one passage described the distance a cartridge travels from a rifle after ejection. Scribbled in Ferrie's handwriting was the notation "50 degrees and 11 feet", indicating Ferrie had test-fired a rifle and plotted the distance of the ejected cartridge.[37]

Author, Paris Flammonde may have offered the most eloquent Ferrie epitath: "This was no Brutus, no Essex, no Burr - This was a twisted, hating, emotionally corrupted phantasizer, costumed in false eyebrows and a bright red wig, probably dreaming of a place in the constellation of some historic conspiracy."[38]

The coroner ruled Ferrie died from a brain aneurysm, despite the presence of two typed, unsigned "suicide" notes. (Whether they were suicide notes or not is a matter of interpretation. Ferrie, who knew he was quite ill, probably saw the end coming and decided to compose his own epitaph). Garrison would postulate that Ferrie could have been force-fed a fatal dosage of Proloid, a thyroid medication Ferrie had been prescribed. It is doubtful that Ferrie could have been fed enough Proloid to be fatal, nevertheless, this theory was bolstered by a member of the coroner's office. Although there were no signs of struggle and the coroner's report noted a "dryness" and "lesions" inside Ferrie's mouth, Deputy Coroner, Frank Minyard described it as a contusion on the inside of Ferrie's lower lip. Minyard concluded this had been caused by "something traumatically inserted into his mouth."[39] Nevertheless, the DA's number one suspect was dead, so Garrison turned his attention to the man he had hoped Ferrie would implicate.

Part Two:

Through the Looking Glass

Chapter Seven

~

Humble Origins

Nestled near the Mississippi border of "Bloody" Tangipahoa Parish is the small town of Kentwood, Louisiana.[1] On March 17, 1913 Clay Lavergne Shaw was born in this rural community where his grandfather had been sheriff and his father, a US. Marshall.[2] Five years later his family settled in New Orleans, where Shaw would later graduate from Warren Easton High School and go on to become the manager of a local Western Union office. During this time Shaw authored several plays including, *Stokers*, *A Message From Khufu*, *The Cuckoo's Nest*, and *Submerged* which was reputedly developed into a feature film, *Men Without Women*.[3]

In 1935 Shaw was transferred to New York City, where he briefly attended Columbia University. He was appointed manager of Western Union's mid-Manhattan area, supervising some 40 branch offices. The young Shaw was restless however, for he soon embarked on several career changes. He did stints in free-lance advertising and public relations, dabbled in the theater, and finally booked lecturers for the Lee-Kiddick Lecture Bureau.[4] In total, Shaw spent seven years in New York, finally enlisting in the United States Army in 1942.

War Years

Shaw once told a reporter that he had been the victim of a typical Army bad MOS classification and was thrown into the Medical Corps as a private. "I didn't even know what a fracture was," he recalled.[5] A short time later he was sent to the Medical Administrative Officer Candidate School in Abilene, Kansas. He came out a second lieutenant and was assigned duty as administrative officer with the 127th General Hospital unit in England. During Shaw's training, he sustained an injury to his back while practicing carrying patients. This injury caused Shaw recurring back pain and numbness to his left leg, which forced him to occasionally walk with a slight limp.[6] Within months Shaw was transferred to Supply where he was made aide-de-camp and later deputy chief of staff to General Charles O. Thrasher. According to Shaw, his unit stockpiled supplies for the Normandy invasion. Indeed, Thrasher was made supply chief for Northern France, Belgium and Luxembourg at the Oise Bay Section Command at Rheims, France where Shaw worked with him, rising in rank to Major. Thrasher's duties also included transferring German POW's to the French government where many were subsequently starved to death.[7] After receiving decorations from France and the US, Shaw was discharged in 1946.[8]

Because Shaw's military record is still classified, this has led to speculation that Shaw's military career consisted of duty in the CIA's precursor, the Office of Strategic Services. This appears not to be the case. However, Shaw's military career had a definite intelligence bent.

Justice Department documents indicate Shaw served in a branch of the Army known as the SOS.[9] A check of an Army Intelligence manual from that time indicates that SOS or Special Operations Section was a sub-division of the Counter Intelligence Group of the Communications Zone Intelligence Division, also known as CommZ. The importance of CommZ in the military intelligence hierarchy should not be underestimated. CommZ's responsibility to direct, supervise and coordinate the activities of the intelligence and counter-intelligence groups and to disseminate this intelligence as appropriate, is not unlike what the CIA was originally chartered to do.[10]

Specifically, the functions of Shaw's group were to:

(a) Prepare estimates, plans, directives, and reports for all matters pertaining to special counterintelligence operations.

(b) Supervise and coordinate special counterintelligence operations throughout communications zone.

(c) Determine requirements for, procure, and employ special counterintelligence units and agents.

(d) Determine requirements for, procure, and issue special counterintelligence funds, equipment, and supplies.

(e) Establish and operate special interrogation centers, if required.

(f) Plan for and supervise the execution of intelligence security throughout the communications zone.[11]

With Shaw's discharge from the service, his intelligence career was far from over. As we shall see, it was just beginning.

Chapter Eight

~

With A Little Help From His Friends

Author John Wilds once noted that Ted Brent was "one of New Orleans principal movers and shakers of his time."[1] When Clay Shaw returned to New Orleans after the war, he was taken under Brent's wing.[2] A self-made millionaire, Brent was the founder and president of the Mississippi Shipping Company, the president of the Louisiana Shipyards, and a director of the Hibernia National Bank.[3] He was also the "Queen Bee" of the New Orleans homosexual underground providing bail and legal representation to members of the gay community who were caught *en flagrante delicto.*[4] For example, when Shaw's lover and Army friend, J.B. Dauenhauer, was arrested in 1946 for committing an "unnatural act," police records show that Brent signed for his bond.[5]

If this pattern sounds familiar, it is because Shaw inherited this mantle after Brent's death in 1953.[6] Recall New Orleans attorney Dean Andrews' Warren Commission testimony that a Clay Bertrand would refer young gay men, in need of legal representation, to his office.[7] Andrews testified that on one occasion in the summer of 1963, Oswald appeared in his office accompanied by a group of "gay Mexicanos" and inquired about having his Marine discharge upgraded. Oswald subsequently visited Andrews to discuss initiating citizenship proceedings for his Russian wife, Marina. More importantly, Bertrand telephoned Andrews the day after the assassination and requested he go to Dallas and represent Oswald. As will be shown there can be little doubt that Shaw was Bertrand and, in fact, we will see the FBI knew of Shaw's use of this alias very early in their investigation.[8]

Getting back to Shaw's return to New Orleans, one of the first things Brent did was appoint Shaw to an executive position at the Mississippi Shipping Company.[9] In 1945, Brent, along with local financiers William Zetzmann, Herbert Schwartz, and Hibernia Bank chairman, Rudolph Hecht, chartered the International Trade Mart.[10] The ITM was a privately supported, non-profit organization established to encourage and promote trade (especially with Latin America) through the port of New Orleans. When the ITM opened its doors in 1948, Brent was its first president and Clay Shaw, its managing director - a post he held until his early retirement in 1965. It was also during this time that Shaw's long career with the CIA began - a career we will look at in detail in Chapter 14. The ITM's sister organization, the International House, was founded earlier and financed with Rockefeller money.[11] Herman C. Brock, the first managing director of International House, was associated with the Morgan family's Guaranty Trust Company of New York.[12] His successor was J. Stanton Robbins, a former assistant to Nelson Rockefeller at the Office of Inter-American Affairs.[13] On its board was Edmund Duane Wingfield, a vice-president of Freeport Sulphur and also a member of the New Orleans Board of Trade which worked closely with Shaw and the ITM.[14] The Rockefeller influence was pervasive at the ITM as well. The principal speaker at the Trade Mart's opening was William McChesney Martin, then a supervisor of the Rockefeller family's trust fund and later the Chairman of the Federal Reserve.[15]

From 1952 through 1955, Shaw employed as public relations director David Baldwin, a CIA operative, who served in India in the early 1950's and used the North American Newspaper Alliance as a cover for his operations.[16] Baldwin's replacement at ITM was Jesse Core, a Shaw loyalist who, not surprisingly, also had an intelligence background in India. In the recently declassified CIA files released between 1992 and 1993, I discovered a brief document on Core. It reads as follows:

CORE, Jesse R.

Chief Consul with USIS in the American Embassy in Madras in 1950, Is friend of David Baldwin former covert agent who was separated in Oct. '52 following serious security breach which involved a Mrs. Lillian Baxter of Calcutta, India, who was also known to subject.[17]

WDSU and the Sterns

In addition to Brent, Shaw was also close to the Stern family. Edith Rosenwald Stern was an heiress to the Sears and Roebuck fortune. Together with her husband Edgar, they owned New Orleans television station WDSU, the local NBC affiliate. In the wake of several police scandals, it was Edith Stern who lobbied New Orleans mayor deLesseps Morrison to bring from Chicago a former FBI man named Aaron Kohn and set him up as head of a citizens watchdog group called the Metropolitan Crime Commission.[18] As we will see, Kohn later led a smear campaign against Garrison, attempting to paint him with a Mafia brush. Suspiciously, prior to Garrison's conspiracy probe, Kohn had always lauded Garrison as a bulwark in the fight against organized crime.[19] In an article for *Back Channels* magazine, author Jim DiEugenio wrote that the "Sterns were good friends of Shaw and were strong supporters of him during the period of his arrest and trial. They promoted his cause by making their local NBC affiliate a media outpost for Shaw's defense and by sponsoring lavish parties for the incoming media representatives. WDSU also worked with long-time intelligence expert Walter Sheridan on the slanderous 1967 NBC special on the Garrison investigation."[20]

Alton Ochsner

By far, Shaw's most telling association was with Dr. Alton Ochsner. Ochsner, a close friend and associate of Shaw's, was in fact president of the ITM's sister organization, the International House. A photograph exists in the New Orleans Public Library showing Shaw and Ochsner conferring in Shaw's ITM office. In a brilliant and highly recommended article entitled, *Social Origins of Anticommunism: The Information Council of the Americas* (Louisiana History Magazine, Spring 1989), Dr. Arthur Carpenter writes:

> [Ochsner] was a celebrated surgeon, wealthy, socially prominent, and an old hand in Latin America... Ochsner's outlook was that of the radical right. He equated liberalism with socialism, thought the federal government infiltrated by leftists, and opposed the civil-rights movement... Further evidence of Ochsner's extremist views came when he endorsed *The Dispossessed Majority* by Wilmot Robertson. "One of the greatest books I have ever read," wrote Ochsner in a blurb

for this volume. What he admired was a frankly racist work. Robertson called upon citizens of Northern European extraction, the "dispossessed majority," to wrest control of the U.S. from usurping racial minorities. The majority's genetic superiority, he argued, justified such a course. .. Similarly, he proposed an American version of apartheid. These views did not make Ochsner a pariah. Indeed, he was one of New Orleans's most esteemed citizens. In the 1960's he was elected to the leadership of both International House and International Trade Mart, the city's chief trade-promotion organizations.[21]

In 1941 Ochsner, with help from Rudolph Hecht and the ubiquitous Ted Brent, formed the Ochsner Clinic.[22] The Ochsner Clinic specialized in catering to Latin American dictators and the ultra wealthy. Ochsner's more notable patients included the Somozas from Nicaragua, Argentina's Juan Peron, Guatemala's Miguel Ydigoras Fuentes and Dallas oil millionaire Clint Murchison.[23] And in the case of the Latin American dictators, the CIA invariably picked up the tab.[24] Ochsner himself was of operational interest to the CIA. A CIA memo from 1968 states that:

> Ochsner was a cleared source (Approved Caution) since 13 May 1955. He was used infrequently as a contact of our New Orleans office in the collection of intelligence information. Last official contact with Dr. Ochsner was on 8 January 1962. Last official contact with Ochsner Clinic was on 8 November 1963.[25]

Together with Brent, Ochsner funded William Gaudet's, *Latin American Reports*.[26] Gaudet published his weekly journal out of a virtually rent-free office at the International Trade Mart. The publication, which usually ran about four pages, was "a survey of political and economic conditions in Latin American countries." But Brent and Ochsner were not the only ones funding Gaudet. Released in 1993, formerly classified payment vouchers from the CIA detail a series of payments, starting in 1949, for Gaudet's services. Admiral Hillenkoetter - at that time Director of Central Intelligence – approved the payments and were contingent upon

Gaudet signing a secrecy agreement "to neither reveal nor exploit his CIA connection."[27] Indeed, Gaudet maintained his silence until a Canadian reporter and investigators from the House Select Committee on Assassinations found him in the late 1970's. In February of 1979, as the HSCA was preparing to release its final report, the Washington Post revealed that Gaudet "was a retired CIA operative who said publicly in a 1977 Canadian TV documentary that he saw Oswald and Guy Banister at a New Orleans garage close to Banister's office."[28] The Post article further states that, "According to a HSCA committee source "he [Gaudet] kept his mouth shut because that's what the agency procedure was. Plus he's paranoid and thought he was going to be killed. And probably more important, nobody ever asked him."" However, the HSCA had plenty they wanted to ask him. In September of 1963 Oswald applied for a tourist card at the Mexican Consulate in New Orleans. A few days later he was issued card No. 824085. After the assassination, the Mexican authorities provided the FBI with a list of all the other people who had applied for tourist cards on the same day as Oswald. Conspicuous in its absence was the name of the person who held card No. 824084, the one next to Oswald's. When the FBI provided this information to the Warren Commission, it inserted a note saying, "No record of FM 824084 located." In 1975, declassified FBI records revealed this to be a lie. The name of the holder was William Gaudet.[29] In 1978, Anthony Summers tracked down Gaudet and interviewed him. Gaudet insisted that he was a victim of coincidence and had no idea why his name was originally omitted from the list of applicants. However, he was quite candid with Summers concerning other matters. For instance, he admitted he had worked for the CIA for over twenty years, had seen Oswald with Banister (in fact Gaudet himself was an occasional visitor to Banister's offices) and that David Ferrie had associated with Oswald.[30]

Outside of New Orleans, Ochsner is best known for his association with Ed Butler and the Information Council of the Americas, or INCA. Ostensibly an anti-Communist propaganda mill, INCA was composed of several members of the New Orleans elite. These included William Zetzmann, Brent's successor as president of the ITM (the ITM was a donator of funds to INCA), as well as Eustis and William B. Reily.[31] The Reily family owned William B. Reily & Co., makers of Luzianne coffee. (It was at Reily's where Oswald found work as a machine greaser in the summer of 1963). INCA and Butler got a lot of mileage from a series of taped debates between Oswald, Butler, and Cuban exile Carlos Bringuier in August of 1963. INCA later released the debates as two LP record albums under the titles, *Oswald: Portrait in Red* and *Oswald Speaks*. Like Ochsner, Butler was also a CIA asset. A CIA memorandum states "Butler, Staff Director of INCA, is a contact of our New Orleans Office and the source of numerous reports."[32] Butler himself boasted of INCA's contacts with the CIA through Deputy Director, General Charles Cabell.[33]

After the arrest of Shaw, however, INCA ran for cover. Butler had all of the organization's files secured and flown to Los Angeles, where he had relocated. Butler reported back that "the records arrived in good order and I have put them under lock and key."[34] On the home front, Ochsner feared his own arrest. In the summer of 1967 he wrote to Butler that he had heard Garrison was preparing a number of arrests, including that of a doctor. "I wondered whether he might mean me," Ochsner wrote, "but did not think he did until Bill Helis, a good friend of mine, who knows Gurvich very well, called me and said Gurvich had told him it was I and he was going to have me arrested as an accessory to the fact."[35] However, Ochsner fought back. He assisted Aaron Kohn in his smear campaign against Garrison, which included sending a copy of Garrison's military medical records to a friend who was the publisher of the *Nashville Banner*.[36] The records, when quoted out of context, seem to indicate Garrison suffered from a host of psychological disorders. But a careful reading of the documents indicate otherwise. After Garrison's discharge from his first tour of duty in 1946, he began to be bothered by severe exhaustion. (Not surprising for someone who flew 35 sorties in an unarmed spotter plane into enemy territory, receiving flak or small arms fire on 5 of those missions. Garrison also helped liberate the Dachau concentration camp, witnessing first-hand the horrors of the holocaust. For his actions, Garrison was awarded the Air Medal and the Bronze Service Star. From Garrison's military record, 413th Field Artillery Group). After returning to active duty in July of 1951, Garrison was hospitalized for his symptoms. The examining doctor recommended discharge from the service for his "anxiety state," suggesting Garrison should collect 10% permanent disability. But Garrison would have none of it. He never applied for or collected his disability, and four years later enlisted in the National Guard. Garrison was up-front on his application and mentioned his previous discharge. Because of this, his record indicates that "Garrison's record had to be reviewed by the army surgeon general (the very top) because of previous disability. On April 19, 1955, the surgeon general of the army found him to be physically qualified for federal recognition in the national army. On April 22, 1955, he was given a waiver of history of separation from the army." The record further states that Garrison resigned from the National Guard on February 28, 1967. However, he asked to be transferred to the army reserve, making him eligible to be recalled to active duty. It appears from Garrison's personal records that he suspected he had suffered, during that time, from a physical condition known as Entamoeba histolytica. He saved an article which quoted former Peace Corps medical director, Dr. Richard A. Smith. Dr. Smith said, "The symptoms of this amebiasis can also be those of appendicitis, peptic ulcer, intestinal flu, or anemia. The anxiety and depression that the disease produces has led some amebiasis victims to seek psychiatric treatment for their physical troubles."

Finally, Ochsner's membership in reactionary organizations was not limited to INCA. In the minutes of a September 5, 1961 meeting of the American Institute for Freedom Project (yet another New Orleans far right group) is Ochsner's name on the list of members in attendance. Next to Ochsner's name is that of former FBI agent, militant anti-Communist and, as we have seen, Oswald associate - W. Guy Banister.[37]

Chapter Nine

~

The Cuban Problem

Woven into the crazy quilt of intrigue that was New Orleans in the early 1960's, was a common thread - Cuba. Castro's march out of the Sierra Maestra and into Havana in 1959 sent shock waves throughout the hemisphere. As Cuba edged leftward, thousands of disillusioned Cuban exiles landed on American shores with many settling in the large urban areas of the South, such as Miami, Dallas, and New Orleans. In March of 1960, President Eisenhower authorized the CIA to train and arm Cuban refugees to overthrow Castro. (As we have seen, much of the training was conducted in the areas around New Orleans, especially north of Lake Pontchartrain). Kennedy inherited this "Cuban problem" and gave the green light to the CIA's plan to invade Cuba in April of 1961. As summarized in the HSCA final report, "The debacle at the Bay of Pigs was not only a military tragedy for the anti-Castro Cuban exiles, but also a painful shattering of their confidence in the U.S. Government. The exile leaders claimed that the failure of the invasion was a result of the lack of promised air support, and for that they directly blamed President Kennedy." - a sentiment shared by the exiles' CIA handlers.[1]

The New Orleans business elite also grew anxious over the red menace ninety miles from American shores. As Arthur Carpenter notes:

> For much of the twentieth century, New Orleans business and political leaders tried to make their city the nations' center for Latin American business. The path to the city's modernization, they argued, traveled through Latin America. After World War II, local business organizations such as International House and International Trade Mart joined with city and state agencies to push the city along that path...By the 1950's New Orleans rested comfortably and profitably at one of the crossroads where North America exchanged its manufactured goods for Latin America's materials and foodstuffs. Latin American goods accounted for approximately 75 percent of the city's imports. Coffee, sugar, bananas, sisal, mahogany - almost all of which came from Latin America - flowed across its wharves in great abundance to be processed locally or shipped into the nation's domestic hinterland. Profiting from this trade were many of the city's leading firms and many of its prominent citizens...Eager to perpetuate and extend this lucrative hemispheric business, the New Orleans elite cultivated and drew close to Latin American rulers...Leading New Orleanians then used a fierce anticommunism to transmute those Latin American oligarchs into guardians of freedom and hemispheric security...These amicable and profitable Latin American relations, seemingly so durable, received an unsettling shock from the Cuban Revolution.[2]

Indeed Cuba accounted for almost 20 percent of the cities' imports.[3] 93 percent of New Orleans sugar imports came from Cuba.[4] What if other Latin American countries fell into the communist orbit? Brazil was the chief exporter of coffee to the Reily Co. Guatemala supplied the bananas for United Fruit. As

Carpenter notes, both countries were on politically shaky ground at the time.

Carpenter also writes in his essay that New Orleans had hopes of further industrialization via the processing of Cuban commodities:

> New York based Freeport Sulphur Company planned to mine nickel and cobalt in Cuba and then ship those minerals to Port Nickel in Plaquemines Parish, about twenty miles down river from New Orleans. There the company was constructing a refinery where an estimated 600 workers were to process the nickel and cobalt concentrates into metals. Production was scheduled to begin late in 1959. The revolution abruptly ended all of this.[5]

However, one of Freeport's directors, with the help of one of New Orleans' most prominent citizens, was not about to let this opportunity slip away. A 1968 report in Garrison's files indicates that in the early 1960's David Ferrie flew Charles A. Wight, a Freeport Sulphur director and vice-chairman of the board, together with Clay Shaw, to Cuba in a Freeport private plane. The purpose of the trip was to set up import of Cuba's nickel ore to a Canadian front corporation, which in turn would ship to the Braithwaite nickel plant. The partnership of Wight and Shaw had a financial interest in the plant and planned to get the ore through the Canadian front. (Canada had no trade restrictions with Cuba).[6] What sounds initially like a fanciful tale, takes on an air of credibility in light of a corroborating report Garrison had received a year earlier from an unrelated source. In 1967, Garrison investigator and New Orleans police detective Sal Scalia interviewed a former newscaster named Ken Elliott. Elliott stated he had information to offer Garrison but did not want any publicity. As an example Elliott stated "that Shaw and two other persons either purchased or attempted to purchase a nickel ore plant in Braithwaite, Louisiana after the company had closed because of the broken trade relations with Cuba. At this time,

David Ferrie flew Shaw and his two partners to Canada in an attempt to receive ore from Cuba through Canada."[7] This information seemed to have been common knowledge among some New Orleanians. In a report prepared by investigators for Shaw's defense team, both Dean Andrews and WDSU reporter, Richard Townley stated that "Clay Shaw is supposed to have had an investment in some kind of firm owned by David Ferrie."[8] While the particulars are somewhat skewed, it clearly suggests a reference to the Freeport venture.

In a separate report, a businessman and Cuban adventurer from Houston recalled how Wight approached him with an offer to assassinate Castro.[9] This is not surprising when one looks at the board of directors of Freeport Sulphur in the 1960's. In addition to Wight, the board is a virtual roll call of stone-age cold warriors. Admiral Arleigh Burke, Chief of Naval Operations under Eisenhower and Kennedy, had been one of the Joint Chiefs of Staff who had been closely involved in the military planning of the Bay of Pigs invasion. In fact, shortly after Castro came into power, Burke was advocating not only the assassination of Fidel Castro but his brother Raoul and Che' Guevarra as well.[10] Also on the board was Robert Lovett, Assistant Secretary of War 1941-1945, Deputy Secretary of Defense, and Secretary of Defense in 1950. In March of 1950, Lovett advocated an all-out, "preventive" war with Russia, telling the National Security Council staff that the cold war "is not a cold war. It is a hot war. The U.S. has to start acting as though we were under fire from an invading army. In the war in which we are presently engaged, we should fight with no holds barred."[11] After the 1960 election, Kennedy tapped Lovett to be his Secretary of Defense. Lovett refused, due to ill health, but recommended one of his peers from the Council of Foreign Relations - Robert McNamara.[12] Other board members were also either closely associated with, or members of the Rockefeller family.[13] In fact, Freeport was headed by John Jay "Jock" Whitney, a multi-millionaire with a history of using corporate institutions for covert purposes.[14] During World War II, Whitney was in charge of propaganda for the Rockefeller-controlled Office of the Coordinator of Inter-American Affairs.[15] Whitney was also second cousin to Tracy Barnes, the head of the CIA's infamous Domestic Operations Division.[16] As we saw in a previous chapter, Barnes was an early suspect in Garrison's investigation. Freeport's desire to eliminate Castro stems directly from the nickel mining venture that Shaw is later involved with. In order to mine the nickel in Cuba and bring it to the Braithwaite plant, Freeport set up a wholly owned subsidiary called the Moa Bay Mining Company. On June 26, 1958 Raul Castro's Second Front rebels attacked the Moa Bay Mining Company and took twelve hostages.[17] All twelve were shortly released unharmed by order of Raul's brother, Fidel. However, after Castro gained power, Cuban nationalization forced the closure of Moa Bay Mining. During its tenure in Cuba, Moa Bay had offices in downtown Havana. Former Alpha 66 leader, Antonio Veciana recalled receiving his CIA training in an office in Havana associated with a mining company.[18] Recall that Veciana worked closely with his CIA officer, "Maurice Bishop," an alias believed to be used by David Atlee Phillips. When the HSCA showed interviewee James Cogswell III a sketch of Bishop/Phillips, he remarked that the sketch resembled a former president of Moa Bay/Freeport Sulphur.[19] He couldn't recall the name but said that he had very powerful connections and came from Texas.[20] Phillips, who came from Texas, often adopted corporate covers while engaging in covert activities and also had an office in Havana.[21]

In light of this, it is also interesting to note the recollections of Jules Ricco Kimble. In 1967 when Garrison took Kimble's statement he recalled that one night in late 1960 or early 1961 he and David Ferrie were drinking at a French Quarter bar named the Golden Lantern (Kimble and Ferrie had known each other for about a year). That night Ferrie introduced Kimble to Clay Shaw and the three of them remained at the bar for several hours. From that time on, Kimble would see Shaw on various occasions at bars or at the ITM. Kimble had in fact heard Shaw being introduced to others as Clay Bertrand. Almost a year later, Ferrie contacted Kimble and asked if he would like to accompany him on an overnight plane trip. Kimble agreed and met Ferrie at the airport, along with a second passenger, Clay Shaw. At this time Kimble learned that his destination was Canada, where they were to pick up another passenger. Along the way Kimble remembered Shaw sitting in the back of the plane, either sleeping or reading a book. When the plane landed in Montreal, Shaw disappeared and Ferrie and Kimble stayed overnight in a hotel in nearby Dorval. The next morning Shaw returned to the plane accompanied by a Mexican or Cuban described as heavy set, 30ish, with a dark complexion. During the return flight, Shaw and the Latin man sat together in the back of the plane. When they arrived back at Lakefront Airport, Kimble left in his car, as Ferrie, Shaw, and the passenger left together in a second car.[22] Shaw's trip to Canada remains an anomaly. Shaw normally eschewed air travel, supposedly because of a fear of flying. In light of the Freeport Sulphur venture, it is not unreasonable to assume that Shaw's Canadian sojourn was somehow connected to Freeport business.

Shaw's Cuban fellow traveler is also an intriguing sidelight. Government records indicate Shaw had an active interest in the plight of prisoners of Castro's Cuba. Take for example the case of Leslie Norman Bradley, a soldier-of-fortune and free-lance pilot who would often fly out of Lakefront Airport. According to CIA memoranda he was once considered for employment as a pilot in Project ZR/CLIFF, but for unknown reasons the offer of employment was withdrawn.[23] In 1959 Bradley teamed with Loran Eugene Hall, John Wilson Hudson, and others to provoke an incident in Nicaragua designed to make it appear Castro was exporting his revolution. The plot was ultimately stopped by Cuban intelligence and many of the principals were jailed, including Bradley and Hall. Both were released a short time later after a top Castro aide, Camillo Cienfuegos, interceded on their behalf.[24] When Bradley returned to the States, the CIA used him as a pilot for one of their proprietaries, Southern Air Transport.[25] While working out of the Houston airport, Bradley renewed his acquaintance with a local man named Sam Kauffroth. In 1966, Kauffroth furnished the following information to the Houston office of the FBI:

> I asked him [Bradley] how he had been making a living since being released from the Cuban prison and he replied that it was pretty rough but that Clay Shaw of the International House was "helping us." He never did clarify who "us" were, but I assumed that he meant the released prisoners. I distinctly recall that I was impressed with the philanthropic activities of this prominent citizen who took the time and trouble to assist these victims of Castro. There was no further discussion on the manner in which Mr. Shaw was helping.[26]

It appears Bradley was not only familiar with Clay Shaw, but David Ferrie as well. According to one of Ferrie's associates, Ferrie used to fly a Douglas 553 for a company called South Central Airlines.[27] Ostensibly, Ferrie flew chickens to Texas, making stops in Monterrey and Mexico City. While in Texas, Ferrie would keep the plane with Bradley and his company.[28] Since Bradley was working for a CIA proprietary, it appears Ferrie was enjoying the CIA's hospitality, not only in New Orleans and Miami, but Texas as well.

In New Orleans, Shaw was frequently seen in the company of Cubans. New Orleans documentary filmmaker, Steve Tyler, told the author of an interview he conducted with a local woman who in the early 1960's was a young New Orleans socialite. She recalled that in the course of attending many of the local social functions (dinners, parties, etc.) she would frequently see Shaw at these affairs, always in the company of well-heeled Cuban exiles. As the evenings wore on and the booze started flowing, the talk inevitably turned to ways of "getting rid of" Castro.[29] According to Tyler's source, one of Shaw's frequent companions was Alberto Fowler. Fowler was a former member of the Cuban invasion team, Brigade 2506 and, like Leslie Bradley, was detained in a Cuban prison. He was released in 1962 and returned to the United States. Fowler later became Director of International Relations for the City of New Orleans and had an office in the ITM. For three months in 1966, Fowler lived in Clay Shaw's house.[30] Fowler's activities in this case are suspicious at best. Immediately after the assassination, he phoned Washington and asked that NBC be notified that Oswald had been filmed passing out pro-Castro leaflets. Fowler later shows up on the board of INCA. His brother-in-law Chico Pipes (also seen with Shaw by Tyler's source) was a close friend of Lloyd Ray, CIA chief of the New Orleans office.[31] Dubiously, Fowler was a temporary investigator for Jim Garrison during his assassination probe.

In late 1966 Assistant DA Andrew Sciambra interviewed Mrs. Carlos Marquez, widow of the former Cuban consul in New Orleans. The consulate had occupied an office in the International Trade Mart, and Mrs. Marquez remembered Shaw as a man who was sympathetic to the anti-Castro cause. In fact, Shaw allowed the consulate rent-free space for several months.[32] Mrs. Marquez also recalled Oswald. She had watched him pass out leaflets in front of the ITM. Then a few days later, she noticed Oswald again, this time walking through the lobby of the Mart.[33]

Shaw's empathy toward the anti-Castro Cuban community may help to explain his membership (with Ochsner) in the Foreign Policy Association. Founded with Rockefeller money, it was the FPA that invited CIA deputy director Charles Cabell to address their group at the International House in late April of 1961. Cabell was one of the high-level planners of the abortive Bay of Pigs invasion who was later fired by President Kennedy.[34] As we saw in Chapter 8, Cabell was also a contact of INCA's Ed Butler. Shaw, as program director of the FPA, personally introduced Cabell at this affair.[35]

The Girnus Allegations

In the summer of 1967, Garrison's office received an anonymous letter from the U.S. Penitentiary in Atlanta, Georgia advising them:

If you would like to place Shaw as Bertrand and Lambert and pickup information concerning Sanchez Diaz, see and talk to Edward Girnus, U.S.P., Atlanta, Ga.

Signed,

Interested and Concerned

A subsequent letter (also anonymous), postmarked Albuquerque and written in a different hand, informed the D.A.'s office that:

If you want information that will definately [sic] connect Shaw and Oswald you should talk to a convict in the U.S. prison at Atlanta, Ga. His name is Gooch Gurinsen [sic] and he works as a clerk in the business office of the prison and is serving time for bank robbery. He has pictures of him and Oswald and some other man took in Mexico City and says he knows Shaw. He laughs about it all the time.

After an exchange of correspondence, assistant D.A. James Alcock, met with Girnus at the Atlanta pen on December 7th. Girnus, who had a diverse 30 year history of criminal activity, laid out a provocative story to Garrison's investigators.[36]

Sometime in April or May of 1963, Girnus was living in Dallas, Texas and through his association with some local strippers, met an acquaintance of Jack Ruby's. Ruby's friend was associated with a rabid right-wing group with access to large amounts of money that they wanted to invest in a gun running operation. Girnus also claimed involvement with a para-military group known as the Democratic Club and was brokering weapons deals with them as well. During the course of his gun running ventures, Girnus made several trips to New Orleans. It was on one of these trips in May or June of 1963 that Girnus met Clay Shaw.

According to Girnus, he was introduced to Shaw at the Alpine Restaurant by a man who owned an apartment house on Exchange Alley. During the course of the conversation, Shaw invited Girnus to his home in Hammond, Louisiana, presumably to further discuss Girnus' gun-running activities. [Shaw did indeed have a home in Hammond.] Girnus didn't make it to Hammond, but met with Shaw about a week later in a downtown office near the Sears Roebuck building. Shaw told Girnus that he knew some people who were interested in buying some guns. Shaw made a telephone call and a short time later two men joined the meeting. According to Girnus, one of the men was Lee Harvey Oswald, who was introduced to Girnus as Lee. Girnus could not remember the name of the other man, but described him as 5' 11", 210 pounds, dark black hair and well dressed in a business suit. The ensuing conversation centered primarily on the living conditions in Central and South America.

At this point in his narrative, Girnus abruptly ended his interview with Alcock, telling the D.A. that he felt they were being bugged and that if they continued he could "get himself into a storm." He told Alcock that he would have someone in Atlanta send him a picture of Oswald and an unidentified person taken in Mexico. Additionally, Girnus was to send an FAA flight plan which he said would be self-explanatory.

As the interview ended, Alcock was able to elicit a few more facts. Girnus added that the last time he saw Oswald was when he drove him to Catulla, Texas in September of 1963. Girnus introduced Oswald to a friend of his who was an ex-Mexican army man. Oswald and Girnus' friend went into Mexico through Laredo, Texas. Their trip had something to do with getting Oswald a passport. [Oswald did indeed travel to Mexico City in late September and attempted to obtain a Cuban visa, but evidence indicates he (or someone impersonating him) traveled there by bus.]

In addition, Girnus said he later attended several parties where Shaw was present. At least one of them was at the Shaw home in Hammond. Supposedly, Oswald was at this particular party.

It is not known if Garrison's office ever received the Oswald photograph, but they did obtain the FAA flight plan.[37] The flight plan itself is a provocative document. It details an April 6,

1963 flight from Hammond, Louisiana to Garland, Texas. Written by someone with an obvious knowledge of planes, the document lists the captain as D. Ferrie and three passengers named, Diaz, Lambert, and Hidell. According to Girnus, Diaz was an anti-Castro Cuban, Lambert was an alias of Clay Shaw's and of course Hidell is the now-famous alias of Lee Harvey Oswald. Because much of Girnus' story does not jibe with the known timeline of events, it appears no follow-up was conducted, despite Garrison's handwritten instructions to his staff to do so. The House Select Committee received the flight plan in 1977 but seemed to do little with it other than to show it to Garrison who barely remembered it. This author tried to track Girnus down and got as far as his son. Edward Joseph Girnus told me his father had left home when he was ten years old and had only talked to him once or twice after he left. He never spoke to him about Oswald, the assassination, Garrison, etc. The son knew of Girnus' criminal career and it was quite clear that the lack of contact with his father suited him fine. The last time Edward, Jr. heard of his father was twenty years ago, when Girnus was sentenced to another stretch in the penitentiary.[38]

The shameful lack of follow-up by the HSCA is unfortunate but typical of the direction Chief Counsel Robert Blakey took the Committee.[39] For now Girnus' story must remain a tantalizing, but uncorroborated lead.

Shaw and Banister

As we have seen, one of the leaders of the New Orleans anti-Castro crusade was the late Guy Banister. He, along with David Ferrie, were both rabid anticommunists with connections to the intelligence community and the anti-Castro movement. As noted, both Banister and Ferrie are indelibly connected to Oswald. However, a couple of points are worth adding here. Banister operative Joe Newbrough recounted to the author an incident that took place in the early 1960's. Banister and Ferrie were meeting in

Banister's office, when Banister asked Newbrough to get Clay Shaw on the phone. Newbrough called the ITM and reached Shaw. Banister told Newbrough to hand the phone to Ferrie, whereby Ferrie and Shaw proceeded to confer with each other.[40] In another incident, former New Orleans States-Item crime reporter, Jack Dempsey (who as stated previously, originally broke the story on the Garrison probe) recalled to me that his friend, the late Jules Fontana, a lawyer from Metairie, had told him he had seen Banister in Shaw's office on numerous occasions.[41] Banister agent Dan Campbell has revealed that Shaw was involved with Banister in a gun running operation to the Alpha 66 exiles in Miami.[42] New evidence seems to support allegations of Shaw's interest in gun-running. A CIA document reports that Shaw and his ITM associate Mario Bermudez traveled together to Cuba in 1959 on a gun-smuggling operation.[43]

Considering Shaw's activities with the Cuban exiles and his associations with Cabell, Banister, and Ferrie, it is hardly surprising that the HSCA's New Orleans investigative team was led to conclude that Shaw was "heavily involved in the anti-Castro efforts in New Orleans in the 1960's."[44]

Chapter Ten

~

PERMINDEX:
Trade Organization or Assassination Bureau?

On December 28, 1956 a press conference was held in the town of Basel, Switzerland. The purpose of the conference was to announce that an "association of American finance companies" was proposing to finance a projected "permanent industrial exhibition" in the city. Known as PERMINDEX, the project was to include a 13 floor office building, an exhibition building, and a 15 floor hotel with 200 rooms. The spokesman for this occasion was a curious choice to represent an association of American finance companies. Ferenc Nagy had been living in America for just nine years, having fled his native Hungary as the Soviets were taking control. Nagy had good reason to flee - he was Hungary's Prime Minister and a devout anticommunist. (He was at one time the erstwhile leader of something called the Anticommunist Countryman's Party). So when Nagy returned to Europe in 1956 to make his announcement, he raised more than a few eyebrows - not the least of whom was the State Department. Between 1956 and 1958, the American Consulate closely monitored PERMINDEX' evolution and cabled dispatches back to the State Department on a regular basis.[1] Nagy's background, combined with the fact that the local investment house associated with the project was considered "second-rate" prompted the Consulate to obtain additional information concerning PERMINDEX. When the American Consul interviewed Nagy and the purported local financier, Hans Seligman, he found the pair to be overly cautious in not divulging the identities of firms financing the project. Their reticence was understandable. Seligman had a reputation of cooperating with the fascists during World War II.[2] In addition, the Seligman financial houses were closely linked to CIA Director Allen Dulles' law firm, Sullivan and Cromwell.[3] More importantly, the Consulate learned, in confidence, that the principal financial source of PERMINDEX was the J. Henry Schroder Banking Corporation. Jim DiEugenio writes in *Destiny Betrayed*, "When [Allen] Dulles's law firm - Sullivan and Cromwell - was still dealing with the Nazis in the late 1930's, the bank he used was Schroder's. When Dulles became DCI, the same bank was a repository for a $50 million contingency fund he controlled. Schroder was a welcome conduit because his bank benefited from the CIA coups in Iran (1953) and Guatemala (1954)."[4] Author Burton Hersh further revealed that the "J Henry Schroder Banking Corporation and the Schroder Trust functioned as prime depositories for CIA monies throughout the fifties and sixties...Like the Kaplan Foundation and a half a dozen others which ultimately served as conduits between the accumulating fronts and the proliferation of committees and congresses and institutes and societies, the banking nexus depended on how many layers of concealment an operation might require. Schroder dealt with sensitive cases, although "There were certainly no biases in that matter," Richard Helms concludes. "Hell, the Agency sloshed money all over the world.""[5] Prior to his role as DCI, Allen Dulles was Schroder's General Counsel. Hersh notes that "the influential Schroder investment banking houses in New York and London remained affiliated, through blood and commercial ties, with descendants of "die Gebruder Schroeder." They included - emphatically - Baron Kurt von Schroeder, Heinrich Himmler's "special angel."[6] In just a little over a month after the original announcement, all references to the "American finance companies" were dropped and the State Department cables were now referring to Nagy's project as the PERMINDEX "scheme."[7]

The addition of George Mandel to the project again started the wires humming between Basel and Washington. A close friend of Nagy, Mandel was a Jewish refugee from Hungary who escaped his country and obtained citizenship in El Salvador. Once there, he engaged in the wartime Jewish refugee racket, extorting money from Jews fleeing the Nazi yoke. He was once expelled from Switzerland for illegal dealings in gold, but was subsequently granted permission to return.[8]

For the next year, the project stalled as public suspicion grew and the local press attacked the integrity of the sponsors and the viability of the project itself. It was also revealed at this time that the New Orleans International Trade Mart afforded the model for PERMINDEX and that a certain Mr. Shaw from the New Orleans Trade Mart has "from the outset great interest in the PERMINDEX project."[9]

The Move to Italy

During the spring and summer months of 1958, Nagy began making overtures to the Italian government to allow PERMINDEX to relocate to Rome. On October 22, 1958, Nagy called his second introductory press conference in as many years. A November 7, 1958 State Department cable summarizes the announcement:

It appears PERMINDEX has formed an affiliate called the Rome World Trade Center (CENTRO MONDIALE COMMERCIALE deROMA) and has leased 37,000 square meters of floor space in buildings of the Italian government originally built for the 1942 Rome World Exhibition... An American, Mr. CLAY SHAW, Managing Director of the INTERNATIONAL TRADE MART of NEW ORLEANS, has been named to the Board of Directors of the Roman affiliate which the news reports said, has been incorporated with a capital stock of 100 million lire... The appearance of Clay Shaw of the New Orleans trade mart as a member of the board of the Roman affiliate recalls the visit to New Orleans in 1957 of a Basel Kantonal Traffic Control Study Group, which included Fritz BRECHTBUHL, Kantonal Councilor in charge of Police, a strong advocate of PERMINDEX during its efforts to establish itself here. The Trade Mart is said to have furnished the model on which PERMINDEX bases itself.[10] [Author's note: The last 3 1/2 lines of this paragraph have been redacted.]

In addition to Shaw, the new board of directors was comprised of the same PERMINDEX bunch (Seligman, Mandel, Nagy) as well as several Italians who can best be described as neo-fascists. These included a former member of Mussolini's cabinet as well as the son-in-law of Hjalmar Schact, financial guru of the Third Reich and convicted war criminal. Others on the board were, as author DiEugenio points out, "a small cross-section of the aging royalists with whom Shaw liked to hobnob on his European jaunts and whose names and phone numbers were kept in his address book."[11]

The Italian periodicals *Paesa Sera* and *De La Sera* both ran a series of articles on the CMC and Shaw in 1967, raising the possibility that the CMC was "a creature of the CIA." The Canadian newspaper *Le Devoir* also ran a similar expose' around the same time.[12]

The credibility and the accuracy of the reporting of the above mentioned journals has come into question. However, one newspaper, that enjoys a better reputation, reportedly published an expose' linking PERMINDEX with the assassination attempts on French President, Charles deGaulle. In the spring of 1962, *Les Echos* (the French equivalent of the *Wall Street Journal*) ran several news and editorial reports of deGaulle's accusations of PERMINDEX involvement in many of the attempts on his life.[13] (Since I have not seen the newspaper articles in question, I cannot comment directly on the veracity of the report). However, it seems quite clear that there was a link between PERMINDEX and the French assassination attempts.

The OAS Connection

Ferenc Nagy was a close friend and supporter of one Jacques Soustelle.[14] A former deGaulle propaganda chief, Soustelle eventually broke with the general over his Algerian policy. Soustelle became a leader of the French OAS, the Secret Army Organization led by former French generals who were violently opposed to deGaulle's policy of Algerian independence. DeGaulle had appointed Soustelle Governor-General of Algeria in the 1950's. When it became clear the French president had no intention of keeping Algeria French, Soustelle went public with his disagreement. He even tried to drum-up support from the CIA. In the early 1960's, Soustelle traveled to Washington and, over lunch, met with CIA officials including Richard Bissell, then Deputy Director of Plans and a key planner in the CIA/Mafia plots to kill Castro. The *New York Times* reported that the cause celebre lunch had been given by the Agency for Soustelle. Soustelle convinced the CIA that "Algeria would become, through deGaulle's blundering, a Soviet base."[15] Soustelle must have indeed been convincing. In 1975, as news of the Church Committee findings was being revealed, the *Chicago Tribune* ran a page one article which read in part:

> Congressional leaders have been told of Central Intelligence Agency involvement in a plot by French Dissidents to assassinate the late French President, Charles deGaulle.[16]

Soustelle fled into exile in 1962 after being implicated in the deGaulle assassination plots. After being pardoned in 1968, Soustelle abandoned politics and returned to his first love - archaeology.

After five years of controversy, the Italians, like the Swiss, had had enough. CMC/PERMINDEX was forced to relocate again, this time to more accommodating environs in Johannesburg, South Africa.

One final point should be made before leaving this subject. In the 1963/1964 edition of *Who's Who in the Southwest* Clay Shaw lists his position on the board of PERMINDEX/CMC in his biography, the last year that he does so. This coincides approximately with the end of CMC's existence in Rome. All told, Shaw's time with the project was about five years. Coincidentally, in 1967, a Garrison informant reported that New Orleans FBI agent, Regis Kennedy had confirmed that "Shaw was a CIA agent who had done work, of an unspecified nature, over a five year span in Italy."[17]

Chapter Eleven

~

East Louisiana Intrigue

On a Wednesday afternoon in late August of 1963 the weather had cooled a bit and Jackson, Louisiana town barber Ed McGehee was taking advantage of it.[1] McGehee shut off his air conditioner and opened the front door to his shop. As he was relaxing in his barber chair, he heard the sounds of a car pulling up and a car door shutting. Although he couldn't see the car, as it had parked just outside his line of sight, almost immediately a young man walked through the doorway and requested a haircut - a young man McGehee would later identify as Lee Harvey Oswald. "A barbershop is a good place for a haircut and information," Oswald said as McGehee started to clip his hair. Oswald asked if there were any jobs available in Jackson. "Well, there are very slim pickens," McGehee said, "All we've got is the hospital which is a mental hospital." (The hospital McGehee is referring to is the East Louisiana State Hospital. Recall from Chapter Five that the East Louisiana State Hospital was where Rose Cheramie made her prophetic statement about Kennedy's death). Oswald queried the barber further, "Do they have all kinds of jobs over there? Such as an electrician job?" After assuring Oswald that there were indeed electrician jobs at the hospital, McGehee referred Oswald to State Representative, Reeves Morgan, who he thought might help in Oswald's quest for employment. He also thought, mistakenly as it turned out, that it would benefit Oswald if he were a registered voter in the parish, and directed him to the Registrar of Voters in the nearby town of Clinton. As Oswald left the shop, McGehee turned his back to wash his hands. As he turned back around, he noticed the car that had arrived just prior to Oswald's appearance, had also left.[2]

Reeves Morgan took notice of the chill in the air that evening and was burning some trash in the fireplace in his front parlor.[3] Morgan didn't receive many visitors to his modest home in rural Jackson. The fact that there was no taxi service or bus routes to his home may have had a lot to do with that. So he would remember well the evening when he saw a car's headlights beaming up his driveway, followed shortly by a knock at his door. When Morgan opened the door the visitor introduced himself as Lee Oswald and asked Morgan if he could assist him in obtaining work as an electrician at the State Hospital. Morgan informed Oswald that he could not help him obtain a job ahead of his constituents, but he did advise him that he would have to take a Civil Service exam and that if he were a registered voter it would give him some extra points on his exam.

After their conversation, Oswald left and Morgan heard the car drive off. A few days after Oswald's visit, Morgan spoke to a Mr. Gremillion, the business manager at the hospital. Gremillion told Morgan that although the hospital budget wouldn't allow him to fill the job at that time, there was indeed an opening for an electrician. After the assassination, Morgan would recognize the accused assassin as his visitor, and contacted the Baton Rouge office of the FBI. The agent who spoke to Morgan thanked him but said, "We already know he has been up in those parts," and ended the conversation. However, several days later, Morgan received a call from someone identifying himself as FBI. Inexplicably, the caller asked only for a description of the clothes Oswald was wearing.[4]

A Memorable Appearance

The next morning found the sidewalks of Clinton lined with local African-American citizens as a voter registration drive sponsored by the Congress of Racial Equality was in full swing. Tensions had escalated recently in this small town, as reflected in the headlines from the Baton Rouge States Times: August 8, 1963, "CORE Worker From New York Held in Clinton;" August 9, 1963, "CORE Members Appear Before Judge;" August 10, 1963, "CORE Worker Seeks To Quash Charges;" August 16, 1963, "Trial of CORE Man in Clinton Postponed;" August 22, 1963, "Tension May Be Receding in Clinton." With such a heightened sense of awareness amongst the townspeople, it is not surprising that a large number of residents took notice of the black Cadillac and its occupants as it pulled into town and parked across the street from the Registrar's office on St. Helena Street.[5] The chairman of the Clinton chapter of CORE, Corrie Collins, was monitoring the drive outside the Registrar's office, when at approximately 10:00 a.m. he noticed the arrival of the car. Thinking they might be FBI, Collins studied the car and its occupants closely. As the car came to a stop, he observed a young white male exit the rear of the car and enter the registration line, while the driver and the other passenger remained in the car. Later, under oath, at the trial of Clay Shaw in 1969 and in his testimony to the House Select Committee on Assassinations (HSCA) in 1978, Collins would identify the driver of the car as Clay Shaw, the passenger as David

Ferrie, and the person in the registration line as Lee Harvey Oswald.[6]

William Dunn, a local farmer and CORE volunteer, would soon join Collins on the sidewalk. He too would testify before the same two investigative bodies, corroborating in full Collins' statements.[7]

Henry Earl Palmer[8] opened his Registrar's office at 8:30 a.m. that morning just as he did every morning that the office was in operation, which at the time was just two and a half days a week: Thursday, Friday, and Saturday morning. By 10:30 he decided it was time for a coffee break and he walked down the stairs from his second floor office, past the line of waiting applicants, and out into the street. He couldn't help noticing Oswald sticking out like a sore thumb, the only white man in a long line of blacks.[9] The second thing that caught his eye was CORE worker Collins eyeing the black Cadillac. As Palmer was purchasing his coffee, one of his companions needled him, saying, "The Feds are watching you." "What do you mean?" asked Palmer. "The black Cadillac, those two men over there." Palmer's coffee shop buddies weren't the only ones who would remember the black car that day. Clinton resident Charlotte Greenup later recalled that "The black Cadillac stayed there for hours and hours."[10] James Bell, a teenage CORE volunteer, when asked later why he would remember the car, replied, "When you're working with CORE, you begin to try to read people and automobiles as fast as you can."[11] Robert Thomas recalled seeing the car with "white men in it."[12] Eddie Lee Spears remembered seeing a black car in Clinton with three white men sitting in the car.[13] Henry Burnell Clark, a twenty-nine year old grocery clerk, stated in an affidavit filed on September 12, 1967, "I stepped out on the sidewalk in front of the Stewart and Carroll store, where I worked, shortly before the noon hour, and saw, coming from the direction of the bank, east of the store, and walking in a westerly direction toward me, a tall man in a dark business suit... He approached facing me, to a distance of about ten or twelve feet from me, and stepped off into the street. He crossed the street and entered a black automobile which had been parked at the curb." From a series of photos, Clark picked out Clay Shaw as the man that he saw. Clark particularly remembered him because, "He reminded me of a movie actor I remembered seeing on the screen, and because he was unusually tall, standing well over six feet."[14] (Shaw, who measured six feet, four inches, did indeed bear a resemblance to actor, Jeff Chandler). He also noticed a stranger using the pay phone that day. He remembered this individual because of his "unusual hair" which "stood up all directions on his head." Clark picked out a photo of David Ferrie as resembling this individual.[15]

With Palmer's curiosity sufficiently aroused, he approached the town Marshall, John Manchester and requested he get a "1028" or license number check on the car. What happened next must have been deemed so potentially explosive, the HSCA felt compelled to take Manchester's testimony in Washington, D.C. in Executive Session, the only Clinton witness required to do so. On March 14, 1978, in Room 2237 of the Rayburn House Office Building, the following exchange took place between Manchester and staff counsel, Jonathan Blackmer:

Blackmer: When Mr. Palmer drew your attention to the car, what, if anything, did you then do?

Manchester: I walked over, and as I would, or any police officer would do, I just checked the car out and I walked over and asked the driver would he please identify himself. He gave me his driver's license, and I looked at his driver's license and I asked him what his business was in town. He told me he was a representative of the International Trade Mart in New Orleans. This meant nothing to me, and I didn't even know what the International Trade Mart was. I asked him was he there - I believe I asked him was he there with the voter registration drive, and he told me he had nothing to do with anything going on in town; any of the activities. I talked with the gentleman a few minutes and passed the time of day with him, and he satisfied my curiosity as to why he was there and he wasn't any part of this, or he wasn't there to cause a disturbance, in other words, and so that is as far as it went. He satisfied my reason for checking him out.

Blackmer: The driver of the car identified himself, did he not, sir?

Manchester: Yes sir, he did.

Blackmer: What name did he give you?

Manchester: He gave Clay Shaw, which corresponded with his driver's license.[16]

Manchester would also identify the passenger as David Ferrie. Manchester reported back to Palmer what he had found out. Palmer testified before the HSCA that "[Manchester] had told me he had gone over and talked to the people in the car, and they were not federal men; that the man was a representative of the International Trade Mart in New Orleans, and I said, "What is he doing here?" He said, "Trying to sell bananas, I guess," and laughed. After that I paid no more attention to the car.""[17]

But Palmer did pay attention to the young white man who waited patiently in line all day. After taking his afternoon break at about 3:30 (and again noting the black Cadillac parked outside), Palmer once again set about processing applicants, when he eventually came to Oswald. Palmer asked for identification and Oswald produced what Palmer described as "a separation paper from the Marine Corps, and it had the address on it, 10-something Camp Street, New Orleans. So I asked him where he lived. He told me he lived at the East Feliciana State Hospital [sic]. And I asked him who he lived with. He told me - I'm not positive about this name - but I think he said, Doctor Pierson." (There is some ambiguity about the name of Oswald's mysterious doctor. Dick Billings, who at the time was a reporter for LIFE magazine, wrote in a journal he kept of the Garrison investigation that, "It was determined by Garrison investigator Lynn Loisel, that Oswald stated that he was living with a Cuban doctor, Frank Silva."[18] Cuban born and from a well-to-do family, Silva was actually on the payroll of Tulane University. The HSCA took these allegations seriously and subpoenaed the hospital for a listing of the medical staff who were employed there in 1963. Ironically, both a Dr. Malcom Pierson and a Dr. Francisco Silva were listed in the records.)[19] Palmer then asked Oswald why he wanted to register and Oswald told him that he wanted a job at the hospital and was advised that he would have a better chance of getting the job if he were a registered voter. Palmer assured him that wasn't the case. "In fact you don't need to be registered at all to get a job at the hospital," Palmer said. "I know people out of Mississippi that are working at Jackson." Oswald thanked him and walked outside and into the back seat of the waiting Cadillac - all duly noted by town Marshall Manchester.

When Palmer closed up at 6:00 that evening, he stopped by the local drugstore. The clerk, Gloria Wilson, standing in the door, noted, "Mr. Palmer, your CORE workers are riding in better cars than you." Palmer asked, "What do you mean?" The clerk answered, "Well that boy that stood in line all day with those Negroes got in the black Cadillac and left with those two men sitting here all day."[20] Again, it should be noted here that throughout the day as Palmer took his lunch and coffee breaks he would study the Cadillac. At the Clay Shaw trial and before the HSCA, Palmer would identify Shaw and Ferrie as the occupants of the car.

Many researchers, subsequently writing about this incident, have tried to build a case for Guy Banister as the driver of the black Cadillac and some have also proposed that Oswald's presence in Clinton was an attempted penetration of CORE in support of the FBI's COINTELPRO operation.[21] One problem with this theory is that the FBI's COINTELPRO against the black liberation movement was not formally initiated until the issuance of J. Edgar Hoover's August 25, 1967 memo, which specifically targeted CORE and other black nationalist organizations.[22] The other problem with this hypothesis (and it's a big one) is that Clinton witness Henry Earl Palmer was personally acquainted with Banister. When Palmer was shown a photograph of Guy Banister by assistant D.A. Andrew Sciambra, at the Shaw trial, he was asked:

Sciambra: Do you know who the individual in that picture is?

Palmer: Yes, I do.

Sciambra: Who is it?

Palmer: Mr. Banister.

Sciambra: Where do you know Mr. Banister from?

Palmer: I knew Mr. Banister in the service in World War II.

Sciambra: Is there any possibility that Mr. Banister could have been the person in that automobile?

Palmer: I am sure I would have known Mr. Banister if I had seen him.[23]

Further information on this point was elicited by HSCA counsel Blackmer during this exchange from Palmer's deposition:

Blackmer: Have you seen Guy Banister any time after 1943?

Palmer: I saw Guy one time at the Legislature down here, it must have been either - I think it was in 1960 I run into him in the Legislature.

Blackmer: And you recognized him?

Palmer: Oh yes, I knew him.

Blackmer: Did you see anyone who resembled Guy Banister in that black Cadillac parked across the street from your office?

Palmer: I couldn't say that anybody who looked like Guy Banister was in that car.

Blackmer: Had Guy Banister been in that car, did you get a good enough look at the car that you would have recognized him?

Palmer: I would have recognized Guy Banister. I knew Guy well enough that I would have recognized him.[24]

Even HSCA Chief Counsel, G. Robert Blakey, knew he was backed into a corner on this point and didn't even attempt to place Banister in Clinton in the HSCA final report. However, he tried to soft peddle Shaw's presence there with this bit of sophistry from the final report: "The committee found that the Clinton witnesses were credible and significant...It was the judgment of the committee that they were telling the truth as they knew it...If the witnesses were not only truthful but accurate as well in their accounts they established an association of an undetermined nature between Ferrie, Shaw and Oswald less than three months before the assassination...[The committee] was therefore, inclined to believe that Oswald was in Clinton in late August, early September 1963, and that he was in the company of David Ferrie, if not Clay Shaw."[25] Blakey later wrote in his 1981 book, *The Plot to Kill the President*, "The evidence we found persuasive was the testimony of six residents of Clinton, Louisiana. It was the committee's considered opinion that the witnesses were honest folks."[26]

Because of the strength of the Clinton witnesses' testimony, Blakey knew he had no choice but to use them. However, when it came to other leads from this area Blakey exhibited a shameful lack of interest. For example, on April 4, 1977 the HSCA received a lead from a private investigator in Baton Rouge, Ronald Johnston, who claimed he knew of two people who had seen Oswald and Shaw together in the Clinton Courthouse. These individuals also maintained that the pair then went to the East Louisiana State Hospital.[27] It would not be until March 10, 1978 that any sort of follow-up investigation was conducted. This consisted of a brief interview with Johnston who told the Committee investigator he would get in touch with his informants.[28] Sadly, there are no records indicating any further HSCA contact with Johnston.

Return to Jackson

This episode did not end that day in Clinton, however. A return trip to Jackson and to the hospital was required.[29] Oswald, now informed of the insignificance of registered voter status, on the next day (presumably) applied for work at East Louisiana State Hospital. Around noon, Bobbie Dedon, a receptionist at the hospital directed a man she would identify as Oswald to the personnel office.[30] Maxine Kemp would offer further proof that Oswald applied for work. Approximately a year after the assassination, Mrs. Kemp was in the personnel office listening to the radio when she heard a report concerning Oswald. Having heard rumors that Oswald applied for work at the hospital, she decided to check the files. Upon checking the applicant files she indeed found a file titled, "Oswald, Lee." She noted the application was on the old type forms that were used in 1963, but she did not look at the information, such as references, etc. She put the file back and later when Garrison's investigators questioned her, she attempted to locate the file, but it was no longer among the existing records at the hospital.[31] Mrs. Kemp did remember that a co-worker, Dale Booty, had also seen this file. When contacted by HSCA investigator Robert Buras, Mr. Booty claimed he could not remember the incident and repeated a mantra common to many witnesses in this case, "I prefer not to get involved."[32]

MK/ULTRA in Jackson?

In 1978, John Marks published his groundbreaking work, *The Search for the Manchurian Candidate*. Using CIA documents he obtained under the Freedom of Information Act, Marks described a massive project undertaken by the Agency to control human behavior. Known as MKULTRA (as well as other code names), the project's most insidious effort at mind control was the administering of LSD to (mostly) unsuspecting victims. Marks also describes how the CIA would fund LSD projects at some of the most influential and prestigious medical and educational institutions. Although Marks does not mention Tulane or East Louisiana State Hospital in his book, it appears that both institutions were conducting research along these lines. In 1975 the General Counsel to the Army, Charles D. Ablard testified before a Senate Committee and said, "We have learned of a 1955 contract with Tulane University which involved the administration of LSD, mescaline, and other drugs to mental patients who had theretofore had electrodes implanted in their brains as a part of their medical treatment unrelated to an Army contract."[33] Also, Dr. Robert Heath, the former Chairman of Tulane University Medical School's Department of Neurology and Psychiatry used LSD and electrode implantation in his research.[34] Most of Heath's subjects were from the East Louisiana State Hospital where a 133-bed ward was assigned specifically for his research.[35]

Direct confirmation of these experiments comes from a former clinical director of East Louisiana Hospital, Dr. Alfred Butterworth who conducted a number of LSD experiments in the 1960's.[36] From 1960 through 1963, Butterworth administered LSD not only to himself but also to criminal patients from Angola Prison. As Marks reveals, Sandoz Chemical would provide the LSD free of charge to MKULTRA researchers. Butterworth admitted that he received his LSD directly from Sandoz for free. In fact while at Fort Detrick, Butterworth worked with the infamous Dr. Sidney Gottlieb, the head of the CIA's Chemical Division. Although Butterworth would not work at Jackson until after Oswald's visit there, he nevertheless remembered that doctors and administrators wanted experience in using these drugs. In fact, instructing other doctors in the use of LSD for the treatment of mental disorders was Butterworth's specialty. Butterworth remembered seeing not only Dr. Silva (Oswald's supposed friend) at Jackson, but Clay Shaw's close associate Dr. Alton Ochsner as well. Butterworth recalled that Tulane University had a psychiatric unit at Jackson and that specifically people from Tulane were using LSD at Jackson. Recall that Dr. Ochsner was on the board of the Tulane Medical School and Dr. Silva was working directly for Tulane. It is also worth noting that a Dr. Rabenet from the hospital would frequently talk about the New Orleans Trade Mart, imparting the impression that he knew people there.[37] Of course the Trade Mart was where both Clay Shaw and his boss, Lloyd Cobb worked.

The use of psychedelic drugs was apparently so pervasive at Jackson, that the doctors nicknamed one of the departments the "Magic Mushroom Unit." Butterworth left Jackson in 1978 eventually retiring to Mississippi. Whatever else Dr. Butterworth might have known, he took to the grave. He passed away in 1995 of prostate cancer.

Before we leave the East Louisiana State Hospital, a couple of points are worth mentioning here relative to David Ferrie. In 1968, Garrison's office interviewed a witness who had attended a function at Dr. Heath's home. At that party Dr. Silva introduced him to New Orleans anti-Castro activist, Sergio Arcacha Smith.[38] The reader will recall that Arcacha was Ferrie's CIA-connected colleague from New Orleans. In Chapter Nine it was pointed out that Ferrie had worked for an airline company called South Central

Airlines. One of the chief stockholders was a Cuban doctor named Abram Diaz.[39] In the 1960's, a Dr. Diaz was on staff at East Louisiana Hospital.[40] It is unclear at this point if it is the same doctor. It appears Ferrie was also closely acquainted with one of the patients at the hospital. Erick Crouchet, a former CAP cadet of Ferrie's, maintained a close relationship with Ferrie throughout the early 1960's.[41] In August of 1963, Crouchet was admitted to Jackson where he remained until November of 1963, just after President Kennedy's assassination.[42]

The Clinton Witnesses Redux

During the HSCA questioning of the Clinton/Jackson witnesses, another important point was educed. Just outside of Jackson is a large tract of land called Marydale Farm. Palmer, Manchester, Morgan and McGehee were all familiar with the unusual farm that employed a fair amount of Cubans. When asked if they knew who owned the land, they revealed a man named Cobb owned it. During cross- examination of Clay Shaw, assistant D.A. James Alcock asked Shaw about this farm. Shaw confirmed that he knew of the farm and that Shaw's associate, International Trade Mart president, Lloyd Cobb, in fact owned it.[43] Cobb was a close associate of INCA's, Ed Butler.[44] (The reader will recall that INCA was the leader of the propaganda smear against Oswald, painting him as a Communist, and that Butler was a CIA asset). Cobb himself was an archconservative who believed that a secret, liberal power structure was running the U.S. government.[45] According to recently released CIA records, the CIA granted Cobb a covert security clearance on October 3, 1963 for use on a "cleared attorney's panel."[46] Cobb's brother, Alvin was a close friend of Guy Banister's as well as a member of the Ku Klux Klan.[47] Lloyd Cobb's, Marydale Farms was a sprawling twelve thousand-acre tract of land that mainly provided dairy products. But Marydale Farms may have served a dual purpose. McGehee, the Jackson town barber, recalled that he used to cut the hair of an imposing individual that he believed to be Cuban. This person told

McGehee that he worked at Marydale Farms.[48] Reeves Morgan also recalled this same individual who he had seen walking the streets of Jackson.[49] From a "mug book" both McGehee and Morgan identified this individual as Lawrence Howard.[50] Likewise, Henry Earl Palmer identified Howard as someone who was associated with Marydale Farms.[51] Howard was an anti-Castro activist whose adventures had led him from Miami to New Orleans and Dallas. Howard also trained Cuban exiles at No Name Key in Florida and associated with those close to the Banister apparatus.[52]

Reeves Morgan recalled a frightening and bizarre incident that occurred at the farm. On the day of the assassination, Morgan noticed the caretakers of the farm rounding up all of the cattle as if they were closing down the farm. When Morgan asked the caretakers what they were doing, he was warned to forget everything he had seen at the farm if he valued his health. Morgan reluctantly revealed this information in an interview with me in 1994. Over thirty years after the incident, it was clear that the fear was still with Morgan.[53]

McGehee also recalled an equally bizarre incident. Shortly after his testimony at the Shaw trial McGehee was at home one night when he noticed someone furtively trespassing on his property. He called the Marshall who arrested the man and took him to the local police station. McGehee followed them to the station and recalled that the man was unusually dressed in that he was wearing a business suit and carried a briefcase. The arrested suspect then asked that he be allowed a phone call. Surprisingly, he called the International Trade Mart in New Orleans. McGehee could only hear one end of the conversation of course, but he remembered the person on the other end of the phone loudly admonishing the caller.[54]

Francis Fruge was a lieutenant with the Louisiana State Police in 1967. At that time he was detailed to work on the Garrison investigation. As part of his duties he participated in the interviewing of the Clinton/Jackson witnesses. In an interview with the HSCA, Fruge commented that the eight witnesses who eventually testified were "completely credible" echoing the committee's sentiments. Fruge elaborated further, stating tantalizingly, "...there were others from the area who did not testify, but who were equally credible and equally enlightening as to the visit of Ferrie, Shaw and Oswald to the area in 1963."[55]

Since the Clinton/Jackson witnesses represent the most credible evidence of a Shaw/Ferrie/Oswald association, it is not surprising that they would come under attack. The first salvo came when disgruntled former Garrison aide, Bill Gurvich and "journalist" Hugh Aynesworth drove to Clinton shortly before the Shaw trial. Their blatant attempts at badgering these witnesses were unsuccessful.[56] The next round was at the Shaw trial. Irving Dymond's cross-examination of the "Country Folk" was virtually ineffective. Even the normally biased James Kirkwood had to concede that "the Clinton people had a strong effect on the press and spectators and one presumed, the jury at the opening of the trial."[57] And finally, author Gerald Posner attempts to deliver the knockout blow, but like his predecessors, ends up swinging at air. In *Case Closed*, Posner writes, "Since Garrison's investigators uncovered the Clinton witnesses, evidently no researcher has gained access to the witnesses' original statements. The author, however, obtained affidavits, handwritten statements, and summary memoranda to Garrison regarding the initial stories the witnesses told the investigators."[58] Posner's assertion that the Clinton witnesses were the discovery of Garrison and his team is false. District judge and later Congressman, John Rarick, spoke to both McGehee and Morgan shortly after the assassination about Oswald's visit. Rarick's findings were printed in a right-wing newspaper based out of Shreveport called, *The Councillor.*[59] The article appeared before Garrison's investigation started.

At the Shaw trial the weather became a factor in determining the credibility of these witnesses and was subsequently picked up by Posner in his book. McGehee recalled he had opened his door and shut off his air conditioner on the day Oswald visited and Morgan remembered burning trash in his fireplace on the evening in question. Since it is typically hot in Louisiana in the summer months, both Posner and Shaw's attorney,

Irvin Dymond, attempted to get mileage out of this. However, it is an argument that is easily rebutted by a cursory reading of the Shaw trial transcript and by talking to the witnesses themselves. (Something Posner conveniently neglected to do). McGehee first testifies that Oswald showed up at his barber shop "along toward the evening."[60] Later he testifies that he remembered talking to the local farmers about the weather and how "we had cool *nights* in the last of August and the early part of September."[61] A bit later McGehee says, "Well, we always discuss the weather in the barber shop - that is about the main topic of conversation - and we have farmers up in Jackson, quite a number of them, and they are always saying wasn't last *night* cool and all like that."[62]

Q. I take it that this was a cool night that you saw Lee Oswald?

A. Yes, the *night was* rather cool.[63]

McGehee always refers to the evening or the nights as being cool. Dymond trotted out weather statistics to try to discredit the testimony and Posner uses this in his argument. Yet both only used the daytime temperature readings of 90 degrees. Fortunately, assistant DA Jim Alcock, while cross-examining Shaw's defense expert, was able to elicit the fact that the evening temperatures dipped into the low 70's.[64] This whole issue about the weather is nothing but a distraction from the relevance of the testimony. Keep in mind that all McGehee said he did was open his door and shut off his air conditioner on a late afternoon or evening he perceived was cool enough to save a few bucks.

    As for Morgan, he testified that Oswald visited his house at night and he describes the weather as "it wasn't cold weather and it wasn't hot weather because when Oswald came to my house that evening I was burning trash out of my fireplace and it didn't feel too bad. It wasn't cold, it wasn't hot."[65] Morgan also had a very good reason for burning his trash - there was no trash pick-up service to his home! It was quite customary for Morgan to burn an accumulation of garbage in his fireplace no matter what time of year. Morgan's son and daughter and Morgan himself confirmed this for me.[66] Morgan's daughter, Mary, also confirmed seeing Oswald that night - she walked right by him on her way out of the house. And as a teenage girl might, she took notice of the young man in her front parlor. She has no doubt to this day that the visitor was Lee Harvey Oswald.[67] Mary's younger brother, Van, himself a young teenager at the time, also recalled the night of the mysterious visit. As is a young boy's wont, Van was "horsing around" by the cedar trees in the front yard of the Morgan house, when he took notice of the car coming up the drive. He remembered being impressed with the look of the car and waited outside while the visitor talked to his father. He noticed that the driver of the car waited as well. He couldn't make out the features of the driver in the darkness of early evening, but remembered one unforgettable characteristic - a shock of white hair. When the car left, Van asked his father if the governor had just paid them a visit. When asked why he thought it was the governor, Van replied that he thought only the governor would come to their house in a <u>black Cadillac</u>.[68]

Chapter Twelve

~

Fourth Estate or Fourth Reich:
The CIA/Media Attack on Jim Garrison

After the suspicious death of David Ferrie in February of 1967, the focus of the investigation now shifted to Clay Shaw. As we have seen, Shaw had come under suspicion early in Garrison's probe. In the fall of 1966 Garrison questioned New Orleans attorney Dean Andrews about his Warren Commission testimony concerning the mysterious Clay Bertrand. Recall it was Bertrand who phoned Andrews the weekend of the assassination and asked him to represent Oswald. When Garrison's assistants combed the French Quarter for Bertrand, the bartender at Cosimo's identified Clay Shaw as Bertrand.[1]

Later in the probe, other Vieux Carre denizens would confirm to the DA's office that Shaw was Bertrand. William

Morris would later state to Garrison's team that he had been introduced to Shaw as Bertrand at the Masquerade Bar, a gay nightclub in the Quarter. In fact, he was introduced to Shaw by Gene Davis, owner of several gay bars in the French Quarter.[2] David Logan also recalled meeting Shaw at yet another raffish French Quarter bar called Dixie's. Shaw subsequently invited Logan to a party on Governor Nichols Street.[3] (At the time Shaw himself owned an apartment on Governor Nichols Street). Logan was also introduced to David Ferrie at this party.[4]

With his suspicions being confirmed almost daily, Garrison decided to call Shaw in for questioning. Two days before Christmas in 1966, Shaw met with Garrison and Sciambra in the DA's office. Garrison found Shaw's answers evasive and in conflict with previous statements the DA had taken from ITM employees and other individuals. (For a full treatment of this issue, see Chapter 6).

On February 24, 1967, FBI records show that an informant for the Bureau had received information that Shaw and Bertrand were the same. The informant called Lou Ivon with this information and the FBI reported that "although Ivon would not confirm this information, [he] appeared very upset and wanted to know where informant developed this information."[5] This FBI memo is revealing in several ways. First, we now know that the FBI had information that Shaw and Bertrand were the same at least four days before Shaw's arrest and resultant notoriety. (As we shall see later, the FBI knew this much earlier). Also, Ivon's reaction, as described in the memo, indicates that the DA's office had already quietly developed the Bertrand information and was concerned about it leaking out.

Perry Russo vs. James Phelan

Shortly after Ferrie's death, a story broke in the Baton Rouge newspapers about a local insurance salesman who had witnessed a discussion of a possible assassination plot in New Orleans. Andrew Sciambra first interviewed Perry Russo on February 25, 1967. Russo stated that in early September of 1963 he attended a party at David Ferrie's house where the plan to assassinate JFK was discussed. Among those present were some anti-Castro Cubans and two individuals, one unkempt and one nattily dressed, who were introduced to Russo as Leon Oswald and Clem Bertrand respectively. Russo would subsequently identify the unkempt "Leon" as Lee Harvey Oswald and Bertrand as Clay Shaw.[6] According to Russo, Ferrie discussed using "a triangulation of crossfire" to kill the president. Ferrie and Bertrand also discussed being in the public eye on the day of the assassination. Ferrie said he would be at Southeastern Louisiana campus in Hammond and Bertrand said he would travel to the West Coast on business.[7] Since there has been some controversy over what exactly transpired at the Sciambra/Russo session in Baton Rouge, some clarification is in order here. On February 25, 1967, Sciambra was dispatched to Baton Rouge to interview Russo. At that time according to Russo and Sciambra, Russo identified pictures of Ferrie, Shaw, and Oswald as the participants in the assassination conversation at Ferrie's. Sciambra took notes on a legal pad and marked the photos Russo identified. The two parties agreed Russo should travel to New Orleans to make a formal statement. After this interview, Sciambra drove to Garrison's house to brief him. On Monday, Sciambra began transcribing his notes, but was interrupted when Russo arrived in New Orleans. Sciambra took Russo over to Mercy Hospital where he was administered Sodium Pentothal™ (commonly known as truth serum) by Orleans Parish Coroner, Dr. Nicholas Chetta. Russo repeated the same information he told Sciambra in Baton Rouge, again specifically mentioning the conspiracy discussion and Shaw's participation in it. Sciambra then drafted the memo from this session in its entirety, therefore making it the first "Sciambra memo." He then went back to transcribing his notes from February 25th interview over the course of the week, only touching on the points not elicited during the truth serum session. During this time, Russo was also put under hypnosis by Dr. Esmond Fatter to further objectify his testimony. Saturday Evening Post reporter, James Phelan, was given a copy of the second "Sciambra memo" by Garrison and then attempted to portray it as representative of the complete contents of the first interview. Phelan's behavior is especially suspect in light of the fact that he took the transcript of the second hypnosis session and used it as proof that Dr. Fatter was planting the name of Bertrand in Russo's head. What the transcript from the first hypnosis session reveals, is that Russo himself first mentions Bertrand. Phelan even went as far as submitting the transcript of the second hypnosis session and the second "Sciambra memo" to the FBI. A copy of that transcript, with Phelan's handwritten marginalia, is in the FBI files at the National Archives.[8] But the FBI was not the first to see the documents. CIA cutout, Robert Maheu, was the first person Phelan called, ostensibly to see if Maheu could Xerox the documents for him.[9]

Curiously missing from Phelan's *Post* article, entitled "Rush To Judgement in New Orleans," was the visit Phelan paid to Russo in Baton Rouge shortly after the memorandum "controversy." At that meeting Russo confirmed to Phelan that he had indeed told Sciambra about the Bertrand/ Ferrie/ Oswald assassination conversation and that he had ID'd Shaw as Bertrand. When questioned on this crucial omission by Mark Lane, Phelan weakly complained that he was bucking a tight deadline and that naturally a point or two may have been lost.[10] As Lane quipped, "It was a Rush to Judgment in New York."[11]

On March 1st, Garrison made a "command decision" and arrested Shaw. Garrison's office had allowed Shaw the opportunity of taking a polygraph test before they arrested him. Shaw refused, on the advice of his attorney Sal Panzeca, explaining he needed to go home first and rest. The DA's office denied Shaw's request and placed him under arrest. While Shaw was being booked, the processing officer, Aloysius Habighorst, routinely asked Shaw if he used any aliases. Shaw's answer – "Clay Bertrand."[12]

After Shaw was released on bond, his attorneys began forming the defense team. The original criminal attorney of record was a lawyer named Guy Johnson. As we saw in Chapter 4, Johnson had a long history of intelligence activity and was a close associate of Guy Banister's. Johnson was soon dropped from the defense team like a hot potato. The reader will recall that a New Orleans attorney, who used to work for Guy Banister infiltrating left wing college groups, revealed in a 1981 interview that "Shaw, Banister, and Guy Johnson made up the intelligence apparatus for New Orleans."[13]

Because of the enormity of the charge, Garrison filed a motion for a preliminary hearing - a move almost without precedent by a district attorney. On March 14 the four-day preliminary hearing commenced before a three-judge panel. Garrison presented Russo as well as a new witness, Vernon Bundy.[14]

The Ordeal of Vernon Bundy

Bundy testified that in June or July of 1963, he was at the Lake Pontchartrain seawall preparing an injection of heroin (Bundy was an admitted heroin addict, more on this later). As Bundy took his position on the seawall a black sedan pulled into the parking area. It should be noted that this is the same description of Clay Shaw's car as described by the Clinton witnesses. It is important to note that the preliminary hearing occurred *before* the Clinton people came to Garrison's attention. The driver, a tall gray haired man, got out of the car and started walking in Bundy's direction. Bundy, fearful that this person may have been a narcotics officer, placed his drugs in a brown paper bag he was carrying and started to walk away from the area. The driver walked past Bundy and remarked to him about the weather. As Bundy retook his position along the seawall he watched as a younger man approached the gray haired man. Bundy continued to watch as the two engaged in conversation for about 15-20 minutes. During this conversation Bundy overheard the young man ask, "What am I going to tell her?" The older man replied, "Don't worry about it. I told you I'm going to take care of it." Whereupon the older man gave a quantity of money to the younger one, which he put in his back pocket. As he did so, some leaflets that were in his pocket fluttered to the ground. After the two departed Bundy walked over to where they had been standing and picked up one of the leaflets. Bundy remembered the leaflets as being yellow in color and had something about Cuba written on it. At both the preliminary hearing and the trial Bundy would identify the men by the seawall as Clay Shaw and Lee Harvey Oswald. He recognized Shaw especially because he walked with a limp. Indeed, as we have seen, as a result of an injury during his military service, Shaw did walk with a limp. The leaflets he identified as the Fair Play for Cuba literature Oswald had distributed that summer.[15]

Once Bundy had been exposed in the preliminary hearing, he was now fair game for Walter Sheridan and NBC (more on Sheridan later). In their attempt to discredit Bundy, NBC aired interviews with two fellow convicts, Miguel Torres and John Cancler. Cancler, a convicted burglar and pimp, appeared first and said Bundy had told him he was going to lie to the DA's office to get out of prison.[16] Torres, whose own record of heroin abuse, burglary, pimping, assault, and suspected murder out rivaled Cancler's, was currently serving a nine year sentence for robbery.[17] He said that Bundy told him he was going to make up a story about Shaw to get the DA to "cut him loose" from prison.[18] After the airing of the NBC special, Garrison invited Mssrs. Torres and Cancler to repeat their stories in front of the Grand Jury. Both pleaded the Fifth Amendment and were subsequently convicted of contempt. Another problem with Torres' story is his accusation that Bundy needed the DA to "cut him loose" from prison. In a recently released memorandum from the New Orleans DA's files, William

Gurvich wrote of his investigation of Bundy. Gurvich states "shortly after my interview with Bundy, I contacted local narcotics officers for background information on him. I also made an extensive inquiry into his criminal history."[19] Of his heroin use Gurvich writes, "[Bundy] uses four or five capsules of heroin daily... This amount is considered sufficient for addiction, but is not an excessive amount as the more heavily addicted use as much as 20-30 capsules daily."[20] Gurvich goes on to write "Bundy claimed he was in Parish Prison at the time because he went there *voluntarily* when he felt himself reverting back to the use of narcotics and feared the consequences of his addiction. Official records corroborate this."[21] Bundy was on probation for breaking into a cigarette machine, but was not serving time. So much for Bundy needing to be "cut loose." Since NBC offered to relocate Perry Russo to California and provide him with a job if he changed his original testimony, one can only imagine what incentives Sheridan offered Cancler and Torres.[22]

    The harassment of Bundy was not limited to Sheridan and company however. At the time of the Garrison probe Nina Sulzer worked in the research department of the Orleans Parish Prison and was later Administrative Assistant in the Sheriff's Department. She was also a friend of Clay Shaw's.[23] On May 22, 1967 Garrison's office took a statement from Bundy's cellmate Arthur King. King stated that on May 18, 1967, "Mrs. Sulzer came up and started talking to Bundy about the case that he was a witness in and she told him that he was riding the wrong horse, that he was on a losing team and Bundy asked her what did she mean and she told him, "You'll see"... She gave Bundy a magazine, which had an article in it about the case in which he was a witness. I remember the article was in *Newsweek* because Bundy wanted to know whether he was going to appear in the *Saturday Evening Post* also, and she told him no, that they all were not big enough for *Saturday Evening Post* . He asked her what she meant and she said, "You'll see." She stood there between fifteen minutes to a half-hour. Mrs. Sulzer repeated that Bundy was on the wrong team constantly. I remember walking to the end of the cell and Mrs. Sulzer had said something to Bundy at which time Bundy told Mrs. Sulzer that he did not take anything from anyone of them, that he'd never take anything from anybody. Mrs. Sulzer asked Bundy what they were doing for you and Bundy said, "There is nobody doing nothing for me." Bundy said he didn't want anybody doing anything for him. He got kind of angry after this and walked off. He told us he didn't know what that woman was talking about. Mrs. Sulzer also said on the outside somebody out there is going to stool on you, *somebody is going to kill you.* She mentioned it again, she said, *"You'll see, somebody will get you out there."* She also said that those people can't save you. She said that whenever he'd get out of here that *he was as good as gone."*[24] [My emphasis] Statements taken from Bundy and his other cellmate, Samuel Davis, Jr., confirmed King's account.[25]

It is interesting to note that Nina Sulzer was one of a trio of prison social workers with unique backgrounds in this case. Former Garrison investigator, Bill Boxley, was given the assignment of providing background information on these three individuals. The author recently discovered this report in a collection of materials Boxley donated to the late Bud Fensterwald. I quote the relevant passages here:

> Mrs. [Ruth] Kloepfer, a Quaker, said that she contacted the Oswalds because Ruth Paine had found the Kloepfer name in a random search of a Quaker directory, and asked her to befriend Marina, a stranger in New Orleans who spoke very little English. Mrs. Kloepfer said that she visited Marina several times. She and H. Warner Kloepfer, her husband, both of 306 Pine Street, are listed in Oswald's personal notebook.
>
> Mrs. Kloepfer also is one of three Orleans Parish prison social workers, with whom connections to the case against Clay Shaw have been uncovered.
>
> In addition to having conferred with Shaw on at least one occasion in Parish Prison (regarding Shaw's interest in inmate, Charles Daniels, whose name appears in Shaw's address book), Mrs. Kloepfer quite possibly is related to the only other person of that sir name appearing in the 1967 telephone directory as living in New Orleans - William Kloepfer, 724 Governor Nichols, an apartment house owned by Shaw.

[Author's note: After William Kloepfer vacated this apartment, the next tenant was David Chandler, a friend of Shaw's and local reporter who, as we will see, assisted in the smear campaign against Garrison].

Another social worker in the prison is Jane Lemman, also a Quaker, whose husband is related to Stephan Lemman, who is (a) General Counsel for WDSU-TV, and (b) according to information supplied to the district attorney, the New Orleans conduit of funds from the CIA to various attorneys who have sought to block this inquiry. [Author's note: Boxley is undoubtedly referring to a May 24, 1967 memo from assistant DA, William Martin, to Garrison titled, "Central Intelligence Agency Connections In The City Of New Orleans." Martin, himself a former intelligence operative, had just interviewed a close associate of his who was ex-CIA and a lifetime resident of New Orleans. From this interview Martin writes, "Mr. Stephen B. Lemman of the same law firm in New Orleans (Monroe & Lemman) is serving as "Special Counsel" to the Central Intelligence Agency and does in fact handle certain matters pertaining to the clandestine payroll of the Central Intelligence Agency in this city. Specifically, our information is that Mr. Stephen B. Lemman will advance funds to Mr. Plotkin (attorney for Gordon Novel) and to Mr. Klein (also an attorney for Novel, as well as Alvin Beauboeuf and Miguel Torres) for the defense of their respective clients now under investigation by this office"].

Completing the triumvirate of Parish Prison social workers is Mrs. Nina Sulzer, wife of Dr. Jefferson Sulzer, a professor of social psychology at Tulane. Mrs. Sulzer approached Vernon Bundy, state's witness in the Shaw case, and told Bundy that he was "on the losing horse" and suggested he read a *Newsweek* magazine, which she gave him. The magazine contained a particularly derogatory article about the investigation. A physical surveillance placed on Mrs. Sulzer after she had attempted to dissuade Bundy's testimony disclosed that on at least one occasion she visited a residence where Shaw was staying and spent approximately three hours with him.

These actions and statements by persons in contact with Oswald, Shaw, and the Garrison investigation strongly suggest a central control over events prior to and after the assassination, with re-entry of some of the principals upon charges having been brought against the defendant Shaw.[26]

Sulzer even accompanied defense investigators on a trip to Dallas in 1967 acting as their transcriber.[27] Not surprisingly, Nina Sulzer was fired from the Sheriff's office just after the Shaw trial.[28]

Almost twenty years later, professional conspiracy refuter, Gerald Posner, tried to discredit the Bundy incident. In the *New York Times Magazine*, Posner reveals with a flourish:

> I discovered a March 16, 1967 transcript of an interview between Bundy and three Garrison investigators. In that talk, only two weeks after Shaw's arrest, Bundy described the "Oswald" character as a "real junkie" and said his name was "Pete." Not once in a 12-page typewritten statement did Bundy mention any unusual walk or gait. By the time of his testimony, he had dropped any inconsistencies, and his memory had "improved" favorably for the prosecution.[29]

This author also discovered a memorandum from March 16, 1967 written by the same three investigators mentioned above. At no point does Bundy waver from his identification of Shaw or Oswald.[30] I also have read the interview Posner cites. Bundy does not say Oswald was a "real junkie" rather he describes Oswald as "dirty" who "*looked* like a real junkie." Again this fits the description of the "Leon" Oswald seen at Silvia Odio's apartment in Dallas and at David Ferrie's apartment in New Orleans. As for being named "Pete," Bundy simply said he overheard Shaw say something *like*, "Hold up Pete." It's possible Shaw could have said "Lee" or something else entirely. Posner also got mileage out of saying Bundy never mentioned Shaw's gait.(The reader will recall from Chapter 7 that Shaw had acquired a slight limp from an injury he sustained during his Army service). Had Posner done his homework he might have found a memo from Assistant D.A, John Volz, also from March 16th, where he writes:

> In order to get a more positive identification, I proceeded with Bundy out of the Prison and milled around the foyer of the Criminal District Court Building near the elevators. As soon as Shaw emerged from the Sheriff's office Bundy said, "That's him, I'm sure of it. He had the same limp when I saw him on the Lakefront."[31]

John Volz was the assistant DA who handled much of the Bundy background work. Once a United States Attorney, today Volz is a prominent lawyer in private practice in Metairie, Louisiana. Although not a fan of Garrison's case, he still feels that Bundy was a credible witness and that Oswald and Shaw were somehow associated.[32]

The three judges ruled unanimously that sufficient evidence existed to require Shaw be bound over for trial. Taking an additional precautionary step, Garrison presented the case to the Grand Jury, a totally unnecessary move that would have meant the end of the case had the Grand Jury returned a No True Bill. However, the Grand Jury indicted Shaw. For the next two years Garrison sought to get Shaw to trial. Countless delays initiated by the defense team, motions for continuance, change of venue, etc., bought time that allowed several penetrations into Garrison's office. Files and trial briefs were stolen and handed over to the defense. Shaw's defense now had the time to hire the infamous Wackenhut Corporation, known as the CIA's CIA, to perform their investigative work.[33] This delay also allowed the defense, the intelligence agencies and a cooperative media to create a general atmosphere that virtually prevented a fair and impartial trial.

The CIA and the Media: An Introduction

As a result of the Congressional investigations of the CIA during the 1970's, one of the more alarming revelations was the CIA's influence and partnering with the U.S. news media.[34] Among other things, it was revealed that about twenty-five news organizations, including the major networks, newspapers and magazines, routinely cooperated with, or provided cover for, the Agency. Close ties were shown to exist between CIA Director Allen Dulles and media executives such as Arthur Hays Sulzberger of the *New York Times*, William Paley of CBS, and Philip Graham of both the *Washington Post* and *Newsweek*.[35] Cover arrangements were also common at the *Saturday Evening Post*.[36] More than 400 journalists, freelancers and stringers were used to spread CIA propaganda virtually unabated until the mid-seventies.[37] According to Carl Bernstein, in an article for *Rolling Stone* titled, "The CIA and the Media," former counterintelligence chief, James Angleton, "ran a completely independent group of journalist-operatives who performed sensitive and frequently dangerous assignments; little is known about this group for the simple reason that Angleton deliberately kept only the vaguest of files."[38] The CIA even ran a formal training program to teach agents to be journalists.[39]

Another important revelation from the mid-seventies came from a former high-ranking staff officer at the CIA. Victor Marchetti was interviewed for an article in *True* magazine in 1975 in which he said:

> I used to attend, among other things, the Director's morning meeting, his morning staff meeting. This was Richard Helms at the time and he held a meeting every morning at 9, which was attended by 12 or 14 of his leading Deputies plus 3 or 4 staffers- the executive assistants to the number one, two and three men in the Agency and also the Press Officer. I often used to take the minutes of this meeting...But during the Clay Shaw trial I remember the Director on several occasions asking questions like, you know, "Are we giving them all the help they need?" I didn't know who *they* or *them* were. I knew they didn't like Garrison because there were a lot of snotty remarks passed about him.
> They would talk in half sentences like "is everything going all right down there...yeah...but talk with me about it after the meeting" or "we'll pick this up later in my office." So after several of these over a week or two I began to ask myself what's going on, what's the big concern. I began to ask around...and one of the other people who attended the meeting...at the time I said, "What's the concern about this trial and this guy Shaw?" I was then told, "Well...Shaw, a long time ago, had been a contact of the Agency...He was in the export-import business...he knew people coming and going from certain areas-the Domestic Contact Service-he used to deal with them...and it's been cut off a long time ago"...and then I was told "well of course the Agency doesn't want this to come out now because Garrison will distort it, the public would misconstrue it."[40]

This information provides a good historical context with which to view new revelations that illustrate the profundity of "help" given to Shaw.

The Media Assault

The first salvo of the anti-Garrison propaganda blitz actually began in May of 1967. On May 6th the *Saturday Evening Post* published the aforementioned article by James Phelan. Then on May 15th, *Newsweek* published an article titled, "The JFK Conspiracy." Written by former *Dallas Times Herald* reporter Hugh Aynesworth, the article is a masterpiece of misinformation. Aynesworth leads off the article by implying that Perry Russo had been hypnotized just "hours before he testified" at the preliminary hearing. What Aynesworth neglected to mention was that Russo had been hypnotized some 50 hours prior to the hearing, in a controlled setting, with both Dr. Esmond Fatter, a court-accredited expert on hypnotism and Dr. Nicholas Chetta, the coroner of Orleans Parish, present.

Since the aforementioned Mssrs. Cancler and Torres were apparently being saved up for the upcoming NBC special, Aynesworth took only a brief swipe at Vernon Bundy, characterizing him as "an unusual witness." Aynesworth's "coup de grace" however was his revelation that two of Garrison's police assistants, Lynn Loisel and Lou Ivon, attempted to bribe and intimidate potential witness Alvin Beauboeuf. The reader will recall that Beaubeouf was one of David Ferrie's companions during his midnight ride to Texas just after the assassination. According to Aynesworth, Beaubeouf claimed that Loisel and Ivon attempted to bribe him if he would testify favorably for the State. Beauboeuf further alleged that both Loisel and Ivon threatened to kill him if he did not testify appropriately. As evidence of the purported bribe, it was reported that Beauboeuf's attorney, Hugh Exnicios, had made a surreptitious recording of the conversation. On the surface these seem like damning charges. However, nowhere in any of

Newsweek's or Aynesworth's subsequent reporting are we given the facts.

Fact One: The New Orleans Police Department and the Deputy Superintendent of Police conducted an internal investigation of the Beauboeuf matter. On June 12, 1967 they issued a 37-page report completely exonerating Loisel and Ivon of any wrongdoing.

Fact Two: Beauboeuf himself retracted his charges, saying in a sworn statement that Exnicios had persuaded him that the "bribery" tape would be an excellent opportunity to make some money. Beauboeuf's wife, the only witness to the purported threat, swore that she had never heard any such threat being made.[41]

Fact Three: The bribe tape was misrepresented. After reading the transcript of the tape provided by Exnicios, both Beauboeuf and his new attorney Burton Klein stated that several parts of the conversation were edited out that would have disproved the offer of a bribe. (Both Beauboeuf and Klein had heard the tape prior to examining the transcript). When asked to produce the tape for the New Orleans Police investigation, Exnicios refused.[42]

An examination of Aynesworth's background might help illuminate the reasons for his obvious lack of objectivity. A graduate of Salem College in West Virginia, Aynesworth began his career as a sports writer in Arkansas in 1950.[43] After a short stint as a UPI reporter Aynesworth started work as the Science-Aviation reporter at the ultra-conservative Dallas Morning News in 1960. However, Aynesworth apparently had other career plans. In 1962 Aynesworth applied for a visa to travel to Cuba. As his application was being considered, Aynesworth contacted the CIA and volunteered his services should he be granted the visa.[44] In fact, CIA records reveal that Aynesworth expressed interest in employment with the Agency.[45] The records indicate that he was given the name of the personnel recruiter for the Southwest region but do not indicate if he ever made contact with the recruiter. The CIA's own background investigation of Aynesworth from 1968 concluded that:

> Aynesworth is considered a good reporter although with a tendency to interpose his own view sometimes and perhaps to sometime lack objectivity. He is considered a Warren Commission man on the assassination and was at one time writing his own book on the subject.[46]

A prime example of Aynesworth's brand of journalism can be found at the Lyndon B. Johnson library. It consists of a rough draft of Aynesworth's *Newsweek* article and a cover letter addressed to LBJ's press secretary George Christian. Aynesworth writes:

> Here is the rough draft copy of the story we discussed this morning...
> I am not offering this for comment of any kind, nor a check of the validity of any part. Simply , its FYI...
> My interest in informing government officials of each step along the way is because of my intimate knowledge of what Jim Garrison is planning...
> I intend to make a complete report of my knowledge available to the FBI, as I have done in the past.

And FBI records do indeed show that Aynesworth had a history of informing the Bureau of developments in the JFK case. In late 1966, Aynesworth was retained by *Life* magazine to give local assistance to their reporters. Aynesworth promptly informed the FBI of the progress of *Life's* investigation, even providing them with copies of internal *Life* memoranda. Aynesworth's only caveat was that the information not be disseminated outside the Bureau.[47]

Other examples of Aynesworth's "objectivity" can be found in the Wegmann Papers at the National Archives. Numerous letters exist between Aynesworth and the Shaw lawyers. Much of the correspondence is on a personal level with invitations being offered to the Wegmanns to stay at Aynesworth's home as well as examples of Aynesworth's attempts at intimidating potential Shaw trial witnesses.[48] These letters continue over a span of about three years, making Aynesworth a virtual member of the Shaw defense team.[49]

Aynesworth was also making use of the D.A.'s files that were stolen by William Gurvich. In December of 1967 Aynesworth reviewed one of the D.A.'s memos that dealt with George Brown of the Texas based Brown and Root. Garrison suspected that Brown was connected to the CIA and Aynesworth duly reported this back to Brown, who in turn informed the CIA.[50] Earlier, in an interview with Shaw's lawyers, Gurvich scoffed and snorted in derision at Garrison's suspicions about Brown, but as we have seen time and again the documentary record vindicates Garrison.[51] CIA memoranda state that Brown had "cooperated closely with the DDP in funding CIA operations."[52]

Aynesworth's own peers took him to task for his dual role as both participant and prejudiced observer. In an article for the *Columbia Journalism Review* titled, "The Clay Shaw Trial: Reporter-Participants," Roger Williams from *Time* magazine's Atlanta bureau and Michael Parks, a reporter for the *Baltimore Sun* wrote:

> At least three members of the Shaw trial press went beyond the normal bounds of journalistic interest in the story, becoming in varying degrees, participants as well as reporters. The three were Los Angeles radio newsman Art Kevin, free-lance writer Jim Phelan, and *Newsweek* correspondent Hugh Aynesworth...
> Jim Phelan and Hugh Aynesworth, both fiercely anti-Garrison, became in effect special advisers to the defense. They consulted frequently with Shaw's attorneys, passing along tips on aspects of the case they knew best from time spent covering it as reporters. The two of them, says chief defense attorney F. Irvin Dymond, were "extremely valuable" to the defense case...[53]

The article also quotes Dymond as saying, "Hugh helped us a hell of a lot, mostly on stuff that did not come out in court."[54] The authors conclude that,

Aynesworth could have chosen between his twin functions of reporter and participant. He could, for instance, have taken a leave of absence to join the defense team and let someone else cover the Shaw trial for his magazine. Failing that, *Newsweek's* editors should have made the choice for him, to protect their own interests and the interests of their readers.[55]

Walter Sheridan and the CIA: The Empire Strikes Back

Following on the heels of the *Newsweek* article, came the most devastating attack to be launched by the media. On June 19th NBC aired an hour long "analysis" of the New Orleans investigation titled, "The JFK Conspiracy: The Case of Jim Garrison." For the job as lead investigative reporter, NBC assigned Walter Sheridan. Shortly after Shaw's arrest Sheridan arrived in New Orleans and began questioning witnesses - perhaps bribing would be a better choice of words. Sheridan questioned Gordon Novel and immediately put him on a $500 a day retainer.[56] He then urged Novel to skip town to avoid being indicted and paid him an additional $750 while Novel was in Columbus Ohio.[57] Dean Andrews was promised a recording studio and Perry Russo was offered relocation to California and a job if he would change his story.[58]

The newly released CIA files present an interesting biography of "reporter" Sheridan. In 1955 Sheridan was security approved as an investigator for the CIA. A month later this was cancelled because Sheridan accepted a position at the ultra-secret National Security Agency. In 1956 he was security approved once again by the CIA so that he could attend their "Basic Orientation Course." After leaving the NSA, Sheridan went to work for Bobby Kennedy's Justice Department in the "Get Hoffa" squad.[59] With this background in the intelligence communities Sheridan was now apparently qualified to work for NBC as a reporter. However, documents reveal that Sheridan did not sever contact with the CIA.

In early May of 1967 the Counter Intelligence office of the CIA issued a memorandum for the Deputy Director of Plans which stated:

> Richard Lansdale, Associate General Counsel, has advised us that NBC plans to do a derogatory TV special on Garrison and his probe of the Kennedy assassination; that NBC *regards Garrison as a menace to the country and means to destroy him.* The program is to be presented within the next few weeks. *Mr. Lansdale learned this information from Mr. Walter Sheridan of NBC.*[60] [My emphasis]

During Sheridan's tenure in New Orleans he enlisted the aid of Richard Townley from NBC's affiliate, the Stern owned WDSU-TV. Townley's loose tongue offered further proof that the NBC White Paper was no more than a deliberate attempt to sabotage the investigation and to ruin Jim Garrison. A recently released FBI memo reads:

> A local FBI agent reported that Richard Townley, WDSU-TV, New Orleans, remarked to a special agent of the New Orleans office last evening that he had received instructions from NBC, New York, to prepare a one hour TV special on Jim Garrison with the instruction "shoot him down."[61]

On June 19th NBC aired their special.[62] In addition to the aforementioned Cancler and Torres, Sheridan also trotted out Dean Andrews and, to help bolster his already weak presentation, the defendant Clay Shaw. Garrison's one time "aide," William Gurvich also appeared, having left the DA's office several weeks earlier. As Garrison noted shortly after the broadcast Gurvich didn't so much as resign as "drift away about six weeks ago" and that since that time he had been in contact with Walter Sheridan.[63] Gurvich also admittedly made off with the DA's master file. The CIA was so smitten with Gurvich that they wanted to make sure he was in touch with Shaw's lawyers. In their enthusiasm to give Shaw's lawyers all the help they could the CIA recommended:

Shaw's attorneys ought to talk to William H. GURVICH. This is an excellent suggestion. It is assumed they have done so, or plan to, but *we should try to assure that they do.*[64] [Author's emphasis]

One other witness Sheridan used makes for an interesting case study of Sheridan's abuse of power. Fred Leemans, the owner of a Turkish bath house in New Orleans, originally stated that Shaw had frequented his establishment using the name of Clay Bertrand. By the time Sheridan and company got to him, he went on the NBC special claiming he had been offered a $2500 bribe by one of Garrison's men in exchange for his incriminating testimony. After the NBC special had aired, Leemans came forward with the truth. In a sworn statement Leemans admitted that part of the reason he participated in the show was threatening phone calls "relative to the information that I had given Mr. Garrison." Leemans also recalled a visit from a man with a badge who stated that he was a government agent. The man supposedly told Leemans that the government was checking bar owners in the Slidell area for possible income tax violations. The man also warned him that "it was not smart" to be involved in the Clay Shaw case "because a lot of people that had been involved got hurt." An anonymous caller told Leemans to change his statement and claim he had been bribed. The caller also suggested that Leemans contact Irvin Dymond, one of Shaw's attorneys. After contacting Dymond, Leemans was introduced to Walter Sheridan. Leemans claimed Dymond offered an attorney and bond in the event he was charged with giving false information to the DA's office. Leemans said his appearance on the show was taped in the office of Aaron Kohn, managing director of the Metropolitan Crime Commission, in the presence of Sheridan and Dymond.[65]

After the program aired, Garrison petitioned the FCC who agreed that the program was biased and granted Garrison a 30 minute rebuttal to air on July 15 at 7:30 P.M. - hardly equal time. Nevertheless, the NBC program aided greatly in the discreditation of the DA's office and potentially contaminated the Shaw jury pool.

In addition to the aforementioned Richard Townley, the local New Orleans news media seemed to have more that its fair share of newscasters willing to flack for the intelligence agencies. Ed Planer, also of WDSU, offered to share information he had relative to the Garrison probe with the FBI.[66] Newly discovered documents reveal that Sam DePino of WVUE-TV was volunteering information to both the FBI and the CIA. In May of 1968, the CIA's Lloyd Ray dictated a memo for file noting that DePino was offering information to the CIA about Garrison.[67] DePino also told Ray that if he could be of any service to the CIA, not to hesitate to call him.[68] Ray discussed DePino with the FBI who confirmed that DePino had talked to the FBI on many occasions and was considered "an eager beaver newshound who calls the FBI frequently."[69]

Noted reporter Jack Anderson also got in on the act when he visited Garrison in April of 1967. After meeting with Garrison for some six hours in New Orleans Anderson reported back, not to the *Washington Post* but to the FBI's Cartha DeLoach. As DeLoach's subsequent memo notes:

> Anderson stated that he went to New Orleans fully prepared to present a hostile viewpoint to Garrison. After listening to Garrison for approximately 90 minutes he began to believe Garrison's story. Anderson describes Garrison as a very convincing talker who has considerable facts at his disposal. Anderson now believes there is some authenticity to Garrison's claims and future plans...
> He stated that at the close of Garrison's six-hour recitation of facts, he (Anderson) was of the opinion that Garrison was not only sincere, but very convincing. Anderson stated that Garrison firmly believed his facts. Anderson then told me that he bluntly asked Garrison why Garrison had not given all these convincing facts to the FBI whereupon Garrison replied, "I got started off on the wrong foot with the FBI." Garrison added, "I would be more than willing to give the FBI everything I have and let them finish the investigation if they so desire."[70]

Of course DeLoach refused Garrison's offer, stating that the FBI would not take over Garrison's "dirty laundry."[71] What is most disconcerting about this memo is that Anderson never once presented these views in his column. In fact, he would discredit Garrison and his probe at every opportunity even positing a "Castro did it" blowback theory, a view 180 degrees from Garrison's.

Following close on the heels of the *Newsweek* article, the CIA immediately decided to employ Aynesworth's article in their propaganda efforts. Boldly proclaiming that "Garrison has been fully exposed in NEWSWEEK, 15 May 1967,"[72] the Agency offered to distribute copies of Aynesworth's hatchet job to anyone so interested.[73]

In addition to the *Newsweek* piece, the CIA was also currently enamored with two other works. One was an article by Arthur L. Goodhart, "The Mysteries of the Kennedy Assassination and the English Press," which appeared in the January 1967 issue of the English legal journal, *The Law Quarterly Review.* Even better, according to the CIA, was a then new book by Charles Roberts entitled, *The Truth About The Assassination.* The CIA gave it a rave review stating, "This gives convincing answers to the major criticisms of the [Warren] Report and shows how the critics have distorted and misread the evidence."[74] Not surprisingly Roberts was *Newsweek's* White House correspondent. In addition to the above items, the Agency also had numerous copies of the Warren Report it was willing to distribute.[75]

Another strategy came from James Angleton's Counter-Intelligence division shortly after a Garrison broadcast on WCBS in New York. The CIA noted that Garrison had claimed that a rash of mysterious deaths seemed to be related to the assassination. Angleton's unit weakly countered by raising the question, "If all of Garrison's statements are true, how come Shaw is alive and unharmed?"[76] The CIA liked this notion so much they suggested passing "this idea to *a press contact who could use it editorially.*"[77]

By late May the CIA was growing even more impatient with Garrison. In response to two Garrison television interviews on May 21st and 28th, Angleton's office once again issued another revealing memo:

> GARRISON has translated the issue into a ward heeler's fight in the worst domestic tradition. This is an unfair contest from the Agency's point of view.
> Both singly and in their totality, GARRISON's allegations warrant timely, energetic counteraction, if only at the level of the Attorney General and among responsible members of Congress.[78]

Two months later just such a plan was devised. On September 26, 1967 a "survey of possible courses of action" was issued. Several steps were outlined including:

Congress

-An effort to block or head off any attempts to put the Garrison *Playboy* interview into the Congressional Record.

- Finding an Agency friendly Senator or Congressman to dissuade Senator Russell Long's endorsement of Garrison.

Other Government Officials

- Induce powerful Washington insider, Clark Clifford, to consider the "problems" growing out of Garrison's charges.

- Persuade former CIA Director, John McCone, to "exert influence in Catholic and Republican Circles."

- Not that J. Edgar Hoover needed any goading to react to Garrison's charges, the CIA nevertheless felt that Hoover was "probably the single most important person to be considered in reacting to Garrison's false charges." The Agency rightly felt that Hoover could be "persuaded on the basic merits of the Agency's position in the Garrison matter." The CIA concluded, "the facts of our case should be pressed not only with the Attorney General and the Department of Justice but with the Director of the FBI as well." Thus one could conclude from this that the FBI's and the Justice Department's complicity in destroying Garrison, came at the CIA's behest.

Mass Media Approaches

This section of the memo is so nefarious, yet important I will quote selected items verbatim.

- "Careful thought should be given to the extent to which Mr. Goodwin or the Director can assure that the newspaper outlets receive a coherent picture of Garrison's "facts" and motives. In anticipation of a trial, it would be prudent to have carefully selected channels of communication lined up in advance."

- "The DCI could take up directly with John Daly, who has recently succeeded to the direction of USIA and is son-in-law of the Chief Justice, the facts of our position on Garrison matter in order to assure that our broadcasts abroad are fully knowledgeable. An indication by the Director to Mr. Rusk would reinforce that action." [Author's note: John Daly was the host of the TV quiz show, "What's My Line" and was indeed the son-in-law of Earl Warren]

- "The Communist Bloc exploitation of Garrison's investigation since March 1967 would by itself constitute a theme to be surfaced and exploited. There is enough known about Oswald's contacts with the Soviets in the USSR and in Mexico City to warrant the suggestion that Garrison's investigation is wittingly or unwittingly designed to cover, exonerate or exculpate the Soviets in the Oswald case." [Author's note: As David Atlee Phillips tried to do in Mexico City, the CIA is, once again, dangerously trying to link the Soviet Union to the assassination.]

- "By selective reading Lane, Weissberg, Epstein and other "assassination buffs" have deliberately turned the Warren Commission Report inside out. The precise status, background, and motivation of each of these individuals ought to be subjected to careful public scrutiny and evaluation." [Author's note: Note the CIA's early use of the diminishing term "buffs" to describe researchers of the case – a smear that continues to this day.]

Apparently after scrutinizing Edward Epstein, the Agency actually liked what they saw. Epstein had earlier written a book on the Warren Commission, called *Inquest*, during which he had become close to the CIA's, James Angleton. Later, Epstein ingratiated himself in the Garrison camp. In their July 13, 1968 issue, the *New Yorker* magazine published a malicious nineteen page anti-Garrison screed written by Epstein. A subsequent CIA dispatch to Chiefs of Station worldwide cautioned against attacking Garrison personally but provided them with Epstein's article instead. The dispatch, which included a copy of the *New Yorker* article, instructed the Chiefs to "use the article to brief interested contacts."[79]

As these repeated and obviously orchestrated attacks on the DA's office continued, Garrison decided to fight back. On July 7 Walter Sheridan was charged with four counts of public bribery and Richard Townley was charged with attempted bribery and intimidation of witnesses. Sheridan's New Orleans attorneys of record were Milton Brener, a former Assistant D.A. under Garrison, now vociferously anti-Garrison and Edward Baldwin of Baldwin and Quaid.[80] Baldwin was the attorney who arranged for William Gurvich's lie detector test, which was proudly displayed on the NBC special. In May of 1967, Baldwin's partner, James Quaid wrote a letter to Richard Helms, then Director of the CIA, requesting that the Agency place his name "on their referral list of qualified attorneys in this area."[81] However, Sheridan's Washington representation is much more illuminating.

Herbert Miller was a former head of the Criminal Division of the Department of Justice working closely with Walter Sheridan. In the aftermath of the assassination Miller was the DOJ's point man in Dallas coordinating the Justice, FBI and Texas investigations.[82] After leaving the DOJ, Miller entered private practice in the Washington firm of Miller, McCarthy, Evans, and Cassidy. The Evans in this case being former FBI Assistant Director Courtney Evans. In 1967 Miller went to work for the CIA representing the Agency's interests in the Hans Tofte case.[83] (Tofte was a long-time CIA covert operative who worked in the Domestic Operations Division with his protege, Tracy Barnes. In 1966 he was fired by the Agency for apparently hoarding classified material in his apartment). While he was representing the CIA in the Tofte flap, Miller found time to interject himself into the Garrison investigation. On May 1, 1967, Miller began offering intelligence on the Garrison investigation to the CIA, advising them of the PERMINDEX angle of the probe.[84] Later that week Miller called CIA Associate General Counsel Richard Lansdale to inform him of the expected arrival in Washington of Alvin Beauboeuf. The reader will recall that Beauboeuf was one of David Ferrie's close friends, having accompanied him on his mad dash to Texas on the day of the assassination. Miller's source on Beauboeuf was Walter Sheridan. As Lansdale notes in his memo, "[the NBC special] is expected to "bury" Garrison because everyone is convinced that Garrison is a wild and dangerous man."[85] Miller went on to assure the CIA that "Beauboeuf would be glad to talk with us or help in any way we want."[86] Garrison would note that after Beauboeuf's Washington trip "a change came over Beauboeuf; he refused to cooperate with us further and he made charges against my investigators."[87] To recap, we have evidence that NBC reporter Sheridan was providing intelligence on the Garrison investigation to a CIA lawyer, a situation that indicates certain sinister possibilities. In fact, a May 11th CIA memo reveals that Sheridan wanted to meet with the CIA "under any terms we propose" and that Sheridan desired to make the CIA's view of Garrison "a part of the background in the following NBC show."[88]

While Sheridan's litigation was pending, Miller began doing double duty as a conduit between Shaw's lawyers and the CIA. In May of 1968 Miller wrote to the CIA's Lansdale:

Dear Dick:

Enclosed are the documents I received from Clay Shaw's attorney, Ed Wegmann.

Best Regards,

Herbert J. Miller, Jr.

The following month Miller provided the Agency with at least two more such packages.

Miller was certainly a very busy man during this time frame. While Miller was acting as a CIA courier for Shaw's lawyers and representing Walter Sheridan, he was also performing similar duties for Gordon Novel. While Novel was fighting extradition from Ohio, Miller came to his aid and was successful in getting an Ohio court to quash Garrison's subpoena.[89] Miller also provided the CIA with the transcripts from Novel's civil suit against Garrison and *Playboy*.[90] After Novel successfully avoided Garrison's extradition he sent a clipping to former CIA Director,

Allen Dulles. In his own handwritten marginalia to Dulles, Novel took great pride in Miller's victory, noting what a great job "Miller the Killer" did for him.[91] It is interesting to note that the supposedly itinerant Novel now had four lawyers representing him: Miller, Stephen Plotkin, Jerry Weiner, and Elmer Gertz. Gertz, who had also represented Jack Ruby was one of Novel's lawyers in his civil suit. When answering a list of interrogatories posed to him by *Playboy's* lawyers Novel stated that payment of legal fees to Weiner and Plotkin were "clandestinely remunerated by a party or parties unknown to me."[92] The reader will recall that it was revealed to a Garrison investigator by a former member of the CIA that Plotkin was receiving his fees from the CIA via a cutout, Stephen Lemman.[93] As for Miller, just a few short years after the Shaw trial ended, he represented President Richard Nixon as his post-resignation attorney.

What brings the Sheridan affair full circle is a friend of Sheridan's, one Carmine S. Bellino. Bellino was a former FBI agent and Kennedy insider who worked with Robert Kennedy on the McClellan Committee in the fifties and was brought on to Sheridan's "Get Hoffa" squad in the sixties.[94] In 1954 Bellino actually shared his office with CIA/Mafia go-between, Robert Maheu.[95] But what is troubling about the Bellino/Sheridan relationship is that Bellino once worked with none other than Guy Banister, performing background checks for the CIA-connected Remington Rand Corporation.[96] In the seventies Bellino became an investigator on the Watergate Committee and did his best to steer the committee away from investigating any CIA involvement in the crime.[97]

CIA Is In The House

One thing the CIA didn't have a shortage of in New Orleans was lawyers. We have already seen that Stephen Plotkin, Stephen Lemman, Burton Klein and Herbert Miller were CIA connected. (It is interesting to note that when Garrison charged Sheridan's partner in crime Richard Townley, Townley was represented by Lemman). But not all of the CIA attorneys were working outside of the investigation, some were actually on Garrison's staff.

William Martin would seem like an odd choice for one of Garrison's Assistant D.A.'s. In the late 1950's and early 1960's he was the Chief Investigator for Guy Banister's and Maurice Gatlin's pet organization, the Anti-Communist Committee of the Americas.[98] After resigning in 1961 and entering private practice Martin soon went to work for Clay Shaw as the Director of International Relations and World Trade at the International House.[99] What is interesting is that during his stint at the International House, Martin began working for the CIA. Actually Martin began providing the CIA information in 1960, however it was during his tenure at the International House from 1964 through 1965 that Martin became a formal contact and source. CIA records reveal that Martin had a "subsequent security status of ad hoc through Secret, dated 9 November 1964, and an NI (a) - Approved, 7 January 1965, Office of Security file no. 388412."[100] The records go on to reveal that the Agency has "always held him in high regard."[101] Supposedly contact was broken off after Martin left International House and went to work for Garrison. It is also intriguing that Martin was the member of Garrison's staff that interviewed Richard Case Nagell. Nagell was the former CIA operative who claimed he had infiltrated the New Orleans CIA/Anti-Castro Cuban cell and had discovered the plot to assassinate the President. Nagell was ordered incarcerated at a mental hospital by a federal judge after he shot up an El Paso bank so he could be in protective custody before JFK's assassination. Nagell begged off any further interviews with Martin after he learned that he was former CIA.[102] After he left Garrison's office Martin attempted to reinitiate contact with the CIA.[103] It is not clear from the record if he ever did.

Other CIA records indicate that another of Garrison's Assistant D.A.'s was interested in employment with the Agency. Robert E. Lee left Garrison's staff in January of 1968. On January 5 he contacted the CIA office with a request for employment.[104]

On January 22 a job interview was set up. Available records do not indicate if the interview was successful.

Although not an attorney, Bill Boxley was one of Garrison's investigators who freely admitted his former employment with the Agency. Boxley, whose real name was William Wood, was first approved for intelligence work in the early days of the OSS, the precursor of the CIA.[105] Active duty in the Army prevented him from accepting that assignment but in 1950 he signed on with the newly formed CIA as Chief Instructor of Clandestine Operations. Three years later a nervous breakdown and a propensity for drink forced an early resignation. After stints as a journalist on various newspapers, Wood, in 1967, once again applied for work at the Agency. According to CIA records he was turned down for the job, and it was shortly thereafter that he showed up at Garrison's office. Garrison assigned him a code name of "Boxley" and he became the resident expert on CIA operations for Garrison. While doing some fieldwork on the Dallas end of the probe, Wood began networking with oil millionaire, H. L. Hunt's organization. Later, suspicions were aroused among Garrison's staff that Boxley may not have completely severed all of his ties to his previous employer. Philadelphia lawyer, Vince Salandria, who frequently consulted with Garrison, immediately pegged Boxley as an infiltrator.[106] When Garrison and Salandria called Boxley and asked him to meet them at Garrison's home he never showed up. Garrison visited Boxley's rented room on Canal Street and found nothing but a neatly pressed shirt laying atop an undisturbed bed. The landlady told Garrison that the shirt had been there for months. She further remarked that she had only seen Boxley once when he first rented the room and had been sent a check every month for the rent.[107] As Salandria noted, there was probably a CIA safe house in close proximity to Boxley's rooms. Garrison now realized why Boxley, who had access to all of the DA's files, was toting an oversized briefcase to work every day.[108]

In the early days of the investigation, Garrison was interested in obtaining information on David Ferrie's putative paymaster, Eladio del Valle. The reader will recall that Ferrie reportedly flew firebombing missions over the Cuban sugarcane fields at the behest of del Valle. Del Valle was a former Cuban congressman turned anti-Castro activist who operated out of Miami, Florida. On the day Ferrie died, del Valle was found brutally murdered in his car in the parking lot of a Miami shopping center. Prior to that, Garrison had sent a part-time investigator named Bernardo de Torres to question del Valle. De Torres was a military coordinator for the Brigade 2506 part of the exile landing force during the Bay of Pigs invasion. He was captured by Castro's forces and detained until Christmas Eve of 1962. He eventually found his way to New Orleans where, according to de Torres, he was approached by Sergeant Duffy of the NOPD and asked to join Garrison's staff. As with many other investigators and volunteers at Tulane and Broad, de Torres' bona fides are suspect. First of all, it was de Torres who showed up at the D.A.'s office in New Orleans very early in Garrison's investigation claiming he had important information.[109] He said he was a private detective who wanted to help and dropped the name of Miami D.A., Richard Gerstein as an entree.[110] Shortly after de Torres was given the assignment to question del Valle, del Valle's brutalized body was discovered in the vicinity of de Torres' Miami apartment.[111] It was later determined that de Torres was filing reports on Garrison to the Miami CIA station, JM/WAVE.[112] Not long after he left Garrison's staff, de Torres went to work for Mitch Werbell's Military Armament Corporation, a large supplier of weaponry to the CIA.[113] The HSCA developed evidence that de Torres was actually a CIA officer with links to Military Intelligence.[114] A well connected anti-Castro Cuban, Arturo Cobos told the FBI that de Torres was "the man to call with contacts on a high level with the CIA in Washington, D.C."[115] The HSCA also came into possession of investigative information, which indicated that de Torres may have been in Dealey Plaza at the time of the assassination, and further, that he may have been involved in an assassination conspiracy, charges which de Torres denied.[116] As for Garrison, he later came to believe that de Torres was one of his earliest sources of misinformation and recalled that whatever information de

Torres provided never went anywhere.[117] In the late 1970's de Torres would be linked to the bombing assassination of Chilean leader Orlando Letelier in Washington, D.C.[118]

As we have seen, de Torres was not the only anti-Castro Cuban to join Garrison's staff. Alberto Fowler, who also assisted in the early days of the probe, was a fellow veteran of the 2506 Brigade. Suspiciously, Fowler worked and lived with Clay Shaw, was a board member of INCA, had a brother-in-law who was best friends with the head of the New Orleans CIA office, and was one of the first people to contact the media just after the assassination to inform them of Oswald's pro-Castro posturing in New Orleans. (See Chapter 9).

Another employee of the D.A.'s office in the early days of the investigation was Raymond Beck. Although not specifically assigned to the assassination probe, Beck nevertheless was in a position to gain inside knowledge - knowledge he would share with the FBI. An FBI memorandum from January of 1967 describes Beck as "a reliable and confidential source" and a former Special Agent of the FBI now employed by Garrison's office.[119] Beck advised the Bureau that a *Life* magazine reporter was now covering the probe and "that it was his belief that [name redacted] was advising Garrison on his investigation."[120] Also revealed in this memo is the fact that Garrison's former Chief Investigator, Pershing Gervais, was also informing on Garrison. The memo notes that Gervais is a PCI (an FBI acronym for Potential Criminal Informant).[121] Gervais would later become Garrison's accuser at a trumped-up bribery and tax evasion trial.

The Mob Smear

The most insidious component of the attack on Garrison has been the attempt to smear him with a Mafia brush. This assault started early in the probe but is still reported as gospel by an ever-dwindling number of "Mob did it" assassination theorists to this day.

As one of this decreasing horde John Davis is undoubtedly the most prolific. In addition to two books dealing with the assassination of President Kennedy (*Mafia Kingfish*, 1989 and *The Kennedy Contract*, 1993), Davis has also written books about the Guggenheims, the Kennedy family, and the Bouviers. In fact, Davis was introduced to President Kennedy through his cousin, former Secretary of Defense, Thomas Gates. By using Davis as an example it will be instructive to look at how these falsehoods spread and to trace their origin.

In both *Mafia Kingfish* and *The Kennedy Contract*, Davis tries to make the case that Carlos Marcello, reputed Mafia don of the South, conceived the plan to assassinate JFK and that David Ferrie, in cahoots with Marcello, masterminded and implemented the assassination and frame-up of Oswald. In addition, Davis contends that Garrison was a corrupt pawn of Marcello, who launched his investigation into the assassination and subsequent prosecution of Clay Shaw as a smokescreen to cover-up Marcello's culpability in the crime.

The last point is key to Davis' (and others) theory, but is ludicrous even on first blush. If Garrison was the tool of Marcello, why did he go after the one person that could lead directly back to Marcello - David Ferrie? (Recall Ferrie worked for a short time for G. Wray Gill who counted Marcello as one of his many clients). Or why even start a probe at all and risk drawing attention to Marcello? From the day Garrison launched his investigation right up until Ferrie's death, Garrison kept the heat on Ferrie. As we saw in Chapter 6, Garrison ordered day and night surveillance on Ferrie, infiltrated an informer into his circle and had his staff question him repeatedly. Indeed, on the Saturday just four days before Ferrie's death, Assistant DA Andrew Sciambra and Investigator Lou Ivon paid a visit to Ferrie at his cluttered Louisiana Avenue Parkway apartment. The reader will recall that Ferrie contacted Ivon the next day and Ivon met Ferrie at the Fountainbleau Hotel. In my interview with Ivon he described Ferrie as "very scared - a wild man." Ferrie confided to Ivon that he had done work with the CIA and had known Oswald. He admitted he knew Clay Shaw and that Shaw too worked for the CIA, adding that Shaw hated Kennedy. Three days later Ferrie was found dead. Curiously missing from Ferrie's admissions to Ivon was any reference to Marcello or the Mafia.

Even Davis seems puzzled about Garrison's focus on Ferrie. In the paperback edition of *Mafia Kingfish* Davis writes, "But what did *Marcello* think about Garrison's pointing a finger at David Ferrie? We can only speculate that if Marcello *had* been involved with Ferrie in a plot to assassinate President Kennedy, he would have been very disturbed over the prospect of Ferrie being cross-examined in a courtroom."[122] [Emphasis in original] Four years later Davis still hadn't figured out the answer, as he asks the same question in *The Kennedy Contract*.[123]

As for Ferrie's compensation as Marcello's assassination guru, according to Davis, Marcello bought him a gas station. One can only speculate on Marcello's words, "Thanks for masterminding the crime of the century, Dave. Oh, by the way here's your gas station." But Davis goes further. He states that Ferrie's gas station was "lucrative."[124] Is there such a thing as a lucrative gas station? In Ferrie's case apparently not. In a memo from police investigator Lynn Loisel to Jim Garrison dated March 22, 1967, Loisel writes: "[I] spoke with the operator of Gulf Oil Company and learned that Dave Ferrie opened his Gulf Service Station located on Veterans Highway in Metairie Heights on January 9, 1964 and closed same station on November 30, 1964." Perhaps Ferrie's gas station was "lucrative" after all, allowing him to retire after just 11 months in service. The real kicker is that Davis implies that Marcello admitted in his Executive Session testimony before the House Select Committee on Assassinations that he did indeed purchase the gas station for Ferrie.[125] Since Marcello's Executive Session transcript was classified and only released after the publication of *Mafia Kingfish* Davis could have only received this information from someone inside the committee. In *The Kennedy Contract* Davis revealed that his source was Chief Counsel, G. Robert Blakey, whose preconceived Mafia solution to the crime is well documented in Gaeton Fonzi's, *The Last*

Investigation. (HSCA investigator Bill Triplett confirmed in an interview, "If a suspect didn't have an Italian last name, Blakey wasn't interested in him").[126] Now that the HSCA transcript has been released, one can now verify the accuracy of Davis' (and Blakey's) claims. Not once in the over one hundred pages of immunized testimony does Marcello ever admit he purchased that gas station or lent money to Ferrie to buy the station.[127] Nor is there any mention of the $7,000 that Ferrie deposited to his account shortly before the assassination that Davis also maintains Marcello was asked about.[128] One final note about Ferrie's gas station. In Garrison's book, *A Heritage of Stone* Garrison quotes an associate of Ferrie's who had just received a free fill-up at Ferrie's station. "Forget it," [Ferrie] said. "The government's paying for it anyway."[129]

In the early 1980's Marcello was indicted under the racketeering statute known as RICO. While Marcello was being investigated the FBI recorded hundreds of hours of surveillance tapes of Marcello that have come to be known as the BRILAB tapes. During the 1981 trial of Marcello three of these tapes were withheld from the court. Davis and others have implied that Marcello incriminates himself in these tapes and the government is covering it up. As much as Blakey would like this to be true, even he wouldn't go out on that limb. In the introduction to the paperback re-issue of Blakey and Billings' *Plot to Kill the President* (renamed *Fatal Hour*) Blakey wrote of his conversation with an FBI official who had heard all of the tapes. "Don't worry. They aren't all that incriminating," the official told Blakey.[130] Furthermore, John Volz the assistant U.S. attorney in charge of the BRILAB prosecution said, "We heard it all; there's nothing on those tapes."[131] Indeed, Volz confirmed that statement when I interviewed him in 1994. Further confirmation came from another U.S. attorney involved in the case, John Voorhees. In a letter to the editor of the *Washington Post* Voorhees writes, "There is no "evidence" on the tapes that implicates Mr. Marcello in the assassination."[132] In 1998 the Assassination Records and Review Board released the BRILAB tapes and, as suspected, there is no incriminating evidence, relative to Marcello and the assassination, contained on them.

Perhaps the most guileful and dangerous charge that Davis and other Mafia theorists posit is that Jim Garrison was a corrupt public official in cahoots with the Mob. This allegation usually breaks down to the following charges:

- That Garrison took a vacation in Las Vegas that was paid for by the Mob.

- Builder Frank Occhipinti, a reputed Marcello associate, gave Garrison a sweet deal on his house.

- Garrison avoided Marcello-owned bars in his Bourbon Street clean up.

- Garrison never considered Marcello or the Mafia as candidates in the assassination.

These charges have been adequately answered in James DiEugenio's excellent presentation, *Garrison, the Media, and the Mob*. I will do my best to summarize the key points here.

In 1967 *Life* magazine published an "expose'" which revealed that Garrison had taken a trip to the Sands Hotel in Las Vegas and had his tab picked up by the management. The owner of the Sands, Mario Marino was, according to *Life*, a Mafioso with ties to Marcello.[133] Garrison provided evidence to the *Life* reporters that the "hospitality" he received was nothing more than the standard loss-leader feature extended to most important personages who visit not only the Sands but most other hotels in Vegas. Garrison provided a copy of his Sands bill to the reporters and pointed out that there was a rather hefty valet and telephone bill that the hotel did not cover. As Garrison noted, "Apparently I am not very highly regarded by the Mafia if they won't even pick up my phone bill."[134] Nevertheless *Life* went ahead with these charges. Chief researcher of that article was Richard Billings, G. Robert Blakey's hand-picked co-author of the HSCA Report as well as their "Mafia did it" tract, *The Plot to Kill the President*. Assisting Billings was local *Life* stringer David Chandler. Chandler was a close friend of the man Garrison indicted for conspiracy, Clay Shaw. In fact Chandler was living in a French Quarter apartment owned by Shaw at the time. Later, we will focus on the actual author of the article, Sandy Smith.

During Garrison's second term as D.A. he purchased a new home in an upscale New Orleans suburb. His critics like to contend that because Occhipinti built the house and that Garrison supposedly got a cut-rate price on the home this somehow proves he was receiving Mob favors. But does it? The fact that the house was built by Occhipinti proves nothing. That was his job. Occhipinti, whatever else he may have been, was a real estate developer who built half of the houses in Garrison's neighborhood. The "cut-rate" price Garrison paid for the house was $60,000. By today's standards that could raise some eyebrows, but the real estate market (and the value of the dollar) was much different in the mid-sixties than it is today. In 1994, Garrison's son, Lyon allowed me and a few others unprecedented access to his father's personal papers. Among other things, Garrison's records show that Garrison took out second and third mortgages on his house just to make ends meet. Apparently the Mafia was only paying minimum wage at the time.

During his first term, Garrison made national headlines as the vice busting D.A. of New Orleans. He successfully padlocked dozens of French Quarter bars that were "clipping" tourists. His detractors like to claim that he shied away from the Marcello run bars as a favor to the "Mafia Kingfish." One only has to look at the *New Orleans Times-Picayune* of the day to see through this charge. Garrison gave the green light to padlocking at least four Marcello connected bars: The Flamingo, The Old French Opera House, The 500 Club and The Sho-Bar.[135] In the case of the Flamingo, Garrison sought to close that bar down for a year and directed his Assistant D.A., Denis A. Barry, to prove in court that the owner,

Frank Sinopoli, was only a front for Marcello.[136]

Finally, the charge that Garrison never considered the mob as a suspect in the assassination is once again the stuff of nonsense. In a 1967 story in *Newsday* the following was written: "Garrison is trying to learn whether the Cosa Nostra and anti-Castro Cubans may have been linked by mob-controlled gambling operations in pre-Castro Cuba...Garrison is trying to determine if there is a thread which binds the Cosa Nostra, anti-Castro groups, the late Dave Ferrie, Oswald and Jack Ruby."[137] In December of 1967, Garrison wrote a four-page memo to this staff entitled "Organized Crime Aspects of the Assassination." In the memo Garrison advises his staff that, "It cannot be denied, for example, that there is evidence which appears to indicate some involvement of individuals who seem to have organized crime connections. Furthermore, we cannot arbitrarily assume that, even if the militant right wing factor continues to develop effectively, involvement of organized crime elements may not be an additional factor as a product of joint interest."[138] Further proof is offered by intelligence operative Gordon Novel. The reader is already familiar with his deposition taken during his unsuccessful libel suit against Garrison and *Playboy* magazine. During the deposition Novel is asked:

Q: What business did you have with Mr. Marcello?

A: I was trying to locate a Mr. Haggeman, who was an arch enemy of Mr. Garrison, and at the time he informed me that Mr. Garrison was considering involving him in the assassination.

Q: Marcello or Haggeman?

A: Mr. Marcello.[139]

In June of 1967, the FBI had information that Garrison was pursuing the mob angle. An FBI source reported that "Garrison believed that organized crime, specifically, "La Cosa Nostra" is responsible along with other Anti-Castroites for the assassination."[140]

What makes these allegations all the more suspicious is that they were virtually non-existent *prior* to Garrison's conspiracy investigation. In fact, the most vociferous sources of these smears, were also once Garrison's loudest champions. The aforementioned David Chandler writing in the November 1966 issue of *New Orleans* magazine declared Garrison "an incorruptible crusader for justice. Which (blush) he is. He really is."[141] Years later Chandler had to concede that he'd "always found Garrison to be honest, a man of integrity with a deep concern for individual rights."[142] Chandler was also the co-author (along with the aforementioned James Phelan) of a 1963 *Saturday Evening Post* article that lauded Garrison as a racket buster - its title: "The Vice Man Cometh."[143] An expose' on organized crime published in the *Saturday Evening Post* in 1964 states that the "city of New Orleans itself, with a record of effective law enforcement in the last few years, is comparatively clean today."[144] This point was also duly noted in Fred Cook's book, *Mafia!*. Cook writes, "The Mob had a history of moving across big city municipal lines to escape the pressure of big city D.A.'s; Capone to Cicero, New York Mob to New Jersey, and Marcello from New Orleans to Jefferson Parish."[145] The *Post* article goes on to relate how a bribe was offered to one of Garrison's assistants from a Marcello lackey. The bribe was refused and reported to the Metropolitan Crime Commission.[146]

The Metropolitan Crime Commission is a citizen's watchdog committee that was organized in New Orleans in the 1950's. At the urging of one of Clay Shaw's close friends, Edith Stern, Aaron Kohn was installed as the managing director of the MCC. Kohn was an ex-FBI man from Guy Banister's alma mater, the Chicago office. In fact Kohn and Banister used to work closely together during Banister's days on the New Orleans Police Department. Again prior to Garrison's probe, Kohn always lauded

Garrison as a bulwark in the fight against organized crime. In the Sunday supplement to the January 17, 1965 issue of the *Times-Picayune* Kohn writes, "The District Attorney for Orleans Parish is the most powerful and most important, single official in the City's processes of law enforcement. The vitality with which the authority has been used by the Garrison administration has been an unprecedented deterrent to crime and organized racketeering in New Orleans." Which brings us to the subject of Aaron Kohn. As mentioned, Kohn was the director of the MCC. Former officers and directors include Shaw's associate, the rabidly right-wing Dr. Alton Ochsner, FBI agent Warren deBrueys, and Oswald's former employer Eustis Reily of Reily Coffee.

In late 1966 a 22 year-old stripper by the name of Linda Birgette was arrested and charged with lewd dancing. Most agreed it was a ridiculous charge, especially in New Orleans, so Garrison wanted to release her. Yet an outraged Kohn insisted she was hooked into the Marcello syndicate and releasing her was tantamount to letting a major felon walk. After Governor McKeithen interceded on her behalf, Kohn recklessly charged that both Garrison and McKeithen had been influenced by the mob. This effectively ended Garrison's relationship with Kohn. Kohn's charges also appeared at the same time Garrison was beginning his assassination probe, which makes Kohn's motivation all the more suspicious. Nevertheless, the important point here is that we now know that all of the mob smears directed against Garrison originated from (or through) <u>one source</u>: Aaron Kohn.[147] When the *Life* magazine articles hit and all of the Mafia allegations were swirling around Garrison's office (effectively sidetracking his investigation) Garrison decided to call Kohn in front of the Grand Jury so he could present his evidence of organized crime in Orleans Parish. As Garrison wrote in a April 17, 1968 letter to Donald Organ, "Mr. Kohn had publicly admitted that it was *he* who made all of this information initially available to Life Magazine. Inside of the Grand Jury room, with the doors shut, Mr. Kohn admitted that he really did not have any evidence of any kind that organized crime was occurring in New Orleans." Kohn also admitted as much in an interview with Garrison and his staff prior to his Grand Jury appearance.[148] When one of the executives of Kohn's Crime Commission appeared before the Grand Jury, he admitted, "No, we have nothing, we have no evidence to put before the Grand Jury."[149] The outgoing Grand Jury concurred when they wrote a blistering criticism of Kohn and his methods in their final report:

> We, the members of the outgoing Grand Jury, have been deluged with defamatory accusations such as being "pawns of the District Attorney," and entering into a conspiracy to "destroy the Crime Commission," and having no redress available while serving as members of the Grand Jury, now wish to acquaint the public with the following:
> Organized crime, as we understand the term, exists in areas that are saturated with corrupt officials. Wherever there is an alert Mayor, an honest and intelligent Chief of Police, with an upgraded police force, and an aggressive District Attorney's Office, organized crime cannot exist. If these officials do not all cooperate and participate in this scheme it cannot flourish because no one official is capable of protecting the illegal endeavors of the so-called "syndicate." A combination without any one official is doomed. To accept Mr. Kohn's view, in this particular area, we must assume the dishonesty of all the aforementioned public officials, plus a dishonest Governor. We, as laymen, acting for the community, can only evaluate what has been sworn to under oath. The allegations of organized crime in this Parish has been fathered by the Metropolitan Crime Commission and published, with their approval, in Life Magazine. When asked for the same files that this Commission gave to Life Magazine willingly, Mr. Kohn first requested assistance. Sgt. Jerry Lankford, one of the most able police officers, was selected for this purpose. Sgt. Lankford holds a degree in criminology and is presently attending Law School in the evenings. Mr. Kohn and his Executive Committee then decided these files should not be given voluntarily to this legally constituted body, so a court fight has ensued. We wish to emphasize that we are not against a properly handled Crime Commission, only against thought-less individuals who, without sufficient foundation, make allegations and then fail to produce proof of these allegations and refuse to give what information they might have to the proper officials.
> The weight of these officials' testimony far outweighs the allegations of one man's fancy. Mr. Kohn, with his limited capabilities, deems himself an authority on this subject. If he is, and has information of such

> magnitude as Organized Crime in this Parish, then he, as a member of a
> civilian community organization, with no power except publicity,
> should give this information to the duly appointed and/or elected
> officials of this community.[150] [Emphasis in original]

Kohn would later be indicted by the Grand Jury and convicted of
contempt of court, his fourth such conviction. After his decision,
Judge Braniff, said, "If Mr. Kohn wants to play cops and robbers,
he is going to have to come up with something in the way of proof,
instead of making a sham of the judiciary."[151] Kohn's conviction
was overturned on appeal.

In 1969, *Look* magazine published an article entitled "The
Persecution of Clay Shaw." The article is an outright attack on
Garrison, rehashing the Kohn allegations. The article carried a
byline by Warren Rogers. What we now know about Rogers is
revealing. In a book written by William Sullivan, who was the
Number 3 man at the FBI for a good part of Hoover's reign, there
is a chapter called "Flacking for the Bureau." Listed as one of the
columnists who would routinely write articles based on material
provided to them by the FBI was none other than Warren
Rogers.[152]

This mob smear is nothing new. Nor is the use of *Life*
magazine by the intelligence community to accomplish these
means. In 1966, Senator Edward Long was a Democratic senator
from Missouri and head of the Judiciary committee. When his
committee started probing the FBI budget and eavesdropping
procedures, Long suddenly became the subject of an expose' in
Life. It reported that Long had received money from Jimmy Hoffa.
It further alleged that Long's probe of the FBI was really a
smokescreen, a sham designed to actually deflect efforts to fight
organized crime.[153] (As we have seen, John Davis and others have
used a similar charge against the Garrison probe). A Senate ethics
committee found no basis to these allegations. Nevertheless the
Life article ruined Long's political career. He lost his 1968
reelection bid.

Like Senator Long, Congressman Cornelius Gallagher was

worried about the FBI's use of emerging technologies to encroach on the private lives of U.S. citizens and Gallagher's Subcommittee on Privacy immediately clashed with Director Hoover. The FBI began intimidating Gallagher, using former Senator Joseph McCarthy's hatchet man and Hoover's fellow homosexual sexcapader, Roy Cohn as a middleman.[154] Failing that, the FBI pulled a "black bag" job on Gallagher's home, making off only with documents.[155] Police contacts of Gallagher's confirmed the FBI's complicity in this harassment.[156] An executive at the Bell Telephone Company also informed Gallagher that the FBI was bugging his phone.[157] But once again it would be *Life* magazine that would attempt to deliver the knockout punch. In the very same issues that ran the Garrison smear, *Life* "linked" Gallagher to New Jersey mobster, "Bayonne Joe" Zicarelli, claiming the two were on the best of terms and had regular "get-togethers."[158] Gallagher denied the relationship and complained to *Life* executives. He considered suing for libel but backed off fearing adverse publicity.

Less than a year later, Gallagher's attorney, Lawrence Weisman, asked that Gallagher meet with him on a matter of the utmost importance. Journalist, Anthony Summers describes what happened next:

> "Weisman explained that he had spent part of the day at Roy Cohn's office. At Cohn's suggestion, he had listened in on an extension as Cohn talked on the telephone with Cartha DeLoach of the FBI. Deloach allegedly claimed the Bureau had "incontestable" proof that a missing New Jersey gambler, Barney O'Brien, had died of a heart attack in the Congressman's house "while lying next to Gallagher's wife." The body had supposedly been removed by Kayo Konigsberg, a gangster linked to Zicarelli. According to Gallagher and his attorney, DeLoach made it clear he had recently been in touch with *Life*. "If you still know that guy," DeLoach was quoted as saying, "you better get word to him to resign from Congress. He's not going to last more than a week after the story hits.""[159]

Indeed in the August 8, 1968 issue of *Life* a story appeared called "THE CONGRESSMAN AND THE HOODLUM." At the heart of the story was a transcript of a supposed eight-year-old wiretap on Zicarelli. According to the story, the transcript showed Gallagher applying pressure to get the local police off of Zicarelli's back:

Gallagher: I got hold of these people [Bayonne Police] and there will be no further problem.
Zicarelli: I hope so, because they're ruining me.
Gallagher: They damn well better not.
Zicarelli: They're doing a job on me like was never done before.
Gallagher: I laced into them.[160]

Despite this smear, Gallagher was reelected, but a 1972 IRS investigation would finally bring Gallagher down. Gallagher was charged with evading taxes and conspiring with another official to do the same. Gallagher felt he had no recourse but to plead guilty and subsequently went to jail for seventeen months.

An investigation by the House Ethics Committee found no evidence that the Congressman had ever been involved with organized crime. Further, *Life*'s source about the supposed corpse in Gallagher's home, Kayo Konigsberg, was in the Mental Center for Federal Prisoners at the time.[161] Konigsberg later admitted that the *Life* story was "a phony" and that the FBI had persuaded him to "frame-up" Gallagher.[162] As for the transcript, again I quote from Summers:

> "There is no evidence that the damning "transcript" of conversations between Gallagher and the Mafia boss Zicarelli ever existed in the files of any law enforcement agency. In 1968 the IRS, the CIA, the Narcotics Bureau, the Secret Service, the New York City Police, the Manhattan District Attorney and the New York Rackets Bureau all pleaded ignorance. As for the FBI, Attorney General Ramsey Clark said he was advised that "the FBI does not have and has not had any transcripts or logs that could be the basis for the quotations in the *Life* magazine story..." Nor have any transcripts turned up in the thousands

of documents that have since been made public. A review of FBI files in Newark, New Jersey, has produced none and agents who worked the Zicarelli case in the sixties said they know of no such evidence."[163]

Which brings us to the author of the *Life* articles, Sandy Smith. Smith was regarded as something of an organized crime expert, having made his name as such for the McCormick owned *Chicago Tribune*. In 1965 former FBI agent turned author, William Turner, submitted a piece critical of the FBI to *Playboy* magazine. No sooner had the article been accepted than *Playboy* editor, Murray Fisher, was paid a visit by two of Hoover's finest, inquiring about the as yet unpublished article.[164] How the FBI found out about the article remained a mystery until years later when Turner received several FBI documents under the Freedom of Information Act. According to the documents, Fisher asked Sandy Smith to look over Turner's article and perhaps lend some of his "expertise" to the piece. But as the documents revealed, Smith was an FBI collaborator who, in the words of the FBI, was "a great admirer of the Director" and had been "utilized on many different occasions" where his value was "inestimable."[165] The FBI would reciprocate by feeding Smith information the Bureau wanted published in the local newspapers and *Life* magazine.[166] The documents showed that no sooner had Smith received a copy of Turner's article than Smith hopped over to the local office of the FBI and gave it to the local boss, Marlin Johnson, who in turn fed it to Cartha DeLoach.[167] Needless to say, *Playboy* killed the article.[168]

Summers writes that former *Life* reporter Bill Lambert, who also worked on the Gallagher story, recalled that Smith was so close to the FBI that he was "almost like an agent." Final corroboration of this sordid mess came from a dying Roy Cohn in 1986. As he lay dying of AIDS, Cohn was informed that Gallagher's wife was still traumatized by the allegation about the gambler O'Brien dying in her arms. Cohn then signed a letter stating that the bogus O'Brien allegation had come directly from DeLoach.[169] Summers closes his section on Gallagher by quoting former Assistant Attorney General, Mitchell Rogovin. "All the leaking to *Life* magazine," he said, was "part and parcel of the retributive mode that went on... This was one of a lot of cases."[170] Another of which, was undoubtedly Garrison's.

I have dwelled at some length on the Gallagher case because of the disturbing parallels to Garrison's situation. First, you have Garrison being smeared as a friend of the Mob in the exact same article as Gallagher, written by FBI asset, Sandy Smith. Second, as with Gallagher, an allegation arose that a supposed gambler, in Garrison's case, Vic Carona, had died in Garrison's home of a heart attack. This is shockingly similar to the O'Brien fabrication put out by DeLoach and the FBI. And third, just like Gallagher, Garrison became the target of a fraudulent IRS investigation, one that Garrison won in court but not before his career as D.A. had been ruined. (It is also interesting to note that the CIA had compiled dossiers on Garrison, Gallagher, and Long).[171] Finally, another familiar thread winds its way through this tapestry. As we have seen, Gallagher had been the object of bugging and electronic eavesdropping by the FBI, with assistance from the telephone company. New evidence indicates this is precisely what happened to Garrison.

In 1977 Garrison met with William Walter. The reader will recall that Walter was the New Orleans FBI clerk who had earlier revealed Oswald's status as an FBI informant and of the presence of a Telex message, warning of an assassination attempt on President Kennedy. Walter, who by 1977 was a banking executive, provided to the former D.A. detailed information regarding an FBI program of wiretapping and surveillance of Garrison. Walter certainly had an impeccable source for this inside information - his wife was the clerk who typed up the daily transcripts of the wiretaps. According to Walter, Special Agents, Chandler Josey and Ed Parent, were both involved in the operation. Josey was later transferred to the security office of the Southern Bell Telephone Company and Parent later went to work for Charles Carlson at Wackenhut. Carlson was the investigator from Wackenhut who was working for Clay Shaw's defense team. Heading the operation was an FBI agent named, Bob Wilson, who was also assigned to tailing Garrison virtually full-time. In order to achieve a level of plausible deniability, the FBI utilized a cutout for the operation - none other than the nefarious Aaron Kohn. The plan, Walter said, was to make it look like Southern Research/Wackenhut was eavesdropping on Garrison while in the employ of Kohn, but it was an FBI operation all the way. Kohn, of course, was a witting collaborator to the FBI's illegal hanky-panky.[172] Of Kohn's collusion with the FBI, there can be no doubt. The National Archives FBI collection is filled with numerous reports from Kohn informing the Bureau of Garrison's nearly every step.[173]

If Walter's allegations are true (and after what we have already seen there is no reason to doubt them) then it is further evidence of the orchestrated attack launched upon Garrison by the intelligence community, a very cooperative and compromised media, and their ubiquitous mouthpiece, Aaron Kohn.

Lest the reader think that the "mob smear" tactic ended after Garrison and Gallagher had left office, nothing could be further from the truth. When the House Select Committee on Assassinations began their investigation in 1976, their first Chief Counsel was former Philadelphia Assistant D.A., Richard A. Sprague. Sprague had just unraveled the conspiracy behind the death of reform labor leader, Jock Yablonski. As Special Prosecutor of Washington County, Sprague had successfully convicted corrupt union boss, Tony Boyle, of Yablonski's murder. When word got out that Sprague was going to actually conduct a real investigation of the President's murder as Chief Counsel for the Committee (with special emphasis on the intelligence agencies), out came the old stand-by. Read into the Congressional Record was a charge linking Sprague to the Mafia that reads not unlike Garrison's own defamation. The allegation was that Sprague had taken several trips in recent years to Las Vegas and it was asked of him who had paid for those trips. It was also charged that Sprague had taken several trips to Fontainbleau Hotel in Miami Beach and a statement was made, "We all know who owns the Fountainbleau," insinuating an association between Sprague and various disreputable individuals. Sprague had his rebuttals to these charges read into the Congressional Record as well. The record affirmed that "Mr. Sprague has been in Las Vegas on one occasion when he lectured at a conference of a National Trial Lawyers Association along with other nationally prominent attorneys. He spoke in the evening of the day he arrived and left the next day. Mr. Sprague has never stayed in the Fountainbleau Hotel in Miami Beach."[174] The controversy arising from these and other spurious charges, as well as political infighting, led to Sprague's ouster, clearing the way for Mafia expert, G. Robert Blakey to take his place.

Before leaving this chapter, a couple of final points should be made regarding Davis,' *The Kennedy Contract*. A modest paperback volume, it was released in 1993 at the tail end of the groundswell of interest in the case generated by Oliver Stone's 1991 film, *JFK*. It is basically a summary of Davis' Marcello theory with a chapter trashing Stone's film thrown in as well. Also included is a chapter on the now discredited Frank Ragano allegations.(Jimmy Hoffa ordered Marcello and Florida Mafia Don, Santos Trafficante to assassinate JFK). But illustrative of Davis' confusion is a passage regarding a conversation Ragano overheard between Marcello and Trafficante:

> "While driving through New Orleans in Marcello's car, Marcello was driving and Trafficante was seated in the front seat and he [Ragano] was in the back, when a radio broadcast related events concerning District Attorney Garrison's escapades revolving around the assassination of President Kennedy. Santos turned and remarked to Marcello, "Carlos, the next thing you know they will be blaming the President's assassination on us.""[175]

Doesn't this remark seem indicative of innocence, therefore disproving Ragano's and Davis' claims?

Another example of this murky writing can be found on page 92 as Davis attempts to reconstruct the shooting:

> "Suddenly a series of shots rang out. The first shot struck President Kennedy in the upper right back six inches below the neckline, and

penetrated to a depth of no more than a little finger's length.

A second and a half later another shot was fired that struck Governor John Connally, who was seated in the limousine to the right of the President, in the upper back at the level of his left armpit, penetrated his rib cage, shattering one rib, then exited from his front chest, pierced and shattered his right wrist, then entered inside his left thigh, where the bullet became embedded in tissue.

Two seconds passed, then, as the presidential limousine slowed to a crawl, a third shot struck the back of the President's head near the top of the skull and exited from the right side. The trajectory of the bullet suggested that it had been fired from the southeast corner window of the sixth floor of the Book Depository. For a fraction of a second the President's head was driven forward, then suddenly it lurched violently back as a fourth shot struck the President in the right temple and exploded out of the back of the head. The shot had come from behind the picket fence on the grassy knoll."

No matter what side of the picket fence you are on in the assassination debate, one point that is without doubt is that the President suffered a throat wound. Autopsy photographs confirm it. Whether you believe it to be an exit or entry wound, everyone agrees it existed. Everyone but Davis I presume. You will note in Davis' reconstruction of events that nowhere is there any mention of the throat wound. I might add that also missing from this reconstruction is any mention of the bystander, James Tague, who was wounded by a missed shot.

Which leads us to another point of controversy in Davis' work - his sources. We have already seen how the Marcello Executive Session testimony was misrepresented, I will cite another example. Listed as a source in both of his JFK volumes is the transcript from the Clay Shaw trial. According to Davis he found this at Southeastern Louisiana University in Hammond, Louisiana. SELU now has a Web site (*www.selu.edu*) where you can look at a catalog of all of their holdings. The transcript is nowhere to be found. In fact the Shaw trial transcript wasn't released until 1993 when the HSCA released their copy to the National Archives. A call to the librarian at SELU quickly confirmed the absence of the transcript. The only trial material they have ever carried is Perry Russo's testimony and the transcript of the 3-day preliminary hearing.

By using gossamer threads to tie Marcello into the assassination, non-existent sources and a baseless and slanderous attack against Jim Garrison, Davis and others who are caught up in the "Mafia mystique" practice a dangerous form of misinformation. Whether intended or not, this plays right into the hands of those who still seek to suppress the truth. One could argue that these authors are confused or have set about to prove a preconceived hypothesis no matter what the cost. However, no such extenuation can be offered to the intelligence community, the major media, and the likes of Sandy Smith and Aaron Kohn.

Chapter Thirteen

~

Trial and Error

Despite all of the governmental misconduct, the attacks on Garrison in the media, and the help Shaw's team was receiving from both of these bodies, Shaw's lawyer's still claimed they could not get a fair and impartial trial. They even had the temerity to plead their case to the Justice Department who were already doing their best to subvert Garrison's investigation. On September 21, 1967, Shaw's lawyers, Irvin Dymond and Edward Wegmann, traveled to Washington, D.C. to meet with Nathaniel Kossack of the Criminal Division of the Justice Department. Shaw's attorneys first played the patriotism card, claiming that if Shaw is convicted then "not only will the Warren Commission and the Commission's Report be completely discredited, but confidence throughout the world in the United States Government will be undermined."[1] The lawyers further warned that "The District Attorney is a dangerous, irresponsible man and must be stopped," and that they are forced "to play with a stacked deck."[2] They went on to request access to CIA files on Ferrie, Novel, Shaw, New Orleans attorney, Burton Klein and themselves! Kossack concluded his memo by saying that Dymond and Wegmann "presented a strong plea for investigative assistance and cooperation to help them refute charges that are otherwise unanswerable."[3]

Knowing little of what was going on behind the scenes, Garrison nevertheless responded to some of these charges and delay tactics in a DA's Answer To Motion For Continuance And Opposition To Change Of Venue:

The State answers and alleges that if an atmosphere exists in Orleans Parish which could prevent a fair and impartial trial, then this atmosphere was created by (1) the notoriety and magnitude of the crime with which the defendant stands charged, and (2) the natural enthusiasm of members of the press and news media to report to the public each and every item they considered newsworthy however obtained, and (3) the conduct of the defendant, Clay L. Shaw, and his attorneys in the following particulars:

(a) The making of a public statement by Clay L. Shaw soon after his arrest in the presence of his attorneys to the various news media which statement was reported on a nationwide telecast and calculated to influence prospective jurors.

(b) The active entertainment and solicitation of the good will and friendship of members of all news media (newspapers, magazines, radio, and television) at the home of Edward Wegmann, an attorney for the defendant, at which time the defendant was publicly interviewed and posed for photographs to be disseminated by the media. Not only were the members of the news media hosted in the home of defense counsel, but they were also given favorable and selective background information on the defendant.

(c) That the attorneys for Clay L. Shaw met with and were in consultation with the producers of an NBC nationwide telecast in June, 1967, which was critical of the charges pending against the defendant, Clay L. Shaw. It had been announced in advance by the reporters of NBC-TV and WDSU-TV that this production was an effort to put an end to the prosecution of Clay L. Shaw and the investigation of the conspiracy to assassinate John F. Kennedy.

(d) The giving of a personal interview by the defendant which was recorded by film and sound and played to a nationwide audience on the aforementioned NBC telecast.

(e) That the attorneys of Clay L. Shaw met and consulted with one Aaron Kohn, the managing director of the Metropolitan Crime Commission of New Orleans, Inc., prior to the previously described nationwide telecast. Aaron Kohn formulated a plan after his consultation with the attorney for Clay L. Shaw and representatives of NBC prior to the production of the NBC telecast to assemble some of the members of the Executive Committee of the New Orleans Metropolitan Crime Commission to watch the NBC telecast and thereafter send a letter to the Attorney General of the State of Louisiana making unsubstantiated accusations against the District Attorney of Orleans Parish in a manner to reflect upon this pending prosecution. The crux of the plan was for Aaron Kohn to release to the news media this letter to the Attorney General in order that it might have widespread local publicity and thereby prejudice local jurors. After formulating such a plan it was indeed put into effect by the said parties, not withstanding the fact that Aaron Kohn has admitted that he has no independent evidence and that the said letter was predicated only upon the baseless allegations of the news media. The real sinister conduct is reflected by the fact that the decision to write the letter was made <u>prior</u> to the actual viewing of the NBC telecast.[4]

As the DA noted, if a prejudicial atmosphere existed in Orleans Parish, Shaw was the author of his own misfortune.

As the heat was being applied to Garrison, his source of outside funds began to dry up. "Truth and Consequences, Inc." was a title coined by a group of fifty businessmen for the private organization they formed to subsidize Garrison's probe. Although the founders were seemingly a trio of altruistic businessmen and friends of Garrison, newly discovered information hints at other darker possibilities.

CIA documents describe Cecil Shilstone as a lifelong friend of both New Orleans CIA Station Chief, Lloyd Ray and his Assistant, Hunter Leake. All three were in the same college fraternity and Shilstone and Ray were members of the same country club. Shilstone, a former Major in the Chemical Warfare Service of the U.S. Army, and the current president of his own chemical firm, also provided the CIA with at least two reports. CIA records note that the "official (but not the personal) relationship ceased in March 1956."[5] Willard Robertson owned a local Volkswagen dealership and available CIA records indicate no Agency contact. However, it was Robertson who recommended fringe CIA spook, Gordon Novel, to Garrison as security adviser to the probe. As we saw earlier, Joseph Rault was on the fateful plane trip from New York with Garrison and Senator Long where the discussion took place that essentially launched the D.A.'s investigation. Although not listed as an Agency contact either, Rault owned his own petroleum company that worked with the Humble Oil and Refining Company.[6] While a source for some early funds, it wasn't long before the flow of money tapped out. Garrison's office had an endless budget problem and while lamenting this fact in a conversation, he noted that the Truth and

Consequences group seemed to have disappeared from the scene completely. Garrison suspected outside pressure and reflected, "All of a sudden one day came and they didn't meet anymore."[7]

As if the full court press being applied to Garrison by the government wasn't bad enough, he had still more trouble from within. In August of 1968 Tom Bethell, one of Garrison's few paid volunteers, met with Shaw attorney, Sal Panzeca. At that time, Bethell provided to Panzeca, Garrison's witness list and summary of expected testimony - in other words, their trial brief.[8] It was shortly after this that Shaw's lawyers announced they were now ready for trial. In January of 1969, when rumors of a leak in the office started to circulate, Bethell admitted his crime to Ivon and Alcock.[9]

By the time Garrison got Shaw to trial in February of 1969, the verdict was almost pre-ordained. It took the jury less than an hour to acquit Shaw. Interviewed after the trial, some jurors felt Garrison had proved a conspiracy but he had not adequately linked it to Shaw or provided a motive. (The two alternate jurors felt differently, however. Though their vote didn't count, they were asked to mark their ballot anyway. Both had voted for conviction).[10] The jurors themselves came under scrutiny from the CIA as soon as they were selected. James Angleton's Counter-Intelligence unit compiled a list of the jurors with background information on all of them and supplied it to the CIA's Security Division.[11] Garrison's witnesses were also fair game for Angleton. While presenting the "Dallas phase" of its case, the State put Dr. John Nichols on the stand to dispute the single bullet theory. After he testified, Angleton sent a memo to the FBI requesting additional information on Dr. Nichols.[12] Some observers have remarked that if Shaw's CIA connections had been brought out in court that may have provided the missing link needed for a conviction. Others have noted that Garrison's case fell apart when State's witness, Charles Spiesel testified.

Spiesel, an accountant from New York City, testified that in May of 1963 he attended a conspiratorial meeting in the French Quarter where Shaw and Ferrie discussed killing the president. On its face, Spiesel's story was too pat - an instant replay of Perry Russo's statements. Under cross-examination the Spiesel time bomb exploded. As Dymond questioned him, Spiesel admitted he would fingerprint his daughter when she would return home from attending college at LSU. He had to make sure she hadn't been substituted for a duplicate, he said. He also testified to being constantly followed, having his phone tapped, and to being hypnotized over fifty times by the New York City Police. Spiesel had even filed a lawsuit against a host of defendants alleging the same. Shaw's lawyers had an easy time discrediting Spiesel, especially in light of the fact they had the stolen trial brief in their possession for the previous six months[13]. But Judge Haggerty felt an important point got lost amid the lunatic testimony of Spiesel. During the trial, Spiesel was allowed to try to locate the apartment where the alleged conspiratorial discussion took place. With the judge, jury, and attorneys in tow, Spiesel led the group to a building in the French Quarter - 906 Esplanade. Shaw, at one time, owned 906 Esplanade. In May of 1963, Shaw also owned the adjoining property at 908 Esplanade and both properties abutted Shaw's residence at 1313 Dauphine.[14]

Ironically, it was Haggerty that hurt the State's case by disallowing the booking card, with Shaw's Bertrand alias, into evidence. Citing the Miranda statute, Haggerty ruled that the booking procedure amounted to an interrogation, and since Shaw's attorney was not present in the booking room with him, Shaw's Miranda rights were violated.[15] In retrospect, it is clear Haggerty made an incorrect decision. The Supreme Court held that the term "interrogation" under Miranda refers not only to express questioning, but also to any words or actions on the part of the police other than those normally attendant to arrest and custody. (Rhode Island v. Innis, 100 S. Ct. 1682 (1980)). At least five other cases have held that biographical information taken at booking is not interrogation for Miranda purposes. But is an alias considered normal biographical information? The federal courts say yes. United States v. Prewitt, 553 F.2d 1082 (7th Cir. 1977) equates an alias with "other identifying characteristics" which are nontestimonial in nature and thereby not subject to Miranda and other Fifth Amendment problems. Nevertheless the damage was done.

It is beyond the scope of this volume to do an in-depth analysis of the Shaw trial. A whole book could be devoted to just this aspect of the case. In fact, one was. *American Grotesque*, by James Kirkwood, is such an obviously subjective and biased treatment, it is of little value. More so now with the release of the Shaw trial transcript.[16]

One point should be made about a different book that attempts to close the case on the entire JFK matter. In *Case Closed*, author, Gerald Posner covers the Shaw trial in less than two pages. He has Perry Russo testifying first, followed by Dean Andrews.[17] Then "to prevent his case from falling apart, Garrison introduced the Clinton witnesses," Posner writes.[18] Posner then has Garrison calling Spiesel to the stand, followed shortly by Marina Oswald and Bethesda pathologist, Pierre Finck.[19] Even a cursory glance at Kirkwood's book will reveal how far off base Posner is here. The Clinton/Jackson people were the first witnesses to appear followed by several New Orleans policemen, then Charles Steele, Vernon Bundy and Spiesel. Russo is called next, some four days into the trial. Dean Andrews, Marina Oswald, and Dr. Finck were not called until days later. No doubt due to the fact all three were defense witnesses, not State witnesses as Posner writes. Whether Posner purposefully juxtaposed witness testimony or if this is just sloppy research on his part, it strains one's credulity to consider that this book was nominated for a Pulitzer.

Garrison himself summarized some of the most salient points of the trial. In an address before the New Orleans Academy of Trial Lawyers five months after the verdict, Garrison outlined several items that he felt were important for the public to understand:[20]

o   Since Shaw was charged by our office we made every effort to give the defendant a fast and speedy trial; however, it is important to note that every delay in the case over a two-year period was caused by the defense and Mr. Dymond so admitted this in his voir dire remarks to the jury. It is also interesting to note that the trial did eventually take place only after our trial brief was taken from our office and turned over to the defense.

o   The attorneys for the defense appealed to the Federal Court for the Eastern District of Louisiana to stop this so-called "reign of terror" and when their petition was denied by this Court, they appealed to the United States Supreme Court which also found no truth in their allegations and refused to stop the prosecution of this case.

o   We have been criticized for using less than credible witnesses when in reality the only convicted felon to testify at the trial was a witness for the defense. We presented a former State Legislator, a civil rights leader, a Registrar of Voters, a town marshal and other law enforcement officers, a postal employee of the United States government and Mrs. Elizabeth McCarthy, one of the most distinguished handwriting experts in the country. The defense answered with Dean Andrews, who has got to be the world's oldest bebopper.

o   Perry Russo was put under sodium pentothal and hypnosis not in order to induce a story into his head but rather to test his credibility, veracity and powers of recall. This is a safeguard that is not unique to my office and is used by many law enforcement agencies all over the country including both state and federal. Also, I might add that the sodium pentothal was administered by the Orleans Parish Coroner under hospital conditions with three other doctors present and not by our janitor as some people would have you believe. I might add that the Coroner was fully convinced of the veracity of Perry Russo's statements under sodium pentothal.

o   The news media have attacked me for what they consider improper methods and accused me of trying Shaw in the newspaper. They have done this in spite of the fact that since the day Shaw was charged I have consistently refused to mention his name publicly. On the other hand, in their zeal to help the defendant I have been personally attacked by every newspaper from the New York Times to the Nairobi Express. N.B.C. put on an hour nationwide television show to criticize me and my investigation using prisoners that I convicted and sent to the Penitentiary. It's really not hard to figure out why I am not the most popular man at the Angola State Penitentiary or the Parish Prison. Every charge that was raised on their program has been investigated and proven to be false.

o   Twice during the trial the defendant moved for a directed verdict which was denied by the judge. This in effect meant that the State had proven a prima facie case of conspiracy.

o   Under Louisiana law the State as well as the defense is entitled to a fair and impartial trial and I submit that if anyone's rights have been violated it has been the rights of the State of Louisiana. This was accomplished by nationwide interference and harassment on the part of the news media.

Garrison is right in noting that the list of defense witnesses is noticeably lacking in character witnesses. Most witnesses were Shaw's business associates from the ITM, who had little or no contact with him outside of the work environment. In addition to Andrews and Marina Oswald, the defense also called Marina's friend, Ruth Payne, Oswald's New Orleans landlady, a meteorologist, a notary public, an FBI agent, a policeman, a reporter, and a handwriting expert, Charles Appel. Appel was called because the prosecution produced evidence that Shaw had signed a guest register in the Eastern Airlines VIP room as Clay Bertrand. This is an often-overlooked aspect of the Shaw trial, but new evidence shines an important light on this event.

The VIP Room Incident

In early September of 1967, the New Orleans D.A.'s office received a tip that a "Clay Bertrand" had signed the guest log the Eastern Airlines VIP Room at the Moisant Airport in New Orleans. Garrison sent investigators to the lounge that photographed the page in question. (The book was subsequently subpoenaed by the State and introduced as evidence at the Shaw trial). On the relevant page was indeed the signature, "Clay Bertrand" preceded by the date of 12/14/66.

A few days later the D.A.'s office took a sworn affidavit from the VIP Room hostess, Jessie Parker. Ms. Parker identified a photograph of Clay Shaw as the man who had signed the guest book as "Clay Bertrand" the previous December. She further recalled that four persons from Caracas, Venezuela and one other individual accompanied Shaw.[21]

Another guest who signed the VIP register that day was a New Orleans resident named Alfred Moran. On November 13, 1967 Garrison's office questioned Moran and he adamantly stated that Shaw was not at the VIP room on the date in question. Moran knew Shaw, he said, and clearly would have recalled his presence.[22] However, newly discovered documents reveal a different story.

The day after Moran's interview he hosted a cocktail party at his suburban New Orleans home. In attendance was Moran's close friend, Hunter Leake of the New Orleans CIA office. During the course of the evening, Moran took his CIA friend aside and told him of his contact with Garrison's office. Moran recalled the occasion at the VIP and said he identified Clay Shaw's presence there. He further expressed the opinion to Leake that Garrison had an "ironclad case against Shaw."[23] First, it is not surprising that Leake was at Moran's party. CIA records reveal Moran had become a DD/P asset in December of 1962.[24] DD/P is, of course, the Deputy Directorate of Plans, the ultra-secret Clandestine Services division of the CIA. Moran was also a contact of Leake's, having some 15 contacts with the DCS from 1963 through 1967.[25] The CIA characterized Moran as someone who "has always been most helpful and cooperative with the Agency."[26] The CIA also urged Leake to make further contacts with Moran with regards to the Garrison matter. And what was the Agency going to do with this information?

> "We have means of getting this information on to Dymond for use in preparing Shaw case without involving Hunter or Agency."[27]

This is an incredible statement. The CIA is admitting in this document that it is illegally feeding information to Shaw's attorneys in order to undermine the State's case. This is one of many confirmations we have seen regarding CIA officer, Victor Marchetti's admission that CIA Director Helms would ask his subordinates at his morning briefings, "Are we giving them [Shaw's attorneys] all the help we can?"

The CIA's underhandedness is further illustrated in the previously mentioned internal memorandum I discovered. The Agency was so concerned about Moran's involvement with the DD/P becoming known that it suggested that his 201 file be modified.[28] A subsequent CIA memo notes that since November 19, 1964 Moran's "contacts for the DDP have been handled by the DCS."[29] This should serve as a bright red flag for researchers. This is direct evidence that the CIA can easily modify anyone's 201 file to make it look like they may have had innocuous DCS contact or perhaps no Agency contact at all.

Apparently Leake's additional contacts with Moran had their desired effect. On December 13th, the CIA issued a memo stating that, "Actually, Moran had not seen Clay Shaw in the VIP room on the occasion in question and recalls that at the time there were one or two other persons present..."[30] At this point Garrison's office dropped Moran as a witness and pursued another lead that would cast serious doubts on Moran's retractions.

Less than a month before the trial, the D.A.'s office issued a Grand Jury subpoena for a Captain Henry C. Spicer. Spicer was a retired Navy Captain who was the Managing Director of International Relations of the International House and Executive Director of the Foreign Relations Association of New Orleans. The reason for the subpoena was a news account in the December 15, 1966 issue of the *Times-Picayune* that reported on a visit by four Venezuelan government and military men with Captain Spicer. It is important to note that the news item was run on the day after the signing of the Bertrand signature and confirms Ms. Parker's account that she had seen Clay Shaw in the company of four men from Caracas and one other man (obviously Spicer).

On January 10, 1969, a representative of Garrison's office visited with Captain Spicer. Spicer allowed the D.A.'s man to view his scrapbook of activities he kept as Director of International Relations. Posted within the scrapbook Captain Spicer's picture with the Venezuelan visitors.[31] (Apparently Clay Shaw was not in the picture. Could he have been the photographer?) Thus the subpoena for Spicer followed on the 14th. But Spicer would never testify before the Grand Jury. It is unknown what subsequently transpired, but Assistant D.A. Alcock interviewed Spicer and was apparently convinced that he could add nothing more to the case and directed Spicer to ignore the subpoena.[32] Certainly in hindsight, this was an area that deserved further investigation.

Nevertheless, in evaluating this whole VIP room situation, the CIA had to concede that "if a reputable handwriting expert can positively identify that the name Clem [sic] Bertrand was written in Clay Shaw's handwriting then certainly Clay Shaw is in serious trouble."[33] Garrison would provide such an expert at Shaw's trial.

Elizabeth McCarthy Bailey was a Vassar educated, multi-degreed attorney whose specialty was document analysis and handwriting identification. By the time of the Shaw trial she had testified as an expert for over 31 years. She was formerly the document expert for the City of Boston Police and the Massachusetts State Police. At the Shaw trial Ms. Bailey stated that the signature on the VIP room guest register matched that of Clay Shaw's. She testified, "I find all of Mr. Clay's [sic] unconscious writing habits in the signature Clay Bertrand. He is a very facile writer with a light pen. All of these characteristics I find in the questioned exhibit...I have concluded that the signatures are the same."[34]

The defense countered with their expert witness, Charles Appel, Jr. Curiously, Appel said he volunteered to appear for no fee because he felt an injustice was being done based on what he heard in the media.[35] However, under cross-examination he admitted he was in fact contacted by Clay Shaw's former boss, Lloyd Cobb. His background is interesting in light of the fact that he also testified for Robert Maheu in his suit against Howard Hughes.[36] Maheu was the CIA cutout in the CIA/Mafia assassination plots against Fidel Castro. Though then in private practice, Appel was a former FBI man. According to author, Curt Gentry, Appel was one of J. Edgar Hoover's closest associates, having become one of his nightly dinner companions at Harvey's restaurant in Washington.[37] Appel's most famous appearance would have to be at the so-called Lindbergh trial. Testifying on behalf of the prosecution, Appel swore that the defendant, Bruno Richard Hauptmann, wrote the Lindbergh ransom notes.[38] It is pretty much accepted as fact today that Hauptmann was framed for the kidnapping and murder of the Lindbergh baby.

Called as a character witness and to confirm Shaw's contention that he was just too busy in the summer of 1963 to make a trip to Clinton and/or Jackson, Shaw's boss at the ITM, Lloyd Cobb testified on Shaw's behalf. The reader will recall from Chapter 11 that Cobb owned a tract of land in Jackson called Marydale Farms. The farm employed a large number of anti-Castro Cubans who all mysteriously left immediately after the assassination. Under oath at his trial, Shaw admitted he had visited Cobb's "farm." In addition to owning Marydale Farms, Cobb, like

Shaw, was also connected with the CIA. Records show that on June 19, 1967 Cobb was granted a Provisional Security Approval for use on a Cleared Attorney's Panel for the CIA's Office of General Counsel.[39] Years earlier Cobb was granted a higher Covert Security Clearance for use on a Private Attorney's Panel for the OGC.[40] Despite the CIA's denials that it was utilizing local New Orleans attorneys (i.e. Plotkin, Lemmann, et. al), these records directly contradict that claim.

Despite Shaw's claims on the witness stand that he was too absorbed in his work to make any trips during the Summer of 1963, veteran researcher and author, Harold Weisberg, developed evidence to the contrary. According to Weisberg's contacts, Shaw rarely worked hard at the ITM and Cobb had actually fired Shaw, giving him the choice between a fine sendoff when he resigned or being given the sack.[41] Weisberg had also found that one James Lawrence had spent about ten weeks (from July to October 1963) working at the Trade Mart handling the leasing arrangements for the new building.[42] This was the work that supposedly kept Shaw so preoccupied during this time frame.

After the Shaw trial, the CIA still maintained their interest in Cobb. A CIA memo, written under the signature of David Atlee Phillips, requested that "priority clearances to contact and talk with identities A and B concerning their suitability and [two lines redacted] availability to act as sponsors for selected [word redacted] broadcasts."[43] Identities A and B are revealed to be Lloyd Cobb and Managing Director of the International House, Paul Fabry, respectively.[44] It is interesting that once again David Phillips is attempting to use New Orleans assets for his propaganda efforts, both of whom, like Shaw, were connected to the International Trade Mart.

As we have seen, an intriguing point about Cobb concerns his brother. According to a private detective who used to work for Guy Banister, Alvin Cobb was in fact a friend of the fanatical Banister.[45] This shouldn't come as much of a surprise, considering that Alvin Cobb was a Ku Klux Klan leader in Shreveport, Louisiana.[46]

Finally, the defense opened a huge kettle of fish when they called Dr. Pierre Finck to the stand. Finck was one of the three military autopsists who performed the autopsy on President Kennedy. His blistering cross-examination by Assistant D.A., Alvin Oser, is still widely quoted as proof of a high level cover-up of the medical evidence.[47] The Federal government was so concerned about Finck's revealing testimony, that they sent one of the other Kennedy pathologists to New Orleans to remain on "stand-by" in case his testimony was needed at the trial. In 1998 the Assassination Records and Review Board deposed Dr. J.T. Boswell and the following exchange reveals the depth of the help Shaw was receiving:

Q: Very early on in your deposition today, you made reference to Mr. Eardley from the Justice Department asking you to go to New Orleans; is that correct?

A: Mm-hmm.

Q: What did he say to you about the reason he wanted you to go to New Orleans?

A: He was really upset. He says, "J, we got to get somebody in New Orleans quick. Pierre is testifying, and he's really lousing everything up." And I called Jim [Author's note: Jim is Commander James Humes, the third JFK autopsist.] to see if he didn't want to go, and he was having - his mother-in-law was ill, and he couldn't go. So they put me on a plane that day and took me to New Orleans, and that was one of the most interesting adventures in my life. I met - do you want to hear all of this?

Q: Yes, please.

A: Carl Eardley sent me to a hotel, and I went into the hotel and registered. I was already registered. I got up to my room, and there was a note on my bedside telling me to meet somebody at a certain place at a certain time. And this was a scary place. This was down around the wharfs, and the federal attorney's office was in a big warehouse down there. And that's - I met somebody on the street. He took me in there, and they told me what was going on. They showed me the transcript of Pierre's testimony for the past couple of days, and I spent all night reviewing that testimony. And it was this bit about the general. Jim said, "Who's in charge here?" And when they asked Pierre in court who supervised and ran the autopsy, he says, "Some Army general." And so that is why - and I never appeared. I spent two days down there and then came home, never appeared in court. *And the government won their case.*[My emphasis]

Q: Actually, the government was the district attorney. So, my next question for you actually was: What was the United States Department of Justice doing in relationship to a case between the district attorney of New Orleans and a resident of New Orleans?

A: Well, they - I went over and met somebody, some lawyer in another firm that night, and I don't know who he was representing. But, obviously, the federal attorney was on the side of Clay Shaw against the district attorney...

Q: What did the government attorney say to you? Did he help prepare potential testimony for you?

A: They were getting ready to. I guess it all depended on what Pierre did that next day or something. I don't know. All I know is that they - he was answering in very strange ways their questions, and, yes, they sent me down and talked to me and tried to get me to agree that he was very strange and that I could do a better job or something.

Many have commented that Garrison's case was a frivolous prosecution as evidenced by the "flimsy" case against Shaw. But even Shaw's own lawyers had to partly concede the merits of the prosecution's case. Approximately two weeks after the verdict, Edward Wegmann wrote, "Had we been unsuccessful in our efforts to secure information with regard to Charles I. Spiesel...the results could well have been a verdict of guilty."[48] Even the presiding judge believed Shaw lied under oath and "pulled a con job on the jury."[49]

From a reading of Shaw's testimony, it is clear that he perjured himself about the arrangements for the San Francisco trip.(See Chapter 6). His further denials about any connection with the CIA and of not having associated with either Oswald or Ferrie - especially in light of the Clinton witnesses - forced Garrison to charge Shaw with two counts of perjury. In addition to the Clinton/Jackson people, Garrison was to present several other supporting witnesses at the trial.[50]

The Tadins, a married couple who appeared as rebuttal witnesses at the Shaw trial, were on the proposed witness list. The Tadins had earlier testified that their teenage son was taking flying lessons from David Ferrie at Moisant Airport. They always took their son to the airport and waited for him to finish his lesson so they could drive him home. The Tadins recalled that sometime in 1964 they were at the airport and had recognized Clay Shaw as he emerged from a hangar door and entered his car. Mr. Tadin asked Ferrie, "Do you have a new student?" Tadin testified Ferrie replied, "No, he's a friend of mine. Clay Shaw. He's in charge of the International Trade Mart."[51]

Betty Rubio worked at Lakefront Airport and knew Ferrie. Shortly before April of 1964, while standing in the ramp office, she noticed a plane taxi up to the office. Ferrie got out, talked to her for a bit, and then went back to his plane, where Clay Shaw met him. Shaw and Ferrie talked for a while and then Ferrie got in his plane as Shaw walked past her toward the terminal building.[52]

Three other acquaintances of Ferrie's, Herbert Wagner, Jim Louviere, and James Laurent, were all prepared to testify that each had seen Shaw with Ferrie, at different times at Ferrie's service station.[53] Court papers indicate the DA's office had additional witnesses to present as well.[54] But it was not to be. In 1971, a Federal judge made an unprecedented move, ordering a permanent injunction restraining the Orleans Parish DA's office from any further prosecution of Clay Shaw. Presiding over this hearing was Judge Herbert Christenberry. If ever there was a judge who should have recused himself from a case it was Christenberry. A week after Shaw's acquittal the following letter was sent to Shaw:

> Dear Mr. Shaw,
>
> Our most sincere congratulations! We shared your anxieties over the past two outrageous years. Should your case have eventually found its way to Federal Court and been allotted to my husband you most certainly would have had a _fair_ trial. He felt we should not risk the possibility of being considered "prejudiced" in advance.
> This is our reason for not openly expressing these sentiments much earlier...
> Our most sincere best wishes for an upward trend of happy events-and for some private and tranquil time to ENJOY!
>
> Caroline Christenberry[55]

Ms. Christenberry was, of course, the wife of Judge Christenberry who wasted little time in blocking Shaw's perjury prosecution.

The ruling was not only unprecedented, but quite possibly illegal. Regarding such injunctions, Federal law states:

"A court of the United States may not grant an injunction to stay proceedings in a State court except as expressly authorized by Act of Congress, or where necessary in aid of its jurisdiction, or to protect or effectuate its judgments." (28 U.S.C.A. 2283)

But it gets worse. It would be Christenberry who would preside over the Federal government's trumped up prosecution of Garrison in 1973. Garrison was charged with accepting payoffs from local pinball operators. The government's case collapsed when their star witness, former Garrison investigator, Pershing Gervais, admitted the whole case was a set up. Garrison also proved in court that audiotapes purporting to be of Garrison accepting bribes were doctored. Garrison was acquitted of all charges. Nevertheless, having spent the majority of his time defending himself, Garrison had little time to campaign and lost his reelection bid to U.S. Attorney, and current New Orleans District Attorney, Harry Connick, Sr.

Shaw would later file a civil action against Garrison, but charges were dropped upon Shaw's death in 1974. In evaluating Shaw's testimony, it is interesting to keep in mind something former CIA Director, Allen Dulles, stated during one of the Warren Commission hearings. When asked by fellow Commissioners if an agent, or a recruiter of an agent would tell the truth about their Agency connection under oath, Dulles said, "I wouldn't think he would tell under oath, no...He ought not tell it under oath."[56]

One has to wonder if, in the history of jurisprudence, there has ever been such a Herculean effort on behalf of the federal government to subvert a legal proceeding? Author James DiEugenio summed it up best in his excellent review of the Shaw case in *Probe* magazine, "The aid given to Clay Shaw's case was munificent and myriad...This aid was granted at the highest levels of these organizations; men like Hoover, Dulles, Angleton, Larry Houston and Ramsey Clark were cognizant and complicit in it...The very fact that this aid was granted, that the risk of clandestine complicity with Shaw's defense was run, clearly suggests that the power brokers in Washington were worried about Garrison's progress."[57]

LET JUSTICE BE DONE

The Final Days

In May of 1973, as Shaw was being treated for an ulcer at the Ochsner Clinic, he was diagnosed with acute lung cancer - Shaw's years of chain smoking had caught up with him. During a subsequent radiation treatment, doctors discovered the cancer had spread to his brain and liver.[58] Shaw's final days were spent at his home - now located on St. Peter Street - in the company of a part-time sitter from Tulane Medical School, as well as an old friend of Shaw's who had temporarily moved in to care for the now bed-ridden and delirious Shaw.[59] Shaw's friend, Donald Dooty, is, himself, an interesting case study. Trained as a Russian interpreter while in Army Intelligence, Dooty also held a law degree from Tulane, as well as a Masters Degree in English Literature. Despite this impressive resume, Dooty did little work as an interpreter, never practiced law, and never taught English literature. Instead, he inexplicably spent most of his time traveling. In an interview with Garrison, Dooty detailed an itinerary that took him from Italy to Chicago, San Francisco, Miami, Houston, Dallas, Tulsa, New York, Havana, Montreal, and finally New Orleans by way of Mexico City in the late 1960's. All without any visible means of income.[60] In light of the fact that Shaw was delirious in his final days, Dooty remains an intriguing choice for the caretaker role.

As in life, Shaw's death was shrouded in mystery. On the night he died, August 15, 1974, a neighbor reported seeing a body on a stretcher being brought *in* to Shaw's house.[61] When Shaw expired, instead of calling an ambulance, the police, or the coroner's office, Dooty called Shaw's lawyer, Edward Wegmann.[62] Wegmann then called William Acosta at the House of Bultman Funeral Home, and asked him to remove Shaw's remains.[63] A Dr. Batson, who was already at the Shaw home when the hearse arrived, signed the death certificate and Acosta set about embalming Shaw's body that evening.[64] No autopsy was performed. Less than 24 hours after his death, Shaw was quietly buried in Kentwood, about 100 miles from New Orleans.[65]

Because of the mystery and lack of proper procedure surrounding Shaw's death, the Orleans Parish coroner, Dr. Frank Minyard, felt an exhumation and a proper autopsy was in order.[66] This set off a firestorm of protest from Shaw's supporters. This charge was led by Edward Wegmann, who recklessly said, "Clay Shaw has been unmercifully harassed by various public officials since December 1966. This harassment and subsequent events unquestionably contributed to his early and untimely death. The scavengers should allow Clay Shaw to rest in peace."[67] Minyard, a publicly elected official, did, indeed, let Shaw rest in peace, and dropped the matter.

Congress Vindicates Garrison

A mere four years later, Congress would conclude that, "[the HSCA] was inclined to believe that Oswald was in Clinton, La., in late August, early September 1963, and that he was in the company of David Ferrie, if not Clay Shaw...[68] [the Clinton witnesses] established an association of an undetermined nature between Ferrie, Shaw, and Oswald less than 3 months before the assassination."[69] The committee added that they "also found that there was at least a possibility that Oswald and Guy Banister were acquainted."[70] They further concluded that the "CIA - Mafia - Cuban plots had all the elements necessary for a successful assassination conspiracy."[71] It is probably the ultimate irony that the U.S. Government's conclusions echoed those of Jim Garrison's a decade earlier. It is also equally ironic that a movie about Garrison would be the catalyst for the declassification of files that would reveal how far government agencies went to protect Shaw.[72]

Chapter Fourteen

~

The Hidden Record

The day after Clay Shaw's arrest, reporters peppered Attorney General Ramsey Clark with questions as he emerged from his confirmation hearing. Neil Strawser of CBS News asked Clark if he had any information regarding the recently arrested Shaw. Clark replied that, "he [Shaw] was involved in an FBI investigation in the investigation in the New Orleans area in November - December 1963."[1] Another reporter shouted, "You say he was checked out and found clear, more or less?" Clark answered, "That's right. That's true."[2] Clark's comments were carried in all the major newspapers. The New York Times added in their piece "a Justice Department official said tonight that his agency was convinced that Mr. Bertrand and Mr. Shaw were the same man, and that this was the basis for Mr. Clark's assertions."[3]

191

They also commented that "Mr. Clark's statement that the FBI had conducted an investigation of Mr. Shaw caused, however, a certain amount of bewilderment in some quarters here."[4] So much so, it took the Justice Department spin-doctors three months to get their story straight. On June 2nd, the Justice Department issued a statement that "Clay Shaw, New Orleans businessman, was not investigated by the Federal Bureau of Investigation during its inquiry into the assassination of President Kennedy...A Justice Department spokesman said that Mr. Clark's statement last March 2, shortly after Mr. Shaw had been arrested...was in error."[5] From the newly released FBI files, we now know this to be a lie - Clark's original statement was, indeed, accurate. An FBI memo dated March 2, 1967 from Cartha "Deke" DeLoach to Clyde Tolson states:

> The AG then asked whether the FBI knew anything about Shaw. I told him Shaw's name had come up in our investigation in *December, 1963* as a result of *several parties* furnishing information concerning Shaw.[6] [My emphasis.]

Hoover himself read this memo as evidenced by his scrawl at the bottom of the page: "I hope a.g. isn't going to peddle this information we send him. H."[7] One has to ponder the significance of this memo. Why, in the aftermath of the assassination, was the FBI investigating Clay Shaw? And who were the several parties who furnished this information? (A further examination of the released files - including the New Orleans field office files - has yielded nothing more on this issue).

Even Clark had to stick to his guns in light of this. In a later interview, Clark admitted, "Yes. Clay Shaw was involved in an FBI investigation. So were other persons now being mentioned in connection with the Garrison investigation."[8] When reminded by his interviewer that the FBI had told reporters that it did not investigate Shaw, Clark replied, "I understand that the FBI information office did indicate that for part of one day recently.

But they shortly received the correct information from their superiors in the FBI."[9]

As noted earlier, the FBI had received information, prior to Shaw's arrest, from a source that stated Shaw was Clay Bertrand. Other FBI documents reveal that *two* sources informed the Bureau of Shaw's alias. A March 2, 1967 letterhead memorandum states:

> On February 24, 1967, we received information from two sources that Clay Shaw reportedly is identical with an individual by the name of Clay Bertrand...[10]

These kinds of reports would continue well into the Garrison investigation. The ubiquitous Lawrence Schiller, on March 22, 1967, generously "shared" the results of his recent research with the Los Angeles office of the FBI. After informing on one of Mark Lane's confidential sources, Schiller volunteered that "three homosexual sources in New Orleans and two homosexual sources in San Francisco have indicated that Clay Shaw was known by other names including Clay Bertrand."[11] Schiller goes on to advise that "rumor in Los Angeles, attributed to Ed Guthman, former Justice Department official, and currently associated with Los Angeles Times, indicates FBI had identified Clay Shaw and Clay Bertrand as being the same person."[12] Lest there be any question on what side of the fence Schiller was on, the memo clarifies that for us:

> Schiller has advised that he is advocate of viewpoint of Warren Commission and is opposed to "irresponsible journalism" of writers such as Lane. Schiller has made favorable comments concerning bureau and work of bureau.[13]

In light of all the FBI reports connecting Shaw to the

Bertrand alias, it might be appropriate to look back at the Shaw trial testimony of FBI agent Regis Kennedy. As an agent of the New Orleans field office, Kennedy, along with Warren DeBrueys, was the bureau's eyes and ears among the shadowy New Orleans intelligence community and anti-Castro underground.[14] On the Monday after the assassination, Dean Andrews called the FBI to notify them of his call from Clay Bertrand. Kennedy was assigned to investigate. But under oath, at the Shaw trial, Kennedy revealed a peculiar bit of information. After claiming executive privilege for most of his testimony, Kennedy was given permission by then Attorney General, John Mitchell, to answer two of assistant DA Alcock's questions. Their exchange went as follows:

> **Q**. Mr. Kennedy, <u>prior</u> to your interview with Dean Andrews, were you engaged in the investigation of the assassination of President Kennedy?
>
> **A**. Yes. I was.
>
> **Q**. Mr. Kennedy, were you seeking Clay Bertrand in connection with your overall investigation into the assassination of President Kennedy?
>
> **A**. I was.[15]

Shaw's association with David Ferrie did not escape the FBI's scrutiny either. Carroll Thomas, owner of Thomas Funeral Homes in Hammond, was a self-admitted close personal friend of Shaw's. In fact, he handled the funeral arrangements when Shaw's father passed away in 1966. While the FBI was interviewing him about another, unrelated matter, Thomas volunteered information about Shaw. He felt that Shaw couldn't be involved with a

Communist like Oswald because "Shaw was always politically conservative."[16] More importantly, Thomas added that he "knew David Ferrie through Shaw."[17] An informant for the bureau, who was also a local news cameraman, reported to the FBI that he had overheard one of Shaw's former secretaries state to a doctor at the Ochsner Clinic that "she had seen Ferrie go into Shaw's office in the International Trade Mart on a number of occasions, and believed Ferrie had privileged entry into Shaw's office."[18] Inexcusably, the FBI neglected to share any of this information with Garrison.

The CIA documents released so far seem to indicate a more than casual relationship between Shaw and the agency. For example, one document, originally released in a slightly sanitized form in the late 1970's, was released virtually intact in 1992. After summarizing Shaw's numerous contacts with the Domestic Contact Service over the years, a more compelling piece of information is revealed on page 4 of the document. Item number 11, originally redacted in its entirety, reads as follows:

> A memorandum marked only for file, 16 March 1967, signed Marguerite D. Stevens, says that J. Monroe SULLIVAN, #280207, was granted a covert security approval on 10 December 1962 so that he could be used in Project QKENCHANT. SHAW has #402897-A.[19]

Note the use of the present tense regarding Shaw's covert security number. Shaw *has* #402897-A. Not had. Not was. Has. One could logically conclude that, at the time this memo was issued (early 1967), Shaw was an active covert operative of the CIA. In April of 1995, I interviewed former CIA officer, Victor Marchetti. The reader will recall that as former executive assistant to DCI Richard Helms, Marchetti had stated that while attending the Director's morning staff meetings during the time of the Garrison probe, Helms expressed great concern over Shaw's predicament, asking his staff, "Are we giving them all the help we can down there?"[20] (As Marchetti has noted, it is not likely Helms was offering to help

Garrison). I showed Marchetti this document and his comments are revealing. As he studied the document, Marchetti would mutter, almost to himself, "That's interesting...He was...He was doing something there." Finally Marchetti explained, "If you're working with DCS, there's no need for a covert security clearance like that. This was something else. This would imply that he was doing some kind of work for the Clandestine Services."[21] I asked Marchetti what division of Clandestine Services did he think would be involved with this project. He replied, "The DOD (Domestic Operations Division). It was one of the most secret divisions within the Clandestine Services. This was Tracey Barnes' old outfit. They were getting into things...uh." Marchetti hesitated, seeming to catch himself, "Uh...exactly what, I don't know. But they were getting into some pretty risky areas. And this is what E. Howard Hunt was working for at the time."[22] Marchetti likewise felt that the use of the present tense in describing Shaw's covert status was significant. "Yeah, that's accurate," he said. "That means he was still active. Three weeks later somebody probably said, OOPS, and changed it to had."[23] Indeed, Marchetti's assessment was right on the money. Shortly after my interview with Marchetti, my colleague Peter Vea discovered a CIA document from 1970. The memo is from Victor R. White, Deputy Director of Security to Martin Lukoskie, Chief, Central Cover Staff and the first paragraph reads as follows:

> Reference is made to your request for a Covert Security Approval on Subject, dated 3 June 1970, for utilization under Project QKENCHANT.

The "subject" being utilized in this instance was none other than E. Howard Hunt.[24]

Also in Shaw's CIA file, is what appears to be a computer printout from the 1960's. It is written in indecipherable "CIAese." Its significance can only be guessed at. I reproduce it here for the reader's edification:[25]

/N **SHAW,CLAY**   **SR S332959**

/A **BERTRAND,CLAY**   **/YM**

/D **SER 1951**

/R **IW   R402897-A**   **2088478 67**

The DCS Reports

In 1994 the CIA released most of Shaw's reports he filed for the Domestic Contact Service. While some of the reports appear to be innocuous, others provide an interesting insight into the DCS career of Shaw and reveal the CIA's use of Shaw and the cover of the International Trade Mart for some of their operations.

The earliest document in the release is dated December 13, 1948 and seems to be a rather routine report about the establishment of a trade exhibit in the Trade Mart by the Czechoslovakian government.[26]

During the spring of the following year, Shaw embarked on a three-month whirlwind tour of Latin America. Shaw's travels took him to such countries as Cuba, Haiti, the Dominican Republic, Puerto Rico, Peru, Ecuador, Colombia, Venezuela, Panama, Costa Rica, El Salvador, Guatemala, Nicaragua and Honduras. In a memo dated June 7, 1949, William Burke, then Chief of the New Orleans DCS office, informs headquarters that "Mr. Clay Shaw was briefed *prior* to his business trip during

March, April and May of 1949."[27] [My emphasis]. Upon his return, Shaw provided information not only on the devaluation of Peruvian currency, but also the political climate there as well. Shaw writes in his report, "...there is a widespread opposition to the Junta government on the part of business leaders, industrialists, etc., and the general feeling among them is that Odria government will soon fall...The man most likely to succeed Odria as the new head of the government is a member of the present cabinet, Lt. Col. Alfonso Llosa, Minister of Public Works. His ascendancy to power, if and when it comes, may have unfavorable results for Peru. He is a brilliant man, but I was told repeatedly, by persons in a position to know, that he is a drunkard and, while drunk, is completely uncontrollable. For example, if he happens to get drunk in a night club, as has happened, the management has to request all the other patrons to leave. I also heard repeatedly that he follows up his sprees with cocaine and has become an addict. While under this drug, it is stated he is completely and utterly unmanageable."[28]

While in Managua, Nicaragua, Shaw conferred with the President and Minister of Finance, noting also that "I heard Gen. Somoza's cattle monopoly bitterly criticized by businessmen in Managua."[29]

Juan and Evita Peron did not escape Shaw's attention either. While meeting with the Minister of Public Works in Buenos Aires, Shaw writes that he was told that "Peron and Evita are each jealous of the other's power and that they maintain separate and independent political organizations."[30] Curiously, both Somoza and Juan Peron were patients and friends of Shaw's close associate, Dr. Alton Ochsner.[31]

In 1952, Shaw received a directory of German firms engaged in international trade. Because 80% of the firms listed were in East Germany, Shaw made the document available to the CIA's Foreign Documents Division.[32]

In August of 1955, Shaw's CIA career seems to take another turn. On August 9th, Burke states in a memo to headquarters, "Both [**name redacted**] and Mr. Shaw, particularly the latter, would be willing to attend the Czechoslovak

Engineering Exhibition at Erno, 11 September to 9 October 1955, as a CIA observer, but ostensibly of course as the representative of [**redacted**] or International Trade Mart, as the case may be, provided the expense could be borne by CIA."[33] Shaw's importance to the Agency was also underscored in this memo. Burke writes, "Messrs. [**name redacted**] and Shaw are both valued sources of this office, and we deem it sufficiently important to compromise a "Y" number to refer you to the reports submitted by Clay Shaw as Y 145.1 and particularly OO-B-54754, Subject: "Observations on International Fairs at Milan, Brussels, Basel, Paris and London/Comments on Western European Economics and Desire to Trade with the Soviet Bloc.""[34]

A memo from 1956 reveals a different methodology employed by Shaw and the CIA to gather intelligence. The Agency at that time was interested in mercury production and shipment of mercury to Soviet Bloc countries. On May 25, 1956, Burke writes, "If we can furnish Mr. Shaw with the names and addresses of producers of mercury in Spain and Italy, he is quite willing to write letters of inquiry to them on World Trade Development Department letterheads, in an attempt to ascertain for us the extent of the Spanish and Italian stocks on hand."[35] The World Trade Development Department was a division of the International House, of which Shaw was the acting director at the time. Burke also writes about utilizing the International House Reference Library to obtain names and addresses of mercury producers in Spain and Italy. A follow-up memo in June addresses the "possibility that Shaw might develop as a source on Italian and Spanish mercury producers."[36] It is interesting to note the use of Shaw as a source of Italian intelligence - especially in light of Shaw's connection with the Centro Mondiale Commerciale in Rome the following year.

At this point the DCS reports end. Indeed, in virtually all of the CIA biographies on Shaw, they note that he stopped being a DCS contact in 1956. That begs the question: Why? If Shaw was a "valued source" just a year earlier, why terminate the relationship? Could it be that Shaw had entered a more covert phase of his intelligence career, perhaps as an operative in Project QKENCHANT? Or was Shaw's 201 file "modified" or his more covert operations handled through DCS as we have seen was possible in the previous chapter? Maybe we will have an answer when all of Shaw's files are released. However, it does not look encouraging that all of his files are even in existence. A CIA handwritten note concerning Shaw reads, "Y # file- 33412 destroyed."[37]

Aside from Shaw's DCS reports a few other CIA documents are worth mentioning here. An April 6, 1967 memo from the New Orleans office mainly concerns itself with an interview of Carlos Bringuier conducted by Alberto Fowler on behalf of Garrison's office. As I noted earlier, Fowler was a veteran of the 2506 Brigade who was captured by Castro's forces during the Bay of Pigs invasion. Fowler was also close to Clay Shaw, having lived at his house for three months, which lends credibility to a statement he made to Bringuier. According to the memo Fowler told Bringuier that "he (Fowler) was impressed by the fact that Shaw, who is reported to have been in intelligence work in World War II in the Army, is now quite calm and assured because he, Shaw, feels that high-ranking Government officials are involved and will see that no harm comes to him."[38] As we have seen from previous chapters, Helms' operatives were obviously performing admirably, providing aid and comfort to Shaw.

The Agency's continuing obsession with Jim Garrison is reflected in two memos from the 1970's. At the time of Shaw's lawsuit against Garrison, a March 4, 1970 memo notes that the "Office of General Counsel (John Greaney) has indicated specific interest in monitoring developments related to this case."[39] Well after the dust had settled on the Shaw case and about two years after Shaw's death, the CIA was still in a bother over Garrison. The catalyst was an article in the June 1976 edition of *New Orleans Magazine*, titled "Was Jim Garrison Right After All?" A memo to headquarters dated June 3, 1976 requested guidance in responding to news media inquiries. The author writes, "As is apparent in the attached copy of a New Orleans magazine article, former District

Attorney Jim Garrison and his Kennedy assassination theories are enjoying a revival of interest by local news media."[40] This was not what worried the Agency the most, however. The memo continues, "We are somewhat more concerned about how we should respond to any direct questions concerning the Agency's relationship with Clay Shaw."[41] Perhaps the author of this memo should have been more concerned about *his* relationship with Oswald's friend, George de Mohrenschildt - for the writer was none other than one J. Walton Moore. Students of the assassination will recognize Moore as the Dallas Domestic Contacts agent who debriefed the worldly and cultured de Mohrenschildt upon his return from a trip to Yugoslavia in 1957. Moore would visit with de Mohrenschildt several times in the following years becoming a frequent visitor to the de Mohrenschildt home. Shortly before his death, de Mohrenschildt said Moore had encouraged him to befriend Oswald. It was at this time that de Mohrenschildt probably discreetly debriefed Oswald at Moore's behest.[42]

Finally, one shouldn't be too surprised that the Warren Commission didn't review any of the relevant CIA files on Oswald, Shaw, Ferrie, et.al. A CIA document reveals that Birch O'Neal of controversial super-spook James Angleton's Counter Intelligence staff, clamped down on any sharing of information. The document, dated February 20, 1964, has O'Neal stating that "the CI staff i.e., Mr. Rocca, has the job of determining which pieces of information should be made available to the Commission."[43] Note that Ray Rocca was Angleton's deputy.

Warren Commission Chief Counsel, J. Lee Rankin was aware of the CIA's withholding of critical information and later voiced his frustration. In an interview with the HSCA, Rankin believed that "hindsight makes it clear that both Hoover and the CIA were covering up a variety of items from the Commission." Rankin expressed approval that the HSCA was devoting considerable time to the CIA/Mafia plots. "Good, good," he said, "That is crucial." Rankin went on to state that the plots would have had "a very direct bearing on the areas of conspiracy which we tried to pursue." Rankin also asked, "Are you looking into the plots on the basis of whether they were covered up by the CIA because some of the very people involved in them could have been involved in the President's assassination." When the HSCA investigator told Rankin they were also looking into charges that Castro might have retaliated for the plots by killing Kennedy, Rankin quickly pooh-poohed the idea asking, "Where is the evidence of that? I think the other approach would be more logical."[44] Even President Johnson suspected the CIA had a hand in JFK's death. FBI records reveal that Presidential Assistant Marvin Watson called the FBI's Cartha DeLoach and stated that "the President had told him, in an off moment, that he was now convinced that there was a plot in connection with the assassination. Watson stated the President felt the CIA had something to do with this plot."[45]

HSCA Chief Counsel, G. Robert Blakey, once referred to the Committee's work as "the last investigation."[46] As such, it is only proper that the HSCA have the last word on Clay Shaw. On September 1, 1977, staff counsel, Jonathan Blackmer, authored a 15-page memorandum addressed to Blakey, as well as staff members, Gary Cornwell, Ken Klein, and Cliff Fenton. Blackmer was the lead counsel for Team 3, the HSCA team responsible for the New Orleans and Cuban angles of the investigation. After an investigative trip to New Orleans, Blackmer concluded in his memo:

> We have reason to believe Shaw was heavily involved in the anti-Castro efforts in New Orleans in the 1960's and [was] possibly one of the high level planners or "cut out" to the planners of the assassination.[47]

A Final Note

In the 1968 *Ramparts* magazine article on the Garrison investigation, Bill Turner closes by writing:

> When news of the assassination probe first broke, Garrison declaimed in a burst of rhetoric, "Let justice be done though the heavens fall!" The heavens are still there, but Washington has come crashing down upon him.

As we have seen, the newly declassified material has confirmed this in spades. To even the most jaded of observers it must seem inexplicable that the myriad agencies of the government would collaborate and spend probably millions in taxpayer money to come to the aid of a retired businessman in New Orleans. With the amount of pressure being brought to bear, it is amazing that the case ever got to trial. Had Garrison pursued a different strategy, it is possible he could have prevailed in a court of law. Perhaps if he had questioned Shaw before the Grand Jury about his associations with Oswald and Ferrie, his West Coast trip and other matters, then the D.A.'s office could have charged Shaw with perjury and presented their strongest witnesses at the perjury trial, possibly obtaining a guilty verdict. But hindsight is always 20-20.

Since Shaw's work for the CIA is always a matter of controversy, it is worthwhile to consider the HSCA testimony of a high-ranking intelligence officer of the CIA, John Whitten. This interview was suppressed until 1996 when the Assassination Records Review Board released his testimony with Whitten's name pseudonymously changed to John Scelso. The questioning covers many areas of the Select Committee's investigation, but the two areas relevant here are the CIA's description of "contract" agents and the illusory nature of the CIA's personnel records. During the interview, HSCA Counsel, Michael Goldsmith elicited the following definition of a contract agent from Scelso:

> **Goldsmith:** An agent is not somebody who you would consider to be a CIA employee?

> **Scelso:** That is right. He is in a contractual relationship of some kind. This is a myth, of course, because there is not any contract, really, but there is an agreement.[48]

So those expecting to see a paper trail back to Langley for the likes of Banister, Ferrie and possibly Oswald are deluding themselves.

While prefacing a later question to Whitten/Scelso, Goldsmith reveals the following important point:

> **Goldsmith:** We recently introduced an employee who, as I mentioned earlier today, indicated that looking at his records, every indication on that record would be that he had retired from the Agency in the mid-50's when actually he had been with the Agency throughout and had continued one way or the other, whether it was to be paid by the Agency or by the State Department, he was still working for the Agency. There was no record of his Agency connection at Langley.[49]

While Whitten felt that maybe some Branch might have some kind of file on such a person, Goldsmith probed further:

> **Goldsmith:** So that it is possible that the personnel file would be purged in some manner, or would be written up in a manner to indicate that he was no longer with the Agency?
>
> **Scelso:** Sure. Very probably yes.[50]

Again, just because the CIA releases a piece of paper saying Shaw's CIA career ended in 1956, based on what has now been revealed, no researcher can definitively say that is the case.

After Garrison's loss to Harry Connick in the D.A.'s election, he went into private practice but was soon elected to a judgeship on the Fourth Circuit Court of Appeals – a position he held until his retirement shortly before his death in 1992.

As the evidence of Shaw's associations and intelligence connections mounts, one can see the official cover story crumble under the weight of its own lies. At the very least I hope this volume has aided in a better understanding of the lives and times of these two men.

Afterword:

GARRISON'S INVITATION TO THE MILLENNIUM BALL:
WHERE DALLAS '63 MEETS THE AGE OF GLOBALIZATION

By Robert Spiegelman*, © 1999
(Footnotes appear at the end of the Afterword)

For the Re-Searchers Among Us

I. Introduction

As the new millennium rushes in, the best efforts of official embalmers to close the books and suture the still open wounds of the 1960s have failed to lay our ghosts to rest. Recent efforts by high-profile luminaries like Seymour Hersh, Norman Mailer and the ubiquitous media accessory Gerald Posner[1] to close the Kennedy case have gone well publicized. To date, the unfortunate truth has been that Oliver Stone's movie *JFK* (1991) marked the high tide of mass outrage over JFK's murder and, by extension, of public interest in Garrison's mode of explanation. For the years

---

* Robert Spiegelman was a technical advisor and script consultant on the Oliver Stone film, *JFK*, and is currently a freelance writer and filmmaker in New York City.

since, JFK has largely been represented as a two-headed media caricature: JFK the Good and JFK the Bad. On the one hand, we are spoon-fed/seduced by a mythic, handsome fantasy prince of Camelot, whose image feeds America's presumed insatiable longing for the glamour of aristocracy. Alternatively, we are scandalized by the incorrigible womanizer who simply got what he deserved -- a prideful arrogance that augurs and merits its own fall.

The ensuing problem is that amidst all this media swill, JFK's actual *political* legacy and its *potential for change* has been steadily eroded, forgotten and engulfed by alternating rounds of character assassination or romanticization, a strategy whose gross effect threatens both to de-fang our outrage and depoliticize our understanding. The question "why" was he killed is not only depoliticized but kept mostly out of bounds. In the main it lies unaddressed or is foreclosed by a well-publicized punditry which debunks conspiracy -- more with the hip nihilism of cliche and sneer than with genuine counter-argument -- while oceans of suggestive evidence and the questions that still gnaw go effectively ignored, suppressed or unasked. This is why Bill Davy's books matter: they continue to uncover fresh evidence and to ask why. And, in so doing, they break new ground.

In spite of all, there remains a stubborn resiliency to JFK's enduring grip on the American psyche. This is most recently attested to by a February 1999 Gallup popularity poll that rates JFK as the greatest US president since World War II, enjoying percentages twice as high the closest two contenders.[2] On the research front, complementary struggles against the floodtides of amnesia, counter-publicity and media distraction continue to battle uphill. But as Bill Davy's book shows, these can nonetheless be truly groundbreaking and exhilarating. The extraordinary dogged work of Davy[3] and like-minded researcher-analysts such as Gerard Colby and Charlotte Dennett,[4] James DiEugenio,[5] Lisa Pease[6] and Professor Donald Gibson[7] have served to re-ignite, refocus and reward fresh attention to the entwined legacies of John Kennedy and Jim Garrison, as they amplify its still reverberating shock waves for those who can still lend an ear. Their work helps preserve that endangered legacy from the rigor mortis of "Cold War relic" and continues to demonstrate, as shown below, its fresh and urgent relevance to the present -- to the emergence of the New World Order.

II. Garrison's Invitation

Until the end of his life, Jim Garrison had a relentless conscience and hungry consciousness that continued to plummet the "why" of Kennedy's murder. Scriptwriter Zachary Sklar, Oscar nominee for *JFK* and editor of *On the Trail of the Assassins*, worked with Garrison late in his life, as a worsening heart condition demanded unwelcomed bed rest. Sklar remembers[8] how Garrison once lay in bed charting a set of converging lines of corporate interest and political alliance which finally would intersect at the Harvard Brahmin, McGeorge Bundy, JFK's national security advisor. Garrison, notes Sklar, was becoming especially interested in the Bundy Brothers, McGeorge and his elder brother William, a former CIA official who was Dean Acheson's son-in-law and held a significant Defense Department post on international security in the Kennedy Administration.[9] (Researchers, of course, have long noted[10] that in the immediate aftermath of the murder, the returning Air Force One was radioed by the White House Situation Room under Bundy's control to fix the lone nut as the sole perpetrator -- this before Oswald was even indicted.) Sklar points out that Garrison had *not* concluded that Bundy himself ordered or coordinated JFK's killing; but rather that, to Garrison, Bundy represented the *type* of high-level player who could well have been materially involved. It is interesting to ponder how Garrison's analysis might have reached this point, and to discern its striking implications for us today.

Jim Garrison's political views evolved out of the practical experience of investigating the New Orleans side of JFK's murder.

It is well known that he brought Clay Shaw to trial but less that he stubbornly maintained his position against an immense array of legal and extra-legal pressures to cease and desist.[11] It all started with his discovery of the double nature of 544 Camp Street (a detective agency/intelligence post). From there, Garrison could not fail to notice that any mention of CIA footprints would result in a quantum jump in the offensive against him and his case -- bugs, spies, character assassination, media disinformation. Though Shaw's precise role in the plot could not be demonstrated beyond a reasonable doubt, Garrison had nonetheless gained a stubborn, practical toehold where before there was nothing. It would prove to be a battering ram that breached the cover-up -- that well-fortified heart of darkness at the core of the American Century -- and lay the foundation for Stone's film, for the declassification and release of countless (and as yet undigested) official files and, most importantly, for significant future probes into our most enduring national mystery.

III. Toward A Better Model of Explanation

At some point in the 1960s, Jim Garrison began to view and seek explanations for JFK's assassination, its cover-up and failure of the Shaw trial that moved beyond the accumulated evidentiary data. He looked into the deeper structures of American power. Certainly by the time of his 1967 Playboy interview,[12] he had already begun to seek their explanations and meanings in the broader historical context of the relentless and seemingly eternal Cold War. Like everyone since 1947, and for the next 30 years, Garrison's grasp of events was imbued by the Cold War. To state the obvious, both his historic prosecution of Clay Shaw and his powerful analysis of Kennedy's murder in *A Heritage of Stone* (1970) took shape during the high tide of American intervention in the Vietnamese civil war. Today, with the benefits of hindsight and the until-recently-unthinkable end of the Cold War itself, it becomes possible to revisit Garrison's analysis and the "why" of the case with fresh eyes. In fact, we can detect that Garrison sensed processes at work in Kennedy's murder that went beyond the Cold War. Not only did he sense the distortions of his/our own Cold War lenses, but was able to peer through that looking glass into a set of underlying historical processes whose traces and agents could be glimpsed in the events of Dealey Plaza, 1963. Garrison dared to be heretical, to hypothesize beyond the given and to change the status quo. Let us surface and explore that hypothesis.

After Clay Shaw's acquittal, Garrison began an intensive analysis of the *politics* of JFK's death. His enduring legacy is to have founded a research agenda based on that analysis. Its most enduring gems are his *A Heritage of Stone* (1970), an article called "The Murder Talents of the CIA" published in *Freedom Magazine* (April - May, 1987) and his bestseller, *On the Trail of the Assassins* (1988), the basis for Oliver Stone's film *JFK* (1991).

In *Heritage*, Garrison states that he is presenting "a model of explanation" to "interpret sensibly the mass of data which has surfaced regarding the assassination;" a model which "explains the available data," serving as a preliminary *"tool of analysis* until or unless another one is offered which better explains the evidence. [13] [My emphasis] Twenty years later, his *On the Trail* would look back "with new information and new insights" and "put together *an informed historical speculation* of what happened to President Kennedy and why."[14] [My emphasis] All this indicates that Garrison was pioneering a paradigm, a mode of analysis. Far from being rigid dogma, it was an invitation to the continued dance of further investigation of critical analysis -- a call to continue in these footsteps. And, as we suggest below, as the global predations of the New World Order expand, it becomes ever more important that we accept his long-standing invitation.

Posing the Why

In the benighted '80s, a widely run Budweiser beer ad campaign coyly demanded that "we," America's unwashed forever-young lager louts, adopt the pseudo-defiant posture: "Why Ask Why?" Jim Garrison was never plagued by this question. He persistently set his analysis of "the why" behind the President's murder in a Cold War context, viewing it as inseparable from its history and political dynamics. One of its central events, he saw JFK's removal as the sine qua non of the Cold War's continuance and longevity as national policy. In *On the Trail* (1988) he states it baldly: "... its purpose was to stop Kennedy from seeking détente with the Soviet Union and Cuba and ending the Cold War."[15]

Yet there is strong evidence that the well-read Garrison[16] had been thinking all along in a still wider context. To wit, his files contain chapter notes for a never-to-be-published manuscript entitled *The War on the Future*. These place the Kennedy Assassination as the centerpiece of three watershed moments in the dark pageant of the postwar American Century. These are: (1) America's post-FDR Counterrevolution against change (vis-a-vis the emerging post-colonial nations); (2) the Kennedy Revolution for peace; and (3) the Establishment's Counterrevolution to reinstate the warfare state (via JFK's ouster). The upshot is that Garrison was hereby linking three powerful trends into an explosive mix: de facto U.S. assault on emerging nationalisms; JFK's ongoing defection from the Cold War; and the restoration of the status quo ante Kennedy -- that is, a re-stabilized warfare state -- via JFK's removal.

It is significant that these three trends converge and come to a head with the Vietnam War. Written in the marrow of Vietnam, *A Heritage of Stone* broaches the idea that Kennedy's killing had economic motivations: "To a warfare state, a war is a market – a market for the services of its military and for the hardware manufacturers."[17] For them JFK's resistance was the last straw:

> There had been his refusal to approve American air support at the Bay of Pigs and his refusal to respond to the Cuban missile crisis by bombing Cuba. There had been the signing of the nuclear test ban

treaty on September 1, ordered by him over the objection of the majority of the Joint Chiefs. Then there had been his initiation of détentes with Cuba and Russia. Now he was blocking a new war market in Vietnam.[18]

For Garrison, it was not surprising that certain leadership circles in America could foment, collaborate or endorse JFK's removal from office because "The Cold War was the biggest business in America, worth eighty billion dollars a year as well as tremendous power to men in Washington."[19] Kennedy, Garrison felt, was building on an opening achieved by Eisenhower, at the end of whose administration, "the end of the Cold War appeared to have come into reach..."[20] The CIA-inspired U-2 incident scuttled the prospect and Krushchev canceled the upcoming Paris peace talks between the two superpowers. Then came Kennedy, who in Garrison's phrase, "was different."[21] He would build on Eisenhower's brief opening to the Soviets and become a conscious de-escalator of tensions, "a president preparing for peace, not war, and he was moving too fast." [22]

In any case, if Garrison is right about the war and the murder having overlapping economic motivations, then it might be possible, for starters, to meaningfully ask, what firms were the specific economic and financial beneficiaries of the war, and then to start investigating the question whether JFK's removal in some way paved the way for their prosperity.[23]

On the Trail of the Who

In Stone's *JFK*, the Garrison figure asks the knowing Mr. X, "How do you think it started?" X answers metaphorically, "I think it started somewhere in the wind."[24] Up close analysis of the real Garrison's writings show his quest, struggles and difficulty in affixing more *specific* responsibility for JFK's murder. Indeed, he wrestled continually with a shifting set of related possibilities that moved through several entwined layers of the power structure. While Garrison's scenarios are roughly drawn and suggestive, they are nonetheless highly informed and well argued, laced with embedded pointers suggesting further development.

For example, Garrison's 1987 *Freedom Magazine* article, "The Killing Talents of the CIA"[25] indicts "a covert part" or "rogue element" of the CIA -- but probably not its "command level" -- as the force that orchestrated or carried out the murder in a de facto coup d'etat. In *On the Trail* he locates the machinery for killing JFK somewhere in the Operations branch of the CIA, carried out in league with unspecified assets and affiliates:

> I believe it was instigated and planned long in advance by fanatical anticommunists in the United States intelligence community; that it was carried out, most likely without official approval, by individuals in *the C.I.A.'s covert operations apparatus* and other extra-governmental collaborators, and covered up by like-minded individuals in the F.B.I., the Secret Service, the Dallas Police Department, and the military...[26] [My emphasis]

A survey across the arc of Garrison's words and writings, however, detects that other non-Cold War currents move in and out of play, and reveals a deeply-embedded hypothesis struggling to be born. For example, at a September 1968 Roundtable Conversation in New Orleans with leading assassination researchers, Garrison posits a category of probable players who were "closely connected with the Pax American organism," which he refined as being "not all military..."[27] Nevertheless, still seeing through Cold War lenses, he added "It's an organism that believes you have to destroy communism all over the earth or it will destroy you."[28] In May 1969, however, Garrison gave his first extensive post-Shaw trial interview (released under his letterhead as New Orleans Parish District Attorney) and defined the CIA more expansively as an arm of the government's warfare interests:

> The C.I.A., it must be understood, had long since ceased to be merely an intelligence coordinating agency and had become, as well, the clandestine arm of *the warfare interests* in the United States government. [29] [My emphasis]

Indeed, because JFK "... had been pursuing an unprecedented and innovative course of détente with regard to the Cold War," he had been "eliminated by the inflexible *cold warrior consensus* hidden within the government, for which it was important that hostile relations with Russia continue."[30] [My emphasis]

Shortly thereafter, Garrison wrote *A Heritage of Stone* (1970) in the relentless hothouse climate of the Vietnam War, whose very legitimacy (especially since the Tet Offensive of 1968) was subject to daily attack and wrenching national debate. This book alleges the "military-intelligence structure's" apparent Kennedy-problem and begins to glimpse beyond the Cold War:

> President Kennedy's program of de-escalation necessarily had a tremendous impact on elements of our military-intelligence structure. From their point of view, we had reached a position from which we were close to military hegemony over the world, and this rich young man, this transient, was undoing it all by the systematic voluntary surrender of our military advantages.

> This steady, ineluctable course toward ending the cold war placed Kennedy on a collision course with the strongest forces in the United States government. His course, if continued, meant the end of the long hayride of billions and billions of dollars of military hardware purchases. It meant the end of the Pax Americana, the new imperialism which had crept into American foreign policy at the end of World War II. It meant the beginning of the end of the dominance of the Pentagon and the CIA over American foreign policy, and, indeed, over much of the domestic policy as well. It meant, in sum, the beginning of the end of *two empires*, one international and the other a bureaucratic structure internal to our government and more powerful than the rest of the government put together.[31] [My emphasis]

Further echoes of these two linked "empires" – one international, the other internal and bureaucratic -- recur in Garrison's subsequent thought. Again, in the *Freedom Magazine* piece, for all its focus on the CIA, Garrison gestures boldly toward a higher plane of authority -- "a more broadly based force" to whose overall interests the CIA-affiliated executors were beholden:

> Even as this crucial point is made – that Kennedy's execution at Dealey Plaza bears the exclusive trademark of a CIA executive action operation – it is essential to keep in focus the enormity of the coup d'etat (designed to assure the reversal of American foreign policy) and to understand, accordingly, that the intelligence component which was utilized acted merely as the agent for *a more broadly based force* of overwhelming strength but screened from sight at the upper level of our government.[32] [My emphasis]

Still speaking generically, the article equates this "broadly based force" to "a higher level" of control:

> It would be unrealistic not to recognize that, while the intelligence group obviously constituted the cutting edge of the assassination project, *other far more powerful elements at a higher level* clearly desired and contributed to the removal of the president. Otherwise, the virtual ratification of the assassination by the US government which followed would never have occurred...[33] [My emphasis]

But there is something more at work. Although Garrison continues to label these elements "cold warriors," he also begins to *see through* the Cold War veils:

> These lofty but well-hidden forces may best be described as the "cold warriors" in our government. By that designation is meant those who had watched with masked alarm the steps which Kennedy had been taking toward détente, toward ending the Cold War. These were men who believe *(or appeared to believe)* – as late as 1963 – in the specter of a united, global communism dedicated to the destruction of the United States. Judging from the massive aid and comfort which the assassins tacitly received in America following their bloody deed, this concealed consensus was rock-hard and fanatically committed.[34] [My emphasis]

Garrison's parenthetical wink intrigues. It is a pointer. The parentheses harbor a tension between a Cold War analysis and something far deeper. What could it mean that these cold warriors "*appeared* to believe" in the global communist conspiracy? Might they have two faces? Might their *use* of anti-communism serve as a cover for other ends? Will the answers help disclose who they were?

IV. GARRISON'S LEGACY AND OUR CHALLENGE

It is high time to revisit the JFK assassination in a revised framework that accepts Garrison's invitation to begin the road toward a "better explanation." Noting that most JFK-researchers no longer ask or analyze the "whys," it seems long overdue to kick-start that enterprise by revisiting Garrison's analyses, deconstructing some of his expressions and parlaying the result into a research agenda that returns once more to the trail of the assassins.

A viable agenda for research would seriously bore in -- *with the greatest possible specificity and depth* -- on a set of intertwined issues and the host of associated questions that they generate. Components of one such agenda are outlined in broad strokes below:

• *Re-examine the actual, elite composition of the so-called Kennedy Administration.*

Evidence and analysis by Colby and Dennett[35] demonstrate that the Kennedy Administration was staffed primarily by Wall Street banker and former Defense Secretary Robert Lovett[36] and thereby composed of first-tier architects of the Cold War and Establishment icons, such as: John J. McCloy (Disarmament chief), C. Douglas Dillon (Treasury Secretary), W. Averill Harriman (Undersecretary of State for Political Affairs) and Paul Nitze (Assistant Secretary of State for International Affairs and Navy Secretary)[37] as well as Dean Rusk (Secretary of State), Walt and Eugene Rostow, McGeorge and William Bundy, Allen W. Dulles (whose hawkish brother John Foster was Ike's Secretary of State)[38] and in the wings, Dean Acheson.[39] Most of their careers were affiliated with Rockefeller financial interests. Indeed, given Nelson Rockefeller's presidential aspirations,[40] the Kennedy Administration was arguably an interim regime, a kind of Rockefeller-Administration-in-waiting. But there is more. Beyond the Cold War and beyond their Rockefeller ties, these men shared a common vision.

The Kennedy Administration was not so much staffed by "Cold Warriors" as by transnational bankers and lawyers with a long-view. They were progenitors, architects and proconsuls for the New World Order. Indeed, its staffers arguably comprised one of the most powerful private men's clubs in world history. Neither mere bureaucrats, political hacks nor presidential appointees, they were American icons. Many were the architects of the Cold War. But beyond the Cold War, they were transnationalists, blue-blooded kinsmen with a shared vision, initially rooted in America's breakthrough to Empire in 1898 and its elevation to world creditor status via the First World War; men who had already defeated détente with the Soviets in the aftermath of the Second World War and midwived the military-industrial complex.[41] Grounded in world-spanning interests and a vision of a world made safe for capital flows, these were geopolitical strategists with an ambitious program of fantasizing and implementing an economic system on the scale of the globe itself. In a word, the fledgling president, vouchsafed to the bigs by an ambitious father, was *dwarfed*. Any president's serious defection from their interests would brand him a maverick, a potential usurper of their world and its entitlements.

The question, then, is whether Kennedy fully or sufficiently shared the values and pursued the core interests of the members of "his" Administration? Did he grow demonstrably estranged on key issues from its key players, or the imperatives of their

216

outside patrons and affiliates? On what issues? From which players? Which affiliates? Was he perceived by them as a dangerous maverick? As finally unsustainable? What interests and values did they hold in common that Harvard-man Kennedy, though seemingly a kindred blue blood, did not?

- *Re-examine the undeclared, ongoing transnational elite war against economic nationalism.*

In the '50s and '60s, transnational commercial interests regarded economic relations with emerging third world nations as a zero-sum game, whereby nationalist economic advances had to be stymied or reversed. Accumulating new evidence[42] suggests that JFK tried to pursue a more nuanced "third way" reformist development strategy --between Wall Street's and Moscow's -- of accommodating emerging nationalist interests and regimes in the Congo, Indonesia, Indochina (including Laos and Vietnam), Latin America and, possibly, in Cuba. The key question is whether this an accurate reading of Kennedy's strategy in the Third World?

For example, how deep was JFK's support for rapid social reform? Did Kennedy's apparent preference for government-to-government as opposed to private development loans invoke the enmity of transnational finance? Was he considered too soft on economic nationalism to be trusted with the core interests of transnational firms? Did this pursuit set him at irreconcilable odds with transnationalist interests and/or with bodies like the CIA whose raison d'etre and dedicated mission was to ensure these interests by any means necessary? Is there evidence, *prior* to JFK, that overt or covert anti-nationalist initiatives were made by the US on behalf of transnational firms such as Freeport Sulphur (in Cuba and Indonesia), United Fruit Company (in Guatemala, Cuba and Latin America) and Tanganyika Concessions, Forminiere and Union Miniere (in the Congo)?[43] If so, the question becomes whether continuance of such policies was either contested by JFK (or like-minded officials) or, at minimum, genuinely thrown into question during his tenure in office. If so, researchers might analyze their boards of directors and to ask whether they had affiliates within the government who defended their interests against Kennedy's policy innovations?

In this vein, the context and evolution of Kennedy's Cuba policy needs to be reviewed. It could be asked, for example, whether it was the loss of Mafia-owned casinos or a host of specific transnational properties -- such as Esso, Texaco and Shell Oil -- that constituted the *main* casualty of Castro's takeover in Cuba and the mainspring of US anti-Castro policies.[44] What, for instance, might it have signified to such business interests for JFK to have "retired" the decidedly corporate-friendly Allen Dulles[45] and his military deputy General Cabell[46] from the CIA? After having refused to order air strikes during the Bay of Pigs invasion (1961), what might it have cost JFK during the watershed Cuban Missile Crisis (1962) to have held out for a naval blockade against the fierce calls for immediate airstrikes, full invasion and hard-line anti-Soviet stances proffered by the potent Messrs. McGeorge Bundy, Paul Nitze, Walt Rostow, Dean Rusk, C. Douglas Dillon, DCI John McCone, John J. McCloy and Dean Acheson?[47] Moreover, did JFK's last "heretical" initiative to open secret back channel negotiations with Fidel Castro via UN deputy William Attwood,[48]-- outside of Rusk's State Department -- cement an irrevocable breach between the President and his elite enemies?

- *Re-examine the original and enduring composition of the warfare state.*

Evidence suggests that only 15 years into the Cold War, JFK was returning to the formerly defeated FDR-Morgenthau-Wallace policy of détente and its vision of postwar cooperation with the Soviets.[49] He was doing so against the very Wall Street-based factions who had defeated it in the first place, who had fought to institutionalize the military-industrial complex as a permanent fixture of national life, and many of whom, such as Robert Lovett, Paul Nitze and John J. McCloy had both served with Wall Street mega-firms and staffed or occupied high posts in the Truman, Eisenhower[50] and Kennedy Administrations.

A viable research probe would query in detail whether, as Garrison maintains, JFK seriously pursued a policy of détente. Then, it would examine whether there is demonstrable evidence of rifts between Kennedy and the "cold warriors" in the Administration?[51] And if there were, it would evaluate whether JFK's detentism was pursued to a degree that seriously threatened, or was seen to so threaten, the current or long-term grip of "the warfare state" and its affiliates over American life, policy and resources? And, finally, it would probe whether any identifiable representatives or affiliates of the warfare state overlap significantly with or have discernible links to officials in the so-called Kennedy Administration, or for that matter, to the Warren Commission?[52]

- *Re-examine the state bureaucracy's post-Kennedy changeover, the state-business stewardship over the war in Vietnam, and the hand of transnational business in the origins of America's intervention.*

Accumulating evidence demonstrates both JFK's overwhelming preference for a *political* solution to the Vietnamese civil war, and his having ordered and set in motion a graduated withdrawal of US ground forces. Evidence also demonstrates resolute backing by the transnationalist business elite for LBJ's turn toward open-ended military escalation in Vietnam and the direct stewardship over the war of its governmental affiliates.[53] Related evidence as early as 1962 *suggests* the expressed, intensive interest by representatives of the transnational elites in favor of military engagement on behalf of their interests in Indochina.[54] Fresh questions arise:

Is there any evidence for Scott's hypothesis that JFK might have been considering a political solution in Vietnam as a quid pro quo for the neutralization of Cuba? In this vein, might there have been a related purpose to the upcoming (slated for February 1964, but never to be held) state visit to Washington of the long-term "Vietnam-Indochina hand" and equally maverick, French President Charles deGaulle[55]?

- *Examine the elite hand in the birth of the Warren Commission as a tool to preempt further investigation and foreclose evidence of conspiracy.*

Evidence gathered by Professor Donald Gibson demonstrates the elite origins of the Warren Commission.[56] He argues that within two hours of Oswald's murder on the afternoon of November 24th, 1963, Eugene Rostow, in the company of at least one other unidentified person called the White House and spoke to LBJ's Press Secretary Bill Moyers, urging him to inform LBJ of his/their view that a presidential commission on JFK's murder be appointed to take charge of the volatile, investigative situation. "Rostow is either the originator of the idea, the first active promoter, or both."[57] Gibson later concludes: "The commission idea comes from Rostow, Alsop and Acheson. It has immediate support from individuals at the Washington Post (James Wiggins) and the New York Times (James Reston). It will be supported by Secretary of State Dean Rusk."

Gibson poses the following research agenda: "Who or what do these people represent? Are these people connected with each other? Are these people in any way associated with those who would direct the Commission once it was established?"[58] It could further be asked whether these people or their representatives could be shown to have had vital interests that JFK, in any of the ways discussed above, was an actual or perceived threat.

To recap: The explosive hypothesis of corporate-state elite involvement in Kennedy's death is latent in Garrison's analysis. For it to achieve undeniable plausibility, sustained and patient research must first explore to what extent, if any, JFK may have defected from their dominant policy currents and overall consensus. And then, it would have to be determined whether there is evidence that he actually crossed the trip wires of their core interests. Without this much, at the least, the augmented-Garrison hypothesis could show that there were specific interests who *benefited* from JFK's demise, but *not* that they had either launched or participated in his assassination.

V. FINALE

With the end of the Cold War and the clear-cut emergence of a globalizing New World Order, it is possible to reexamine both the Cold War and a salient moment, JFK's premature death, with truly fresh understanding, in ways that Garrison sensed and opened up, but did not fully articulate. Garrison's own broadly caricatured analysis permanently invites us to fashion "a *tool of analysis* ...which better explains the evidence." The road to a better explanation requires that researchers seriously revisit and reconstruct an in-depth, cold-eyed, demythologized history of the *context* of JFK's murder: namely, to use Scott's phrase, to investigate the "deep politics" and dynamics of the Truman, Eisenhower, Kennedy and Johnson Administrations.

This is clearly a major undertaking of collaboration, sharing and discussion. But if *any* of the foregoing agenda holds water, then there are compelling, *democratic* reasons for researchers to attempt it. In any case, however uncoordinated or scattered it may appear to date, that work is already well underway. We have at hand both the strip mining and deconstruction of the sedimentary past and its gradual reconstruction into a common vision and agenda. We, in fact, have no less than an emerging paradigm, a "better explanation" of Jim Garrison's Cold War "why." Among its wellsprings are John Stewart Martin's and Carl Marzani's[59] long-out-of-print but seminal exposes of the Cold War's fomenters; the unpublished, but forever-fertile research masterpiece of Peter Dale Scott, *The Dallas Conspiracy* (1971); and Scott's long out-of-print, kindred volume on Vietnam, *The War Conspiracy* (1975). More recent equally-invaluable research sources are the searching in-depth political studies of America's leading political-economic elites by Professors Phillip H. Burch,[60] Frank Kofsky[61] and Jerry Sanders,[62] as well as the surprisingly valuable mainstream study of America's so-called "wise men" by journalists Walter Isaacson and Evan Thomas.[63] This said, however, it should be underscored that the cutting-edge for this new paradigm is currently being honed in the aforementioned work of James DiEugenio, Lisa Pease, Donald Gibson, Charlotte Dennett and Gerard Colby and, of course, in that of Bill Davy.

VI. EPILOGUE

Waxing preeminent, former Secretary of State Dean Acheson titled his memoirs *Present at the Creation* (1969). He was "not only present at the creation of the postwar world," as his liner notes assure us, but "one of its chief architects." By 1967, Jim Garrison became the Prometheus to the Achesonian Olympus. He would shortly come to believe that the Cold Warriors destroyed JFK for Cold War imperatives, bringing one of the lesser deities, Clay Shaw, to the bar of mortal justice. His mission – to bring down the cover-up and steal the divine fire of truth for us mortals -- was driven by a deeply personal credo: "Let justice be done, though the Heavens fall." For this, Garrison was severely punished, outcast and hounded to his dying day by the oracles of power, the New York Times and Washington Post, even through to their mean-spirited, parting obituaries. But for all this, it is thanks to authors like Bill Davy that Garrison's true legacy of challenge lives on. That contested arena -- Acheson's Creation versus Garrison's Justice – still harbors the keys to the labyrinth that is John Kennedy's murder.

[1] Posner's strange brief as official undertaker of conspiracy theories regarding the '60s assassinations is shown not only by his *Case Closed* (1993) on John Kennedy case, but also his *Killing the Dream* (1998) on the murder of Dr. Martin Luther King. Will further prosecution briefs against RFK, Malcolm X and Walter Reuther round out his bibliography?

[2] The Gallup poll results for the week ending February 8th was reported by CNN on President's Day, February 15th, 1999.

[3] See William Davy's self-published *Through the Looking Glass*, 1995.

[4] See Gerard Colby and Charlotte Dennett, *Thy Will Be Done*, 1995, especially Chapter 27 which details and highlights tensions between JFK and the Rockefellers.

[5] See James DiEugenio's seminal study of Garrison, *Destiny Betrayed* (1992) and his article "Dodd and Dulles Vs. Kennedy in Africa," (*Probe*, Jan-Feb, 1999).

[6] See Lisa Pease's articles in *Probe*, "David Atlee Phillips, Clay Shaw and Freeport Sulphur" (Mar.-Apr. 1996) and "Indonesia, President Kennedy & Freeport Sulphur" (May-June, 1996)

[7] See Donald Gibson's *Battling Wall Street* and his articles in *Probe*, "The Creation of the 'Warren Commission'" (May-June 1996) and "Kennedy vs. the Early Globalists" (Jan.-Feb. 1998) and "Clay Shaw, Freeport Sulphur and the Eastern Establishment" (Nov.-Dec. 1996).

[8] Author's interview with *JFK* scriptwriter Zachary Sklar, February, 1999.

[9] See Phillip H. Burch, *Elites in American History*, p. 197. Burch notes that in the months after JFK's death, William Bundy was moved from his Defense post to replace the pro-Kennedy political-solution-for-Vietnam advocate Roger Hilsman as Secretary of State for East Asian Affairs. Soon thereafter he became a director of the Council on Foreign Relations and, more recently, served as editor of its preeminent policy journal, *Foreign Affairs*.

[10] Though this *proves* nothing about Bundy per se, examples include Vincent Salandria who stated that Bundy was "in control of the White House Situation Room" (*Speech at COPA Conference*, November 1998, p.15). Robert Groden and Harrison Livingstone write that Col. L. Fletcher Prouty had told them "it was Bundy" (*High Treason*, p. 20). They also cite William Manchester to aver that those on Air Force One "were told" that a lone man did it from the White House Situation Room either by McGeorge Bundy or an aide, the former US Moscow-based naval attaché, Commander Oliver Hallett. They report that the Situation Room was manned by military personnel and received much of its information from the Pentagon-based Defense Intelligence Agency (DIA).

[11] See Jim DiEugenio, *Destiny Betrayed*, 1992.

[12] See Interview with Jim Garrison, *Playboy Magazine*, October 1967.

[13] See Garrison, *Heritage of Stone*, p. 185.

[14] See Garrison, *On the Trail of the Assassins*, p. 277

[15] Ibid.

[16] Author's interview with Zachary Sklar. Having worked as Garrison's editor for *On the Trail*, Sklar has vivid memories of Garrison's extensive bookshelves whose contents went well beyond that of his purely legal collection.

[17] See Garrison, *Heritage of Stone*, p. 178.

[18] Ibid., p. 179

[19] Ibid.

[20] Ibid.

[21] Ibid.

[22] Ibid.

[23] See, for example, Fletcher L. Prouty, *JFK: The CIA, Vietnam and the Plot to Assassinate John F. Kennedy* (1992), p. 290. Among the chief beneficiaries of the war, Prouty points to the alliance of Bell Helicopter, the major helicopter manufacturer and nominal employer of Oswald acquaintance Michael Paine, with Textron and the First National Bank of Boston. Scott names several beneficiaries in his unpublished *The Dallas Conspiracy* (1971) and out of print *The War Conspiracy* (1975).

[24] See *JFK*, The Documented Screenplay, (Applause Books, 1992), p. 180

[25] See Jim Garrison, "The Murder Talents of the CIA," *Freedom Magazine* (April-May 1987), p. 277

[26] Ibid.

[27] See transcription of the *Roundtable Conversation*, New Orleans Athletic Club (September 1968), p. 126

[28] Ibid.

[29] Interview with District Attorney Jim Garrison, Release of the Office of the District Attorney, Parish of New Orleans, May 27th 1969, p. 1.

[30] Ibid.

[31] See Garrison, *Heritage of Stone*, pp. 72-73

[32] See Garrison, "The Murder Talents of the CIA," *Freedom Magazine* (April-May 1987) p. 7.

[33] Ibid.

[34] Ibid.

[35] See Colby and Dennett, *Thy Will Be Done*, pp. 337-339. McCloy and Lovett had administered the wartime War Department under the patriarchy of War Secretary, Henry L. Stimson. McGeorge Bundy helped Stimson compile and write his memoirs. C. Douglas Dillon was the son of Wall Street financier Clarence Dillon, boss of Dillon, Read, whose high-octane firm provided Stimson's replacement, the hawkish Defense Secretary James Forrestal and his younger protege Paul Nitze.

[36] Lovett became a board member of the Rockefeller Foundation as of 1949 and Secretary of Defense in 1951. In 1950, with Dean Acheson and Paul Nitze, he helped spearhead NSC-68, the top-secret Cold War manifesto as national policy and ground the military industrial complex as a permanent fixture of US life.

[37] Nitze was appointed Navy Secretary to replace the TFX scandal-tainted Fred Korth, a notable Texas bank president who, amazingly, had been divorce lawyer for Marguerite Oswald, mother to the alleged assassin.

[38] Allen Dulles was a partner and operative of the Wall Street mega-law firm Sullivan and Cromwell among whose senior partners was elder brother John Foster Dulles, the former president of the Rockefeller Foundation (1946) and Secretary of State, who represented Rockefeller interests such as the Standard Oil Company of New York (Esso). In the mid-30s, Allen served as general counsel and a director of the Wall Street based J. Henry Schroder Bank, a corporate partner in Schroder, Rockefeller & Co. During the wartime, Dulles was close to the board of the transnational, Nazi-dominated set of private central bankers who comprised the gold-laundering Bank for International Settlements. Its American president, William McKittrick, was an informant for Dulles, who then headed the Swiss HQ of America's OSS.

[39] While formally returned to corporate law, the Wise Man Acheson was always on tap: called in as a hawkish senior advisor during the Cuban Missile Crisis; among the first to call for the Warren Commission (see footnote 41) and a member (with Bundy, Dillon and McCloy) of LBJ's Senior Informal Advisory Group on Vietnam (see Philip H. Burch, *Elites in American History*, p. 210).

[40] Nelson Rockefeller, JFK's most feared electoral opponent, announced his Presidential bid in November of 1963. His first major speech held that Kennedy was "jeopardizing the peace and demoralizing America's allies with a weak, indecisive foreign policy." (cited in Colby and Dennett, *Thy Will Be Done*, p. 411)

[41] The deep origins of the military-industrial complex does not lie in the demands of helmeted yahoos and hormonally driven generals; but in the radical, focused and pioneering work of internationalist bankers and lawyers and the financial and industrial interests they represented.

[42] A growing body of research shows the opposition of JFK's accommodationist strategy toward economic nationalist regimes like Congo, Indonesia and the opposition to it by transnational corporate interests and the CIA. For example, in *The Dallas Conspiracy*, Peter Dale Scott notes that JFK backing the emergent "third way" nationalist leadership of Juan Bosch in the Dominican Republic, whereas in 1965 LBJ dispatched 25,000 US Marines to prevent Bosch's assumption of power via popular election. Jim DiEugenio's "Dodd and Dulles Vs. Kennedy in Africa," (*Probe*, Jan-Feb, 1999) provides a case study of JFK's opposition to Allen Dulles and transnational interests in the Congo. A related study by Richard Mahoney notes that JFK was unique in establishing a

"common ground between Africa ideals and American self-interest in the midst of the Cold War." (*JFK: Ordeal in Africa*, p. 248)

[43] The Pan-Africanist leader of Ghana, Kwame Nkrumah, who then helped turn Africa's Gold Coast into a center of nationalist agitation wrote: "Belgian financial domination of the Congo, because of the close connections of Belgian banking institutions with such international houses as Rothschild, Lazard Freres and Schroeder, in their turn linked with the Morgan and Rockefeller groups, was shared with British, French and American finance." See Nkrumah, *Socialism in Africa* (1962), p. 39.

[44] See Morris H. Morley, *Imperial State and Revolution: The United States and Cuba, 1952-1986*, 1987.

[45] Shortly thereafter, Ellen Lansing Dulles, Allen's Germanophile sister and booster for the Bank for International Settlements, was "retired" from her State Department post. Secretary Dean Rusk distanced himself from JFK as he told her, "The White House has asked me to get rid of you."

[46] Cabell, Garrison notes in *On the Trail*, was brother of Dallas mayor Earl Cabell. Near the time of his being fired, Cabell was introduced by Trade Mart Manager Clay Shaw for a speech to the Foreign Policy Association of New Orleans.

[47] For a summary of players and positions, see the National Security Archive's online "Selected Glossary on the Cuban Missile Crisis,1962"at: http://www.seas.gwu.edu/nsarchive/nsa/cuba_mis_cri/cmcnames.html.

[48] Author Anthony Summers has written that McGeorge Bundy was "the aide most concerned with the Attwood negotiations." See Anthony Summers, *Conspiracy*, 1981, p. 425.

[49] Garrison was first and most consistent in the advocacy of this position. It has been generally supported, for example, by in-depth analyses such as Philip H. Burch in *Elites in American Life*, Peter Dale Scott in *The Dallas Conspiracy* (1971) and L. Fletcher Prouty's *JFK: Vietnam, the CIA and the Plot to Assassinate John F. Kennedy* (1992).

[50] C. Douglas Dillon, for example, served as an Undersecretary of State in the Eisenhower Administration and vetted such nationalist leaders as the Congo's Patrice Lumumba for compatibility with US interests.

[51] Gibson informs us of a "serious rift" between JFK and John McCloy "over how to organize and pursue peace and arms negotiations," citing as evidence two New York Times articles published on June 30, 1961 which undermine the received portrait of the two men acting as "close collaborators" in the peace process. See "Establishment Radicals and Kennedy" in *Probe*, November-December 1998, p. 12.

[52] Peter Dale Scott's *Dallas Conspiracy* shows that one Commission lawyer, Albert Jenner, was counsel for Henry Crown, the leading stockholder in then

number one defense giant General Dynamics. Some time after his service on the Commission, Jenner was elevated to the board of directors.

[53] Scott's *The Dallas Conspiracy* (1971) details the role and words of a Socony Mobil representative William Henderson in promoting America's armed intervention to stabilize the region for business. See William Henderson, ed., *Southeast Asia: Problems of United States Policy*, (1963), pp. 253-254

[54] See, for example, Peter Dale Scott's "The Vietnam War and the CIA-Financial Establishment," in Mark Selden, ed., *Remaking Asia*, 1975.

[55] DeGaulle, whose nationalist agnosticism vis-a-vis NATO infuriated US military circles, was himself the target of seventeen assassination attempts, some of them over his decision to pull France out of its long colonial war in Algeria, just as it had left Vietnam prior to the Americans entry.

[56] See Gibson, "The Creation of the 'Warren Commission'", *Probe*, May-June 1996.

[57] Ibid., p. 30

[58] Ibid.

[59] See John Stewart Martin, *All Honorable Men* (Boston: Little, Brown, 1950) and Carl Marzani, *We Can Be Friends* (New York: Topical Books, 1950).

[60] See Phillip H. Burch, *Elites in American History*, 1980. A tour-de-force study of the elites and factions that comprised every presidential administration from the New Deal through the Carter Administration. The chapter on the Kennedy-Johnson Years is a must read and gold mine for serious researchers.

[61] See Frank Kofsky, *Harry S. Truman and the War Scare of 1948*, 1995. A remarkable study of the action by elite players within the Truman Administration to scare the nation into support of massive peacetime expenditures for war.

[62] See Jerry Sanders, *Peddlers of Crisis*, 1983. A remarkable study of elite players like Paul Nitze and Eugene Rostow and the Committees on the Present Danger which combined to give us NSC-68 to institutionalize the Military-Industrial Complex, Cold War and Arms Race as permanent fixtures for our times, and who destroyed the SALT Talks and détente to perpetuate those institutions and wage undeclared war to finally bring down the Soviets.

[63] See Walter Isaacson and Evan Thomas, *The Wise Men*, 1986. A richly detailed study of the prime American "architects" of the postwar world -- Dean Acheson, Robert Lovett, John McCloy, Averill Harriman, George Kennan and Charles Bohlen -- and such fellow-travelling potentates as Paul Nitze and John Foster Dulles.

Appendix A:

~

James Alcock's Closing Argument

MR. ALCOCK:

May it please the Court and Gentlemen of the Jury:

Gentlemen, let me being by thanking you on behalf of the State of Louisiana and the District Attorney's office,first of all for serving on this Jury. I realize that it has been a personal sacrifice and certainly a sacrifice on the part of your employers as well as on the part of your families, and we do appreciate it and I am sure the City of New Orleans appreciates it. Let me also thank you gentlemen at the outset for your kind attention.This has been a long tedious trial,oftentimes there have been some rather technical points gone into.There have been experts that have testified in this case, and I realize as a layman -- and I am a layman also -- that sometimes this testimony became a little tedious and sometimes a little difficult to understand and sometimes a little difficult to follow, but I certainly do appreciate the attention that you have given to these witnesses.

Gentlemen, this is what is known as the State's Opening Closing Argument. I will attempt during the course of this argument to try to piece together for you the various bits and pieces of evidence as it unfolded from the witness stand. We have here parts of a puzzle, if you will, and I am going to attempt in this argument to bring these pieces of the puzzle together and to give you a clear image of just what the case is about. Naturally, during this argument I am going to highlight those things which I think most favorable to the State of Louisiana and to the prosecution in this case.Mr. Dymond and whoever else might argue for the Defense, in their argument will highlight those that they figure most favorable to the Defendant. Now, Mr. Dymond will have a rebuttal argument, the State will have its rebuttal argument. It may seem on the surface somewhat unfair that the State is given two arguments as opposed to one for the Defense attorney, but I submit to you that the State carries a heavy burden, and that is proof beyond a reasonable doubt. Therefore, the Legislature of this State and most states throughout the United States accord to the prosecution two arguments.Therefore, you will hear from the State twice.And then after Mr. Dymond and Mr.Wegmann, if Mr. Wegmann should argue, you will hear again from the State of Louisiana. Gentlemen, at the outset of this trial the State made what is known as an opening statement, and in that opening statement, which is not -- and I remind you again, is not --evidence in this case, the State outlined in thumbnail fashion, schematic fashion, blueprint fashion, what it intended to prove during the course of the trial.The State was required by the law of Louisiana to make this opening statement; Defense Counsel was not required to make an opening statement. However, in this case, as is sometimes the situation, Defense Counsel chose to make an opening statement, and in his opening statement, gentlemen, he made certain promises to each and every one of you. One promise that comes to my mind most readily and most clearly is this: that his client, Clay Shaw, not only did not conspire with David W. Ferrie or Lee Harvey Oswald, but did not know either David W. Ferrie or Lee Harvey Oswald, and further, gentlemen, never laid his eyes on either one or both of these men. Gentlemen, I submit to you that within four hours of the beginning of this trial that promise was broken. That promise, gentlemen, lay shattered, broken, and forever irretrievable in the dust of Clinton, Louisiana. With that promise being broken, gentlemen, the Defendant before the Bar, that man right there (indicating), was a proven liar unworthy of your belief, and the Judge will charge you that if any witness, either for the State or for the Defense, lies on any material issue, you may disregard his entire testimony. And there can be no more material issue in this case than whether or not the Defendant, who is charged with having conspired with two men, did in fact know those two men and was in fact in association with those two men. So I submit to you gentlemen, within four hours the promise was broken and the Defendant was proven a liar.

Now, gentlemen, the State opened its case in Clinton, Louisiana. We heard from some six or seven witnesses from Clinton, Louisiana. These people are not involved in this case directly. These people, gentlemen, had nothing to gain by coming to the City of New Orleans and testifying, perhaps an environment strange to them. I doubt if any of them had ever testified in any criminal prosecution before, and certainly not in a criminal prosecution of this significance or notoriety, not in a criminal prosecution in a courtroom filled with reporters from all over the world. Gentlemen, by this testimony from these people who had nothing to gain, the State proved certain important and crucial elements of its case. The first man to take the stand was Mr.Lee McGehee, the barber from Jackson, Louisiana. He testified that Lee Harvey Oswald entered his barbershop and received a haircut from him in late August or early September, 1963. Now, there was nothing great or significant about this gentleman except the fact that his testimony also adduced these facts: Lee Harvey Oswald was interested in gaining employment in the East Louisiana State Hospital at Jackson, Louisiana; Mr.McGehee directed Lee Harvey Oswald to Reeves Morgan, who was then the State Legislator for East Feliciana Parish. Lee Harvey Oswald arrived, gentlemen, or at least Mr. McGehee deduced he arrived in an old battered automobile and there was a young lady in the automobile. Now I want to at this time make it abundantly clear that the State does not claim that it identified that woman at all. The State is certainly not coming before this Jury and saying that it was Marina Oswald, now Marina Oswald Porter, that drove him. I wish we could have identified her, I wish we could have brought her into the courtroom and presented her to you. But nevertheless he did appear on that occasion. And Mr. McGehee did something else, he mentioned the name of Henry Earl Palmer, and not the necessity but the fact that it would serve Oswald well if he should register to vote in the area, since he was sending him to the State Legislator, and he mentioned Clinton, Louisiana. Now, after this, gentlemen, and I submit as a direct result of this,Lee Harvey Oswald went to the home of Reeves Morgan, again in the City of Jackson, Louisiana, or, as he put it, somewhere close by the city or on the outskirts of the city. He went into Mr. Morgan's home and at first introduced himself as Oswald. You recall Mr. Reeves Morgan saying that he mentioned the name of Oswald Chance, an acquaintance of his, asking Lee Harvey Oswald if perhaps he was related to Oswald Chance because of the similarity of the name Oswald. He also mentioned the possibility of Lee Harvey Oswald registering to vote, and the place to register to vote, gentlemen, was Clinton, Louisiana. On the way out of the door, he had more than just the name Oswald, because Lee Oswald told him his name was Lee Oswald and he was from New Orleans, Louisiana. After the assassination when Mr.Morgan saw Lee Harvey Oswald on television, he had a conversation with Mr. McGehee. Mr. McGehee confirmed the fact that the man he sent to his home was the same man he, Mr. McGehee, had seen on television -- Lee Harvey Oswald. Mr. Morgan went one step further. Mr. Morgan went one step further. Mr. Morgan called the Federal Bureau of Investigation and told them of the presence of Lee Harvey Oswald and got the response, "We know he was in the area." Gentlemen, I submit with just these two witnesses the State has proven beyond any doubt that Lee Harvey Oswald was in fact in the Jackson-Clinton area in late August, early September, 1963. Now, gentlemen, there was at that time in the City of Clinton certainly an unfortunate confrontation. The situation was not normal. People unfortunately were suspicious of their neighbors and even more suspicious of any strangers that might have been in the town of Clinton in late August or early September, 1963. There was a voter registration drive going on. The lines had been drawn, CORE workers on one side, perhaps the Registrar on the other side, some people attempting to get people to register to vote, others perhaps on occasion attempting to prevent these people from voting. Gentlemen, we are not talking about a normal time in a small country town in the State of Louisiana, we are talking about a critical time, a time of tension, a time where everyone of necessity, everyone by nature becomes much much more observant of the things around him than he or she might be on other occasions. One day, gentlemen, in that time period a black Cadillac pulled up just close to the Registrar'soffice in the City of Clinton.There were many people present. One of the persons present, gentlemen, was Mr. John Manchester, Town Marshal of Clinton, Louisiana. Now certainly, gentlemen, if there was anyone who was keenly aware of the explosive or possibly explosive situation at the time, it was Mr. Manchester. And unfortunately sometimes these confrontations do explode, sometimes from persons not native to the area but from outside agitators for either side coming in and taking advantage of a tense situation and exploding it. So he was keenly aware, as the only local law enforcement agent in Clinton, Louisiana, at the time. He by his nature and certainly by his duty

during that time was observant of any and all strangers that came into town. By his nature and duty he was equally observant of all strange automobiles that came into town. On this morning, gentlemen -- perhaps it was toward noon, I don't recall the specific time but certainly let me say at this time it is your memory of the facts that is important, it is not my appreciation of the facts or Mr. Dymond's appreciation of the facts, it is your appreciation of the facts -- he went up to this black Cadillac car for a specific reason. He wanted to get a 1028 on it as they call it, he wanted to get some form of identification. Where were they from? Were they possible troublemakers? Could they in any way inflame an already tense situation? He was keenly aware of this, gentlemen, and he went to this car and inquired of the man behind thewheel where he was from. "We are from the International Trade Mart in the City of New Orleans." Now I wonder how many people in the City of Clinton, Louisiana, up until that point had ever heard of the

International Trade Mart in the City of New Orleans. Mr. Manchester said that this was the first time he had ever heard of it. But he went further, gentlemen, and he positively and unequivocally and under oath identified that man there (indicating) as the driver of that automobile, the man who said he was from the International Trade Mart in the City of New Orleans. Have you ever, gentlemen, thought of the probabilities of approaching a man in a strange town and having him say he is from the International Trade Mart in the City of New Orleans unless he is or unless he is in some way connected with the International Trade Mart? And we all know that in the summer of 1963 he was connected with the International Trade Mart in the City of New Orleans. John Manchester positively identified the man, the Defendant before the Bar, as the man in the car. And again, gentlemen, the State – and I want to make this abundantly clear at this time -- the State is not wedded to the proposition, the State is not bound by the proposition, and the State is not asking you definitely to believe that that black Cadillac on that day belonged to Jeff Biddison, a long-time friend of the Defendant, but it certainly is a curious coincidence that the Defendant knows Jeff Biddison, has used Jeff Biddison's car, and it was a black Cadillac, 1960 or '61, and, as the witnesses said, a brand new or apparently new automobile, shiny automobile. But the State is not saying necessarily that that was Jeff Biddison's automobile, because the State -- unfortunately no one on that occasion got the license number of that car so we could check it down and tell you positively and stand behind it as to the owner of that automobile.

Henry Earl Palmer testified, gentlemen -- and this is the man that Oswald was referred to by the barber, Mr. McGehee -- he testified that he arrived at his office and it was his duty to register those attempting to register during this drive. Most of the registrants in line were Negroes. However, there were two white men, or white boys as he called them, in that line. One of these white boys in that line was Lee Harvey Oswald. Mr. Palmer told you of going back and forth getting coffee, told you of seeing these two men in that line, one of whom he positively identified as Lee Harvey Oswald. Mr. Palmer also told you that he told some law enforcement officer to get a 1028 or an identification on the black Cadillac. And Manchester told you that when he assured Palmer that the people in the black Cadillac, the two men in the black Cadillac, were not troublemakers, they were from the International Trade Mart, he made a ittle joke up to the effect that, "They are no trouble, Henry Earl, they must be here to sell bananas." And this was testified to by Henry Earl Palmer, who also saw that black Cadillac, who also said that the Defendant before the Bar fit the general physical characteristics of the man behind the wheel of that Cadillac, the man who John Manchester positively identified under oath on that stand, and he also said, gentlemen, that the other man in the automobile had bushy eyebrows and when Mr. Sciambra showed him a picture of David Ferrie, he said he looked similar. I am not trying to fool this Jury at all. He did not positively identify David Ferrie, nor did he positively identify the Defendant, but he said the man had the same general characteristics of the Defendant. You recall that when Mr. Palmer first came the black automobile was not there. You recall though that throughout the day as he made his trips the automobile was there the entire time until he left his office at 5:45 p.m. You will recall further that when he left his office Oswald had already been to him, Oswald had firmly identified himself as Lee Harvey Oswald attempting to register to vote. And here is further corroboration of both Lee McGehee and Mr. Morgan, because Oswald was curious about the necessity of registering to vote to get the job at the East Louisiana State Hospital, and he was assured that that was not necessary. He was turned down on his voting registration because he could not show sufficient residence in the Parish of East Feliciana. Gentlemen, there again can be no doubt at all that Lee Harvey Oswald was in the barbershop, in Reeves Morgan's house, and he was in that voter registration line and he attempted to vote in Clinton, Louisiana, in late August or early September. Now, gentlemen, that was essentially what you heard, and again from one side of the confrontation. The lines had been drawn. But there were also CORE workers who were attempting to have their people register, and I submit to you that they were just as conscious, maybe more so conscious than John Manchester as to strangers in town, as to strange automobiles in the town, because they also were aware of the fact of a possible conflagration, a possible explosion of a tense situation. Corrie Collins took the stand in this court room under oath and positively told this Jury some very important things, and I submit he had no reason to lie to this Jury. He saw that black Cadillac pull up with three individuals in it, two in the front seat, one in the back seat, and Corrie Collins positively said the man in the back seat got out of that automobile, went in the voter registration line and stood in that line to vote, and that individual positively was Lee Harvey Oswald, the man named as a co-conspirator with the Defendant. But he said even more than that. He corroborates the fact that John Manchester was then in that area, he corroborates the fact that John Manchester went to the window of that automobile and spoke to the driver of the automobile, and this is exactly what Mr. Manchester said, and that is when the Defendant told him they were from the International Trade Mart. Corrie Collins went further. Corrie Collins was in a position to better see the individuals in the automobile, and under oath and in a strange court room and in a strange city he positively and unequivocally and without any hesitation whatsoever pointed out the Defendant before the Bar as the man who drove that automobile, and he identified a picture of David Ferrie as the man in that automobile. And he was conscious, gentlemen, of who was in the City of Clinton, what they were doing there, and what their reason was for being there. He made a statement, gentlemen, that I think we can all remember. There were, because of the voter registration drive, many Federal people apparently present, FBI, perhaps the Justice Department, and, frankly, he and Mr. Dunn, who testified after him, thought that perhaps the parties in the automobile were from the Justice Department or the Federal Bureau of Investigation. When he saw John Manchester go to the car and inquire of the driver or speak with the driver, he made the statement, "They must be trading with the enemy." Because, gentlemen, at that time perhaps, and unfortunately so, at that time Mr. Manchester was probably the enemy to Corrie Collins and to William Dunn. Mr. Dunn took the stand, gentlemen, and he corroborates the other witnesses in this case concerning the incident in Clinton, Louisiana. He was with or certainly saw Corrie Collins. He recalled the statement of Corrie Collins to the effect that they must be trading with the enemy. Gentlemen, this man had no reason to come into this courtroom and lie to you or to this Court. This man was concerned like the rest at that time because of the tense situation, and he positively identified the Defendant before the Bar as the driver of that automobile, the same automobile, gentlemen, that Lee Harvey Oswald left to get in the voter registration line and to wait for his turn to talk to Mr. Palmer, and Mr. Palmer confirmed the fact that Lee Harvey Oswald did in fact talk to him. And as further corroboration, gentlemen -- and I hope not to be too long, I don't want to go down and list witness by witness by witness and give you a recapitulation or summary of everything they said, because you outnumber me, you heard twelve times as much as I did, and certainly it is what you heard, and it is your appreciation of the testimony, and it is the weight that you want to give to the witnesses on the witness stand that counts, not what I say. Mrs. Dedon confirmed the fact that Lee Harvey Oswald did eventually go to the East Louisiana State Hospital and ask her for directions to the Administration Building, and the Administration Building was where the Personal Office was where a man would attempt to seek employment at the East Louisiana State Hospital. Mrs. Kemp testified that she saw Lee Harvey Oswald's application in the files of the East Louisiana State Hospital. And there is something -- there is something curious about this, and it is another coincidence perhaps. She said that the file card had "Harvey Lee Oswald." Gentlemen, there is only one person in this courtroom during this trial who ever admitted to calling Lee Harvey Oswald "Harvey Lee Oswald," and that was the

Defendant before the Bar when he gave his interview the night after he was arrested. Now, what has the State shown by the presentation of these witnesses from Clinton, Louisiana? I think it has demonstrated, I think it did demonstrate beyond a reasonable doubt at that juncture the Defendant was a liar totally unworthy of your belief, that in fact he did know Lee Harvey Oswald, that in fact he did know David W. Ferrie.

Gentlemen, after the evidence from Clinton, Louisiana, the State put on the stand certain police officers who had arrested Lee Oswald, certain evidence as to the distribution of Fair Play for Cuba Committee Leaflets. You saw these leaflets. Marina Oswald testified that she put the stamp on the leaflet, "A.J. HIDELL." You have seen the leaflets. The interesting one and the significant one, gentlemen, was June 16, 1963. Officer Gaillot said that he asked Lee Harvey Oswald, who was passing the leaflets out, to leave the Dumaine Street wharf. But what is critical here, gentlemen, is the fact that he seized some leaflets and they were identical to the ones taken from him on Canal Street, the one identified by Marina Oswald on June 16, 1963. And they were significant for this reason: because the latter part of June, 1963, a State witness by the name of Vernon Bundy saw the Defendant and Lee Harvey Oswald on the Lakefront in this city, and, if you will recall, he said that he wrapped up his narcotics outfit in leaflets that said "FREE CUBA" or something of that nature. I showed him the leaflet taken from Lee Harvey Oswald earlier that same month, one of the leaflets taken from him earlier that same month, and he said it appeared to be the same. Now let's consider the testimony of Vernon Bundy. Gentlemen, I want to make one thing abundantly clear. I do not apologize for Vernon Bundy or any witness that the State of Louisiana put on during this case. You take your witness, gentlemen, as you find them. It would be fine if we had a lot of bank presidents come before you and tell you how they overheard the Defendant conspire to kill the President of the United States, but you are not going to find too many bank presidents associating with Lee Harvey Oswald and David Ferrie and those of his stripe. Vernon Bundy took that stand, gentlemen, and we elicited from him at the outset that he was on the Methadone program designed to help addicts rid themselves of the habit of drug addiction. This man told Defense Counsel and the State from the witness stand that he had been shooting narcotics for a long, long, long time. And he took this witness stand, gentlemen, and he said that he had gone to the Lakefront of this city, and that when he was on the seawall preparing his narcotics for injection, a black car pulled up behind him. Now, gentlemen, perhaps it is difficult -- I know it is difficult for me, and I know it must be difficult for you -- to put yourselves in the frame of mind of Vernon Bundy or any drug addict on the Seawall. He is concerned with only one thing, and that is shooting the narcotics, protecting the narcotics and not letting the police sneak up on him and arrest him before he could dispose of the narcotics. The moment that car pulled up, gentlemen, you can be assured, and you were assured by Vernon Bundy, that his attention was riveted on that automobile as it was on the occupants of that car, who left the car and walked along the seawall. And his attention was riveted for a good, good reason, and he told you that reason: he did not want this man to run up on him all of a sudden before he could jettison or throw his narcotics out into Pontchartrain Lake, because without the evidence the man could not be charged with possession of narcotics. And he riveted his attention to that man. He saw another man walk from the other end of the seawall or from the other direction. They met, and he in this courtroom and under oath positively identified the Defendant as the man that got out of the black Cadillac. Coincidentally, the Defendant was seen in a black Cadillac in Clinton in late August, early September, 1963. He saw him get out of that black Cadillac, approach the other man whom he positively identified as Lee Harvey Oswald. He appeared to give him a roll of money. The State did not prove, and I am not attempting to tell you here that it was definitely and positively and beyond any possible doubt a roll of money. He appeared to give him a roll of money, that is, the Defendant gave Oswald what appeared to be a roll of money, and when Oswald put this item, which appeared to be a roll of money, in his pocket, he dislodged some of these leaflets, the same leaflets that he had been distributing on the Dumaine Street wharf earlier that month, maybe a week or a week and a half before this incident. And let us recall, gentlemen, that Vernon Bundy was seated on the top wall, or the top step rather, of the seawall. His position was down, and there is something that he noticed, something that frankly might have frightened him, as he said, somewhat. It was the strange gait or apparent limp of this man whom he identified as the Defendant before the Bar. Vernon Bundy graphically demonstrated to this Court and to this Jury while he was on that witness stand when he made that Defendant walk back to that door and then walk forward. Is there anyone in this courtroom or anyone on this Jury that did not notice the peculiar gait of the Defendant? The Defendant himself on the witness stand admitted that he had the affliction in 1963 as a result of a dislodged disc in his back. This was but further corroboration of the testimony of Vernon Bundy in this case. Again, gentlemen, when the Defendant makes the statement under oath that he did not know Lee Harvey Oswald, he is proven a liar and unworthy of your belief.

Gentlemen, again the State apologizes for none of its witnesses in this case, and I don't apologize at all for Mr. Charles Spiesel. Mr. Spiesel took this witness stand under oath and testified that one night he was in Lafayette in Exile, and he saw a man whom he thought he served in the military of the United States with. He asked this man about the ferry service, and perhaps there was a breakdown in communications, because he thought the man said something about ferry, but what he was saying was his name, "Ferrie" -- F-e-r-r-I-e rather than f-e-r-r-y. He went back to the bar, gentlemen. Subsequent to this, this man David Ferrie, whom he positively identified, a young male and two women asked him to go to a party in the French Quarter. He testified that David Ferrie's eyebrows were not as thick or as heavy as they appeared in the picture. You heard Perry Russo testify that oftentimes David Ferrie's eyebrows were not as thick as they appeared in that picture.

240

You heard him also testify that there were occasions when David Ferrie's hair was not as mussed up or as unsightly looking as it was on some occasions. They went to an apartment, gentlemen, as he recalled it at the intersection of Dauphine and Esplanade Avenue in the City of New Orleans. They walked up, as he recalled it, two flights of stairs and went inside. There was a man who appeared to be the apparent host, and Mr. Spiesel positively identified that man as the Defendant before the Bar. And he said here something else very interesting: It was not the Defendant's apartment but rather two people he knew, I think he said teachers, I am not sure, from North Carolina. The Defendant took the stand and said that he knew many, many people in North Carolina. What are the odds, gentlemen, of Mr.Spiesel going to this party and having the host tell him that the apartment really belonged to two people from North Carolina? Fifty-to-one, since there are fifty states. During the course of the evening when the two girls left with the young man that was with David Ferrie when they first approached Mr. Spiesel in the bar, the conversation turned to President John F. Kennedy, and the sentiment was hostile and certainly anti-Kennedy. The suggestion was made that he ought to be killed. Was it made in jest? We don't know. At first, frankly, Mr. Spiesel did not take this conversation seriously. However, he did later on become somewhat alarmed. The consensus of those at the table was that the President should be shot with a high-powered rifle from some distance away. He posed the possibility of the man doing the shooting getting capture or killed before he could escape from the scene of the shooting. It is at this point apparently that the Defendant injected himself into the conversation, although I assume he must have been part of the consensus spoken about by Mr. Spiesel earlier, and he inquired of David Ferrie of the possibility of flying this man to safety after the shooting of the President. And again, that is something that is curious and significant, because, if you will recall the testimony of Perry Russo, the principal portion of the conversation entered into by the Defendant was that which concerned exit or availability of escape, and this is the same portion of the conversation at this party in which he injected himself at that time. Why does he remember the Defendant Clay Shaw and David W. Ferrie and no one else at the party? First of all, I submit, gentlemen, you have been here a long time, but if you had only been in here one day, one hour, or for ten minutes, and seen the Defendant before the Bar, he is not the type of person that you would readily forget. Because of physical stature, because of his hair and his general appearance and demeanor, Clay Shaw, gentlemen,is not easily forgotten once you had seen him, and he was not forgotten by the witnesses who positively put him in the presence of Ferrie and Oswald. And there is another reason why Charles Spiesel remembered the Defendant before the Bar. You will recall he was looking for some work in the City of New Orleans. You will recall that David Ferrie volunteered to help him in this regard, volunteered to speak to this man who had a lot of pull, power or ability to help someone seeking a job, and that man was Clay Shaw, the Defendant before the Bar. You will recall that he attempted to contact the Defendant before the Bar, Clay Shaw, by telephone, but was unsuccessful. Although he never saw the Defendant again after he left the party until he came into this court room, he did, however, see David Ferrie. There were the reasons that Mr. Spiesel remembered the Defendant, his friends from North Carolina, and he remembered David W. Ferrie at that party. We went with Mr. Spiesel, gentlemen, down to the French Quarter of this city in an attempt to locate that apartment. Gentlemen, the probabilities are almost astronomical that this man could pick out an apartment house, not living in the City of New Orleans that was -- that the apartment house next to it was identical. He picked out 906 Esplanade as one of the possible apartment houses. The very next apartment, 908 Esplanade, which is identical in appearance on the outside, was owned at that time, by the testimony of the Defendant, by the Defendant Clay Shaw. The probabilities, gentlemen, of that ever happening again are almost uncalculable. Who is Charles Spesel? I know Mr. Dymond will spend much time on Mr. Spiesel. I would just like to call to your attention certain basic facts. Gentlemen, we are dealing here with truth, and this man was never convicted of anything in his life. This man holds a responsible job in the City of New York. This man's employer knew of the suit he had filed against the City of New York and other defendants. This man's employer knew he was coming to the City of New Orleans to testify in this case. This man permitted Charles Spiesel to leave his work and to plead his case in the Federal Court. Charles Spiesel prepares corporate and personal income tax returns. Charles Spiesel has a very responsible job. Charles Spiesel has dealt in the formulation of spinoff corporations, and this is exceedingly complex work. He told you how down here in New Orleans he formed a system for certain jukebox companies while he was down here. He told you how he was in the militray service of the United States and graduated with an honorable discharge, and of his college background. And most importantly, gentlemen, he told you he had never been convicted of anything. And I submit, gentlemen, that Charles Spiesel told you the truth in this courtroom. The coincidence of North Carolina, the coincedence of picking out the same exterior appearance of an apartment next door to an apartment owned by the defendant, are too much to overcome.

Gentlemen, sometime toward the middle of September, 1963, Perry Russo went to the apartment of David Ferrie. Now, for some time, at least for the summer of 1963 and into the early fall of 1963. David Ferrie had become obsessed with the assassination of President Kennedy during that time period. He went to his apartment house one day and he saw a stranger in that apartment house on the porch, sitting, as he recalled it, in the dark cleaning a rifle. This man had what appeared to be at least a two or three-day growth of beard. He was introduced to this man as Leon Oswald. He positively identified this man as Lee Harvey Oswald, but it is interesting to note that the first time he saw Lee Harvey Oswald he was doing something which apparently had become a habit with him, as testified by his wife or former wife, and that was to sit on the porch or in a dark room and clean and stroke his rifle. Marina Oswald Porter saw him do it many times at 4907 Magazine Street in this city, and this is exactly what Lee Harvey Oswald was doing when Perry Russo first met him. There is something else. Perry Russo and Lee Harvey Oswald apparently did not get along. To Perry Russo, Lee Harvey Oswald was an introverted person, a person that liked to be left alone, did not like to be part of a group or socialize or talk too much, he liked to sit and read. Again, gentlemen, this is corroborated completely by witnesses of the Defense. We have the testimony of his own wife who said he was not a talkative person, did not like to join but liked to sit on the porch and read. We have the testimony of Ruth Paine, another Defense witness, who said the very same thing. After this initial encounter, gentlemen, Perry Russo one night went to the apartment of David W. Ferrie in this city, 3330 Louisiana Avenue Parkway, and there was a gathering there. Some may call it a party, some may call it a meeting, some may just call it some people getting together and talking. You can put what label you choose on it. During the course of this get-together or meeting or gathering, David Ferrie paced nervously back and forth with clippings about President John F. Kennedy, and he railed and he raved against the then President of the United States. When this party broke up, gentlemen, when this party was reduced in size to four people, David W. Ferrie, the Defendant before the Bar using the name Clem Bertrand, Leon Oswald or Lee Harvey Oswald, and intermittently Perry Raymond Russo, who said himself the discussion, gentlemen, got much more serious. We hear such things as triangulation of cross-fire. We saw David Ferrie or heard that David Ferrie used this symbol (demonstrating) for triangulation of cross-fire. We heard such things as a discussion of the necessity of using three but at least two people in the shooting of the President of the United States. We also heard that one of these persons would have to be a patsy or a scapegoat or be sacrificed so the others could get away. Again during the course of this meeting, during the course of this discussion, the Defendant spoke up, again and again he spoke up as he had done in June of that same summer, about availability of exit and about escape and about the possibility of the man doing the shooting getting killed. It was discussed that perhaps direct flight to Cuba might be possible, it was discussed that this might not be feasible or possible or safe and that maybe a flight to Mexico and then on to Brazil where extradition could not be had (would be necessary). It was decided, gentlemen, during the course of that meeting that some of the participants in this conspiracy would not be at the scene of the shooting, some of the participants in this conspiracy would make themselves obvious at other locations so as to make an alibi more believable, so as to form an alibi for themselves. The Defendant was going to the West Coast. If you will recall, gentlemen, the testimony of the Defendant on this witness stand, he knew by mid-September when this meeting allegedly took place that he was going to the West Coast of the United States. David W. Ferrie was going somewhere to establish an alibi. David W. Ferrie ended up in Houston, Texas, and you heard Mr. Rolland testify about the bizarre activity of David W. Ferrie in that ice rink I submit that you gentlemen use your own experience, apply your own common sense. Would you if you went to this skating rink repeatedly, as many as five times, go up to the manager of that skating rink and keep introducing yourself or interjecting your name in the conversation? I submit you wouldn't unless you had a purpose, and he had a purpose, and that purpose was to let everyone know that I am David Ferrie and here I am in Houston, Texas. And the Defendant in fact did end up on the West Coast, and Lee Harvey Oswald did in fact end up in Dealey Plaza in the Texas School Book Depository, and he did in fact take a gun with him to the Texas School Book Depository as the State alleged, and the State frankly had to prove it circumstantially. This conversation was characterized during Russo's testimony by himself -- and I don't deny it, I don't deny the State's own witness characterized it as a "bull session," characterized it as never having referred to any of the participants as "conspirators." But, gentlemen, his characterization, my characterization is not important, it is your characterization that counts. And when you do consider that point, I fervently ask you to consider the fact that David Ferrie did end up in public making himself known, that the Defendant before the Bar did end up on the West Coast of the United States, and how in the world is Perry Russo going to know that the Defendant was going to the West Coast of the United States? How in the world could he know this? How in the world could he dream this up? And that one of the participants in this conversation, in this conspiratorial meeting, ended up in the Texas School Book Depository in Dallas, Texas, and did in fact take a gun into that Depository on that morning. That certainly, gentlemen, throws an entirely different light on this conversation. This conversation was not -- did not take place in a vacuum, but everything said in this conversation was actually carried out by all of the participants of that conversation. The State showed you in the testimony of Mr. Frazier that Lee Harvey Oswald did in fact take a package with him into the Texas School Book Depository on the morning of November 22, 1963. Breaking a ritual that he had with Mr. Frazier of returning on weekends, he returned home the night before the President was assassinated, and he carried a package approximately two feet or over long. He told you that he had broken down his own rifle in the military service, and it broke down to as low as twenty inches. He identified a package taken by Lee Oswald into the Depository on that fateful morning. Lee Oswald told him that it was curtain rods. Lee Oswald is not our witness, Lee Oswald is a named conspirator with the Defendant. Now let's see what the Defense's own witnesses had to say about these curtain rods. Mrs. Paine categorically testified that she heard no mention of curtain rods that morning, but she did testify to the fact that she went to the garage and found strangely that the garage light was left on, and there was Lee Harvey Oswald where Lee Oswald had kept his gun. Marina Oswald testified, and, as I recall the testimony of Mr. Frazier, Lee Oswald said his wife, Marina, got him curtain rods to take to the Texas School Book Depository, to his apartment in Oak Cliff, and his wife categorically testified that she did not bring him any curtain rods ever for his apartment in Oak

Cliff, that he never asked her for curtain rods, that she never saw curtain rods in anyone's possession least of all the possession of her husband, Lee Oswald. I submit to you, gentlemen, that when he rode to work that morning he took the gun from the garage, and when the police came there the following day they were unable to find it in the package it was in or the wrapping it was in because he had taken it that morning. Marina Oswald also testified that she did in fact see him go to that garage on numerous occasions that night.

So, gentlemen, this conversation taken by itself, and frankly and honestly styled or categorized or classified by a State witness as perhas a "bull session," certainly turned out to be more than any bull session. Gentlemen, Perry Russo saw Leon Oswald or Lee Oswald once or twice more in the apartment of David Ferrie, and the last time he saw Lee Oswald in that apartment Lee Oswald was going somewhere, apparently making a trip, and he said he was going to Houston, Texas. Now I want you to recall the testimony of the Defense's own witness, Ruth Paine, who testified that when she spoke to Lee Oswald just before taking his wife and baby back to Irving, Texas, he told her he was going to look for work in Houston or Philadelphia, Pennsylvania, as Perry Russo corroborated. What are the probabilities of that coming about unless it really happened, one witness living in New Orleans, one living in Irving, Texas today, and she said Houston, Texas, and Perry Russo said he said he was going to Houston, Texas.

Perry Russo, gentlemen, said that he had seen the Defendant on the Nashville Street wharf when President John F. Kennedy spoke there in 1962. He recalled the Defendant specifically, because the Defendant apparently was not looking at all times at the President of the United States, who was making a speech, and that he was positioned somewhat back towards the end of the crowd, and this is where Perry Russo saw him first. The Defendant took the stand and admitted he was at the Nashville Street wharf. When did Perry Russo make this statement that he was on the Nashville Street wharf? Perry Russo made this statement on the very first contact by Mr. Andrew Sciambra of our office, February, 1967.

How on earth did Perry Russo know that the Defendant, Clay Shaw, was on the Nashville Street wharf unless as a matter of fact he saw him on the Nashville Street wharf? How did he know that the Defendant was standing in the rear of the crowd unless he had seen him in the rear of the crowd, and how did he know that he was not always looking at the President but appeared to be looking at others, unless he saw that? Now, Mr. Dymond's argument will be the Defendant admitted all this. Gentlemen, the Defendant sat here and heard the testimony of Perry Russo. Is it logical to you that the Defendant would admit this knowing that this corroborated 100 percent the testimony of Perry Russo? And at first blush when you think of it, it sounds like a fairly good argument, but I want to remind you gentlemen that he well knew that the State had rebuttal witnesses, that the State had a right to rebut the case of the Defense, and he didn't want to get caught flatfooted in an obvious lie, because they didn't know who we had for rebuttal witnesses. He also well knew that there were probably many cameramen in and around the Nashville Street wharf on that occasion, and should the Defendant lie, he would be caught in a picture lying. Gentlemen, ask yourselves, how could Perry Raymond Russo know in 1967 that he was on the Nashville Street wharf when the President spoke there unless he saw him? He also saw the Defendant at David Ferrie's gas station out on the highway, and he testified to this. Mr. Dymond will say that the State's case rises or falls upon the testimony of Perry Raymond Russo, and essentially I agree, but where is Perry Russo corroborated? He is corroborated by the fact that David Ferrie and Lee Harvey Oswald and the Defendant were acquainted, were seen with each other and knew each other, contrary to what he says and contrary to what he said in his opening statement. He is corroborated by the fact that in fact he was on the Nashville Street wharf. He is corroborated by the fact that their own witness -- that their own witness -- said that he was going to Houston, Texas, and in fact that is exactly what Lee Oswald had told him, they were going to Houston, Texas, or he was going to Houston, Texas. He is corroborated by more than that. Remember, gentlemen, that during the course of this meeting, during the course of this conspiratorial meeting, the Defendant used the name Clem Bertrand, C-l-e-m Clem Bertrand.

Gentlemen, Mr. James Hardiman, a postman of long service in this city, took that witness stand and under oath positively testified that when he was delivering letters addressed to Clay Shaw at 1313 Dauphine Street, at 1414 Chartres Street from 1313 Dauphine Street, at that very time he delivered at least five, or enough to call his attention to the fact that he had delivered letters to Clem Bertrand, the same name used by the Defendant in this conspiratorial meeting. And, you know, it is a strange thing, and perhaps it is just another coincidence, but, gentlemen, these coincidences just can't keep piling up without painting a true picture. Who lives at 1414 Chartres Street? Jeff Biddison. How long has he known the Defendant, Clay Shaw? Twenty-three or twenty-six years, I can't recall. Now, was there any evidence presented that Mr. Hardiman knew that the residents of 1414 Chartres Street even knew the Defendant before the Bar? Why would he pick that address and come into this Court and say he had delivered letters to Clem Bertrand to that address unless in fact he had done it? 1414 Chartres Street meant nothing to Mr. Hardiman other than the fact that that was the address that he delivered letters to Jeff Biddison, but he did not know, gentlemen, of the relationship or the association of Jeff Biddison and the Defendant before the Bar. He testified that the letters were addressed directly, that is, to 1414 Chartres Street, and -- I don't want to confuse the Jury -- that the letters were first addressed to 1313 and then forwarded to 1414, because that is not the way I recall the testimony. They were addressed directly to 1414, but these letters only arrived -- these letters were only delivered to that address at the same time that this man was delivering mail addressed to Clay Shaw at 1313 and forwarded to 1414. And what fantastic explanation does the Defendant give to this under oath and expect you to believe it? He is trapped. He cannot deny that there was a cancellation of a change of address on September 21, 1963, because it is right there in the record. 1966, I am sorry. Which again is an interesting date, because, gentlemen, this is before the investigation of the District Attorney's office even became public. In fact, it is before the District Attorney started his investigation. The Defendant said -- and this is the most curious statement I have ever heard in my life -- he said he did not execute a change of address for the delivery of mail from 1313 to 1414 Chartres Street. He was sure on this point. Yet he executes a cancellation of something that doesn't exist, and the only reason he admitted doing that was because it was right there in black and white in that record, and I submit to you, gentlemen, that that mail was in fact delivered during that time, and you will also recall that the Defendant actually took up residence at that location for a week or two before he could get back into his 1313 address. Is this just another coincidence? How common is the name Clay Bertrand? Is this just another coincidence, gentlemen, along with the many other coincidences, or does this begin to give us a picture?

Gentlemen, Mrs. Jessie Parker took this witness stand, and you will recall that she was the hostess at the VIP Room, the Eastern Air Lines VIP Room at Moisant International Airport. She testified that on December 14, 1966 – again before any mention in the public media of the investigation by the District Attorney's office – the Defendant, whom she positively identified, came into that room with another man and signed the VIP book "Clay Bertrand." The Defendant took the stand and positively denied this act, positively denied the use of any alias in his life with the exception of the use of a name for writing a play. She remembered the Defendant, among other things, because of his pretty hair, as she put it. The Defendant, gentlemen, signed the book, for what reason we don't know. I think it is reasonable to assume that perhaps he might have been signing it for someone to come later on as a message. I don't know why he signed the book, but I believe Mrs. Parker that he did sign that book "Clay Bertrand," and when he signed it, he looked over at her and kept looking at her, and he wasn't seated but standing at this time when he signed that book.

He was not signing his own name but signing a fictitious (name) or alias. Does it seem logical to you that he would use his normal handwriting on this occasion? Does it seem logical to you that he might not try to disguise his normal handwriting on this occasion? You have heard from two experts who have conflicting opinions as to whether or not that signature "Clay Bertrand" was made by the Defendant before the Bar, but we have a woman, gentlemen, who saw him make it and who took a lie detector test on that very point. The Defense put on an expert who examined photographs of the questioned signature, admitting frankly that this was not the best procedure to follow, but there is something else about the expert of the Defendant that should be taken into consideration. Can there be any doubt in the mind of any juror here that this man, Mr. Appel, on that witness stand did not say that he had a fixed opinion about this case before he rendered his judgment or decision on that handwriting specimen? He had a fixed opinion. He was coming down, as he put it, for the cause of justice.

"Do you know anything about the case?"

"No."

"Well, what are you talking about 'justice'?"

"Well, I was coming down here because of justice, I didn't want an injustice done."

You know that this man had a fixed opinion when he rendered his decision on that point. The State's expert frankly admitted she intended and hoped to get paid. The State's expert did not have a fixed opinion in this case. The State's expert did not have time to give you a blow-up of the questioned signature next to the true exemplar or sample signature, but I found it entirely curious that the expert for the Defense blew up but one, one sample out of thirteen, D-30 through D-34, for you gentlemen to view. You had an opportunity, at the request of the State, to view D-30 through D-43. You had an opportunity to view Mr. Appel on the stand, and you had an opportunity to view Mrs. McCarthy on the stand. I submit, gentlemen, that Jessie Parker was telling the truth when she testified that the Defendant signed the VIP book.

I see I am going much longer than I had anticipated. Gentlemen, yesterday on rebuttal you heard from Mr. and Mrs. Tadin. They testified that they in fact saw the Defendant and David Ferrie at the airport, and they knew David Ferrie because they were concerned about him being with their son, who was deaf. Mr. Tadin also, since he works in the French Quarter as many as six nights a week, also had seen and knew the Defendant before the Bar, and as soon as he saw him with David Ferrie, he commentedtohiswife exactly who he was, and his wife took the stand, gentlemen, and said that they were in fact together. Mr. Dymond brought out that the first time they came to us was yesterday. I was somewhat disappointed that they hadn't come to us sooner, but I don't think, gentlemen, that they were lying, and it is up to you to weigh their credibility. Mr. Tadin made one of the truest statements made throughout this trial. Using a cross-examining trick, Mr. Dymond asked Mr. Tadin, "Do you ever lie?" If Mr. Tadin had answered, "Never", I doubt if many of you gentlemen would have believed him, but he answered modestly that yes, yes, he lied, that most people lied, but that was telling the truth, and that he knew he was under oath and he was telling the truth, and as he told the truth this man was proven a liar again and again and unworthy of your belief. Mrs. Jessie Garner took the stand for the Defense, the landlady of Lee Harvey Oswald, and there crept into the record a very curious thing. David W. Ferrie was over at the apartment of Lee Harvey Oswald one night shortly after the assassination. She couldn't recall whether it was the night of the assassination or shortly after the assassination, and I submit it was shortly after the assassination. How did David Ferrie know where Lee Harvey Oswald lived in the City of New Orleans? You would have a different proposition if David Ferrie were a Dallas resident and after the announcement on television and so forth he went to the home of Lee Harvey Oswald in Dallas, but how did he know where he lived here in New Orleans four months before?

And Mrs. Garner, again a Defense witness, a woman that they vouch for, said that Lee Harvey Oswald's apartment was filthy, that the sink was torn up and the toilet was torn up and it was generally filthy, and that the mattress was filthy, and yet they want you to believe that this man literally carried a Norelco shaving outfit along with him, never had a beard, despite the fact that Marina Oswald herself testified that there were days that Lee Harvey Oswald did not shave. Marina Oswald, frankly, gentlemen, could not recount to you the movements of Lee Harvey Oswald -- and for good reason. How much did Lee Harvey Oswald confide in his wife? Before coming here to the City of New Orleans she didn't even know where he was employed, had no telephone number to contact him. Coming to the City of New Orleans, gentlemen, she knew one language, and that was Russian; she was pregnant, expect a baby. Lee Oswald had told her never to go into his belongings, and she abided by that. Gentlemen, she attempted one day pathetically to find her husband by going to the coffee company where she thought he might have worked, and it was the wrong one. And you know why it was the wrong one, because Lee Oswald never told her where he worked, he never gave her a phone number, he never talked about anybody he met at work, he never told her about the post office box, he never told her where it was located. She did not have a key to the post office box. Frankly, gentlemen, she didn't know what Lee Harvey Oswald was doing. And there is one other point I would like to bring out in connection with her testimony. She on the witness stand said the farthest back she would put the firing of Lee Harvey Oswald would have been approximately one month before they left the City of New Orleans, and they left the City of New Orleans on September 23. That would have made it August 23,1963. Lee Harvey Oswald was fired from the Reily Coffee Company July 19, 1963. This is how much Marina Oswald knew about the activities of Lee Harvey Oswald.

Gentlemen, I haven't gone into all of the testimony of all of the Defense witnesses. Presumably, Mr. Dymond will highlight their testimony, and I will be back in front of you again for I hope a period not this long, to rebut his arguments about what their witnesses said. So I at this time will not go into the testimony of many of the Defense witnesses. I think that the State generally has proven its case beyond a reasonable doubt, and has proven him an absolute liar and unworthy of your belief, and absolutely guilty in this case, and I will ask this Jury, after serious deliberation for both sides, to return a just verdict, and I feel that verdict will be guilty as charged. Thank you very much.

Appendix B:

~

James Alcock's Rebuttal

MR. ALCOCK:

May it please the Court:

Gentlemen of the Jury, it is now my function to rebut the arguments of Mr. Dymond, Defense Counsel in this case. I took down many notes during the course of his argument, and I intend to cover these matters just as quickly as I can and still cover them thoroughly enough to familiarize you with the particular elements
involved. We heard an awful lot of the unbelievability of the State's witnesses. We heard an awful lot about the State's witnesses coming forward at the last minute. Did Defense Counsel explain to you in his argument how Perry Raymond Russo could have known that the Defendant was on the Nashville Street wharf when the President of the United States spoke there in 1963 unless he had in fact seen the Defendant on the wharf that day? He didn't mention that one time in his argument, and I don't blame him, because there is no way he could explain it other than the fact that Perry Raymond Russo did see the Defendant on the Nashville Street wharf. Is that corroboration of Perry Russo? Certainly it is. Did he mention the probability that that mailman, this "old mailman" as he

termed it, would have delivered the letters to Clem Bertrand --
another coincidence, gentlemen -- the same name that this man used
during the conspiratorial meeting -- to a long-time friend of the
Defendant before the Bar? What are the probabilities of this man
delivering such letters to such a man? Did he answer that for you?
He did not. Is this just another coincidence, a long-time friend of
the Defendant, the Defendant's mail going to that house? Did he
cover for you the implausible explanation given by the Defendant
that he filed a cancellation of change of address but did not file any
original change of address? He did not. And again I don't blame
him, because he could not explain it to you. Did he say anything
about Charles Spiesel mentioning the fact that the couple
that owned the apartment were from North Carolina, and that his
Defendant admitted knowing many people in North Carolina? Is
this just another coincidence? Did he explain to you how Perry
Raymond Russo on the last time he saw Lee Harvey Oswald in the
city of New Orleans mentioned that Lee Harvey Oswald said that
he was going to Houston, Texas, and his own witness, Ruth Paine,
corroborated Perry Raymond Russo when she said the last thing
Lee told her when she left the city was that he was going to either
Philadelphia or Houston, Texas? Was that explained to you at all in
Defense Counsel's argument? I submit it was not. As far as the
Defendant's trip to the West Coast, the fact that he knew it before
mid-September and certainly could have said it in this meeting in
mid-September, that he was going to the West Coast – is this just
another coincidence, that Perry Raymond Russo would know that
the Defendant was going to the West Coast of the United States?
Gentlemen, we can only accept these things as coincidences so
long, and then they become hard fact and they give us a pattern.
And David Ferrie was in the public eye in Houston, Texas. Did he
mention the fact that David Ferrie went to the home of Lee Harvey
Oswald on Magazine Street in his argument? No. Did he mention
the fact that Mrs. Jessie Parker took a lie detector test on
whether or not she had –

MR. DYMOND:

Your Honor, I object to that. Counsel well knows that that is not arguable evidence.

MR. ALCOCK:

That was in the record, Your Honor.

THE COURT:

What was the statement made?

MR. DYMOND:

About a woman taking a lie detector test.

MR. ALCOCK:

That is in the record, Your Honor. The results may not be, but it is in the record.

THE COURT:

The Law Review article, the American Law Review article states that it cannot be made part of the record if it got into the record -- if it didn't get in by testimony, got in by a statement of Counsel.

MR. ALCOCK:

Your Honor, I submit to the Court that you allowed me to call Mr. Krubbe, Captain Krubbe, who administered the test.

THE COURT:

You didn't use the word "testimony," you used the word "interview." I purposely told them not to use the word "testimony."

MR. ALCOCK:

Well, gentlemen, I will leave it to your memory and to your recollection of the testimony. Did Counsel mention the fact that though the trip to Oregon may have been prearranged, there may have been solicitation by the people in Oregon to have the Defendant speak before them? Did he mention the fact that in the letter of Mario Bermudez, that a friend of the Defendant on behalf of the Defendant was soliciting a speaking engagement between the 21st of November, 1963, and the 23rd of November, 1963, and that date just happened to be November 22, 1963, the date on which the President, or the former President, of the United States, was shot down in the streets of Dallas? Answer. He mentioned to you, in passing, the testimony of Clinton, Louisiana, the eye-witness testimony in Clinton, Louisiana, and read a passage from a decision of the United States Supreme Court. I submit that if we had come before this Jury with a wholly circumstantial case, with no eye-witness identification, he would have been up here screaming, where are your witnesses, where are the people who actually saw the Defendant in person in the presence of Lee Harvey Oswald and David Ferrie? This is direct evidence as opposed to circumstantial evidence, and it is stronger evidence, and Counsel knows it is stronger evidence. What is his answer to the identification under oath of John Manchester? It is 76 and cloudy in Clinton, Louisiana. What is his answer to the identification, positive identification, of Corrie Collins? It is 72 and raining in Clinton, Louisiana. There were two gentlemen that recalled this incident because of the coolness of the weather, and that was the barber who left his door open because it was unseasonably cool, and Reeves Morgan, who was burning some things in his fireplace because it was cool. And you heard their witness testify that the temperature went all the way down to 60 degrees on some occasions. So their answer to you is to disregard this eye-witness testimony because they brought this man in with a temperature chart. And, gentlemen, there was something that struck me, as Mr. Dymond would say, right between the eyes. He got up and said it was an insult to him personally as an Officer of the Court because the State put Charles Spiesel on the stand, and I explained to you gentlemen that you are entitled to all of the evidence in this case, and the State finds its witnesses where it can. Has Charles Spiesel been convicted of perjury? Has Charles Spiesel been conflicted of getting on a witness stand and lying? He has not. Has their witness, Dean Andrews, been convicted of perjury? Not about any subject but about the subject of Clay Bertrand. And they have the gall to infer that we abused you by bringing Charles Spiesel before you, and they put Dean Andrews on the witness stand. And then, gentlemen, I could not believe my ears -- and from the murmur in the courtroom I think there were many, many others, who believed as I believed -- Mr. Dymond would have you believe that Dean Andrews rose from the muck and mire of lies that he has spun since 1963, and laid bare his soul to this Jury and finally told the truth, and I wrote something down at this time. Mr. Dymond wants you to believe that now he was telling the truth, and I wrote down, "Now telling the truth." Why? This man who admitted he lied before the Warren Commission under oath, "shot the bull" as he put it, but lying nevertheless; admitted he lied twice before the Orleans Parish Grand Jury; and this, gentlemen, is their witness, and when they put a witness on this stand, they vouch for his credibility, his believability and his truthfulness, and they have the gall to assault the State and impugn the State for putting Spiesel on the stand. Was he convicted of perjury? No. Was their witness convicted of perjury? Yes.

MR. DYMOND:

Your Honor, we are going to object at this point. Counsel knows very well that the conviction about which he talks is presently on appeal and is not technically a legal conviction until it is final, and I think it is misleading the Jury.

THE COURT:

That is correct. It is on appeal as I understand it.

MR. ALCOCK:

Well, that is correct, Your Honor, but again, gentlemen, I will leave it to you. A jury composed of men such as yourselves found him guilty of perjury. But I could not believe that Mr. Dymond would think that this man cleansed his soul before this Jury, and now, gentlemen, some five years later has finally decided to tell the truth, this man who is a habitual liar, their witness. I told you in my opening argument, gentlemen, that Perry Raymond Russo's appreciation of the conversation was not important. It is your appreciation of the conversation that took place in the presence of Lee Harvey Oswald, participated in by Lee Harvey Oswald, the Defendant, and David Ferrie. He called it a "bull session." How many "bull sessions" did Lee Harvey Oswald participate in here in the city of New Orleans concerning the killing of the President of the United States? If nothing had ever happened as a result of this conversation, if none of the items brought up had ever reached completion, there may be an arguable point, but when the Defendant ends up on the West Coast, Ferrie ends up where he ended up, Lee Oswald ends up in the Texas School Book Depository and the President of the United States is killed by a triangulation of fire, gentlemen, I submit that was a conspiratorial meeting and he was a conspirator to kill the President of the United States. And again when Russo saw Oswald for the last time, he was going to Houston, and their own witness confirmed that. And it is another interesting and curious thing, gentlemen, it is like a two-edged sword, it is like picking and choosing. They want you to accept Perry Russo's characterization of this meeting as a "bullsession," because he has got a college degree in some law school, and yet they want you to believe he is a complete liar as far as the Defendant being at that meeting. You can't have it both ways. You can't say, accept this man for this because it helps my case, but don't accept him for this proposition because it hurts my case.

Gentlemen, I certainly would not come before this Jury and state unequivocally that Mr. Cobb was lying to you, or even Miss Moore, but I submit to you, gentlemen, that to go back that far and to recall three months and to be able to come before a jury such as yourselves and positively state that this man was never away from work is humanly impossible. But there are some very curious things about the testimony of both Miss Moore and Mr. Cobb. Both of these witnesses couldn't wait to inform this Court and this Jury that after working hours they did not know the Defendant and had nothing to do with him. It seems as if the De-fendant led two lives, a veritable Dr. Jekyll and Mr. Hyde. After hours he consorted with the likes of Lee Harvey Oswald and David Ferrie. And, you know, there is another curious thing to this case, gentlemen. This man of this position, this so-called pillar of society, did not have one character witness to take this stand and to vouch for his good character, and I find that rather curious and rather strange. The State never attempted to hide the fact that Vernon Bundy was a user of narcotics. Mr. Dymond wants you to believe it was completely implausible for this man to go to the Lakefront to shoot narcotics, and I submit to you, gentlemen, it is not as implausible as he wants it to sound, because if I am shooting narcotics and positioning myself on the seawall without obstructions too close by, isn't it obvious that I can see the approach of any possible police officer or any possible person who would disturb me and deprive me of my narcotics before I could throw them into the water? I don't think that was implausible at all. Do you want to know that the other side of the coin is? He is going to shoot narcotics at home, risk the fact that the police might arrive, confiscate the narcotics and charge everyone in the household with possession of narcotics, including his mother. Because there is constructive possession of narcotics as well as direct possession of narcotics, and his mother or whoever else was in the household including his brother, could just as well have been charged with possessing narcotics.

Mr. Dymond seemed to find not too much fault with the testimony of Mr. Hardiman other than the fact that he said he must have been completely mistaken because he fell for an old defense trick. The name "Clem Bertrand" came to him, because shortly after -- this is no long period of time – recall this, gentlemen, that these letters to Clem Bertrand were delivered in the fall, the early fall of '66, and the Defendant was arrested in March, or March 1 in 1967, and the name "Clem Bertrand" was flashed locally and nationally, and this is why he recalled it. And again, gentlemen, what are the probabilities of this man picking out a house, not knowing that Jeff Biddison was a close friend of the Defendant's? Does this corroborate again Perry Raymond Russo when the name "Clem Bertrand" was used? Mr. Dymond wants you to believe that because the name was used once in this conspiratorial meeting, the Defendant would forever forget this name and never utter it in public again. Well, I assume the Defendant didn't write the letters to himself, someone else was writing to him, and we must remember that the Warren Commission had reported -- we must remember that it was the feeling that there was a lone assassin and no one else was involved. So the risk, gentlemen, wasn't as great as Mr. Dymond wants you to believe it was. And again at this time, and in conjunction with the testimony of Mr. Hardiman, the Defendant took the stand and said he executed the cancellation of the change of address. And yet what was he canceling? Thin air, because he said he never issued the original change of address. And we know why he canceled that, we know why he admitted to canceling that, because it was right in this record in print in black and white and he couldn't get around it.

Mrs. Parker testified that she saw the Defendant sign that book. She took an oath and took the witness stand and said she saw him sign the book. Now, you have heard from two handwriting experts. And I don't criticize their expert for being from Washington, D.C., I don't criticize their expert for having worked with the Federal Government -- my father did for a long time -- but I submit that his testimony proved that he had a fixed opinion before he even examined it. And here is another thing, and I elicited this from him during cross-examination. Mr. Dymond wants you to believe that the State's expert did a hurry-hurry, rush-rush job, but I specifically recall Mr. Apel testifying that he made his judgment after but two hours of analyzation of the handwriting specimens, and the State's witness testified that it took her four hours to make the analyzation, so I fail to see here where the State's expert did not perform an adequate analyzation of that handwriting sample. And there was another thing -- and I certainly do not fault Mr. Cobb, but we must remember that Mr. Cobb was a witness in this case for the Defense, and Mr. Cobb is the one that contacted the handwriting expert whom they placed on the witness stand, and the mere fact that this witness does not want compensation does not in any way make his opinion more weighty than the opinion of one who is expecting a fee in this case. If anything, it should prove to you, gentlemen, beyond any doubt that he had a fixed opinion before he even attempted to analyze that handwriting.

Mr. and Mrs. Tadin took the stand, and Defense Counsel wants you to believe that Mrs. Tadin took the stand solely and only because her husband insisted she take the witness stand. She said that she wasn't looking forward to coming here, she didn't want to get involved. And, unfortunately, gentlemen, this is a malaise or sickness that besets our society today. I know that you are familiar with examples of people not wanting to get involved. But did she ever testify from that witness stand that she was not telling the truth, that all she was doing was parroting the words of her husband, that she was forced to come up here and testify? She testified -- in fact, I asked her at the end of the testimony whether she was telling the truth, and, frankly, she was somewhat indignant at my question and said, "Of course I am telling the truth." She would not have taken an oath and taken that witness stand unless she was telling the truth. And here is something else you must remember. Her husband knew the Defendant before the Bar and recognized him in the presence of David Ferrie, and this is something Mr. Dymond said they were going to prove to you in the opening statement, that his client never laid eyes on either Lee Harvey Oswald or David Ferrie.

And now we come to Perry Raymond Russo and the much maligned Sciambra memo. Andrew Sciambra, the Assistant District Attorney, went to Baton Rouge, Louisiana, and interviewed Perry Raymond Russo. During the course of the conversation, Perry Raymond Russo related the events that transpired at 3330 Louisiana Avenue Parkway, the conspiratorial meeting. This was testified to by Andrew Sciambra and Perry Raymond Russo. This is not all in Mr. Sciambra's memo, but if you will recall his testimony, this was not his first memorandum on the subject but rather his second memorandum. The first memorandum or the second memorandum says something about the Defendant, Clay Shaw, being on the Nashville Street wharf in 1962, and then in 1964 the Defendant is with David Ferrie at David Ferrie's gas station. Gentlemen, why on earth would the District Attorney's Office for this parish bring Perry Raymond Russo down from Baton Rouge, Louisiana, to New Orleans, Louisiana, to talk to him if he had not related that in fact there was this conspiratorial meeting. What significance would there have been by just the Nashville Street wharf thing -- meeting -- or the Nashville Street wharf presence of the Defendant and the 1964 presence in a gas station? Why would we have called this man to our office had not in fact Andrew Sciambra returned from Baton Rouge and verbally conveyed to Jim Garrison about the events that transpired in that apartment on Louisiana Avenue Parkway? Mr. Phelan read this memorandum and became upset over the absence of the conspiratorial meeting in the body of the memorandum, and I don't necessarily disagree with the fact that he became upset. At first blush it looks somewhat alarming. But who made the arrangements for Mr. Phelan to go to Baton Rouge and talk to Perry Raymond Russo? And this is after Mr. Phelan had expressed grave concern about this omission in this memorandum. Andrew Sciambra arranged for that meeting. Does it seem likely or plausible to you, gentlemen, that Andrew Sciambra and Mr. Garrison would send this man up there to confirm the fact that it wasn't said? The District Attorney's Office sent him up there because they knew that Perry Russo did say to Andrew Sciambra and did relate the events in that meeting. Now here is the most curious thing in this case: They want you to believe Jim Phelan as to whether or not Perry Russo said, "I did not mention the conspiratorial meeting until I got to New Orleans," and this is what is curious about it. You remember Mr. Phelan took the witness stand and said, "I took along Matt Herron, a photographer." I asked Mr. Phelan, "Why did you take Mr. Matt Herron along with you?" "I took him along as a witness, as a witness to what transpired." Matt Herron was in there the entire time according to the testimony of Mr. Phelan. The Defense, gentlemen, subpoenaed Matt Herron (exhibiting document). This is the return on the subpoena, and on this side it reflects personal service, which means that this subpoena for this trial was physically put in the hands of Matt Herron. Now, why didn't the Defense call Matt Herron? Why didn't they call this man who was supposed to be Mr. Phelan's witness to what took place in Perry Russo's apartment? I submit they didn't call him because he didn't corroborate Mr. Phelan. And as far as the point about how much time it took Mr. Sciambra to compose this memorandum, he said approximately from seven to ten days. Counsel makes much of the fact that there were not that many days between the date the memorandum is dated, the 27th, and the 5th of March or whenever it was that Jim Phelan saw Jim Garrison in Las Vegas. And I remind you again this was not the first memorandum but the second memorandum.

And now, gentlemen, Jim Phelan came back on the scene of this case in the employ of NBC, the National Broadcasting Corporation, in May of 1967, or approximately that time, came to the city of New Orleans to compose this white paper, came to talk to a man who testified in the preliminary hearing, who had already given his testimony under oath and who was obviously a witness or to be a witness in this case, that you gentlemen have heard. I want to ask you this one question: Was Mr. Phelan a law enforcement officer? Was Mr. Phelan or NBC working for the Defense? They say not. Mr. Dymond made much about the scavengers who wanted to make money on the death of our President. Well, what about NBC? What about those scavengers that came down here and attempted to suggest to a State witness that he was wrong? Not only did they attempt to suggest it but they suggested a possible name of another person that he might have misidentified the Defendant for. Now what are they saying in effect, gentlemen? They are the Judge and Jury. NBC is going to decide whether this man is guilty or innocent, they are not going to leave it to a jury such as yourselves. They are going to make that decision, they are going to come down here and wreck the State's case because they believe -- they believe -- they don't trust the Jury composed of a cross-section of citizens of this city. I say thank God that we have the jury system and a jury such as yourselves. I don't want NBC passing upon my innocence or guilt at any time, because they have got that old dollar motive. They are scavengers, and they tampered with the State's case because they didn't think you were proper or worthy to pass upon the innocence or guilt of this man.

Gentlemen, I feel that I have covered essentially most of the main points that Defense Counsel brought out in his argument, and I

don't intend to keep you much longer. I just ask you to bear in mind what the State has proven in this case from that witness stand, how it has shown, gentlemen, that within four hours of this case the Defendant was proven a liar and unworthy of your belief; how it was shown that he conspired with David Ferrie and Lee Harvey Oswald to kill the President of the United States. And when I sit down, gentlemen, and when I stop talking -- and certainly my talking to you now is insignificant, because it is your voices that are the most important, and I do concur with Mr. Dymond, this is certainly an important case. Thank God it got to a jury such as yourselves despite the efforts of the Jim Phelans, the Walter Sheridans, and the Friends of NBC, because this is where it belongs, and whatever your verdict is, you have got the right to make that verdict, a verdict which squares with your conscience, and I submit to you, gentlemen, when this case is considered in its entirety and you consider the coincidences, the many coincidences that keep cropping up in this case, the firm testimony under oath in this case, I feel sure, gentlemen, that when you deliberate and consider this that you will return a just verdict, and that is what I am asking for. Whatever that verdict be, make it a just verdict, and I feel that that verdict should be "Guilty as charged."
Thank you.

Appendix C:

~

Jim Garrison's Closing Statement

THE COURT:

Do I understand, Mr. Garrison, you wish to address the Jury?

MR. GARRISON:

Yes.

May it please the Court:

Gentlemen of the Jury, I'm not going to dignify Mr. Dymond's personal inferences about my staff, because I think you've seen them for some days, and I think you've seen me here, and I'll leave it to your judgment whether or not we would take advantage of any human being in order to try and get any gain of any sort; and I'll address myself to the remaining issues of the case which have been posed by Mr. Dymond.

Now, I know you're very tired. You've been very patient. This final day has been a long day, so I'll speak only a few minutes, and I'll probably make one of the shortest closing arguments that's been made in this Court, because I think most of the issues are clear to you, and I feel that you probably have an understanding of the case by now. Mr. Dymond posed, in his last argument, one final issue which in a sense raises a question of what we do when the need for justice is confronted by power. So, let me talk to you about whether there is Government is a great deal like a human being; it's not necessarily all good, and it's not necessarily all bad. We live in a good country, and I love it, and you do, too. But, we have, nevertheless, a Government which is not perfect, and there have been indications since November the 22nd of 1963, and that was not the last indication, that there is excessive power in some areas of our Government -- that the people have not received all of the truth about some of the things that have happened; some of the assassinations that have occurred; and particularly with regard to the assassination of John Kennedy. Going back to when we were children, I think most of us, probably all of us here in this Courtroom, thought that Justice came into being automatically; that virtue was its own reward; and good would triumph over evil; that it occurred automatically. Later, when we found that it wasn't quite so, most of us felt that, hopefully, that at least Justice occurred frequently of its own accord, but now I think that almost all of us would have to agree that there's really no automatic machinery, not on this earth at least, which causes Justice to happen automatically. Men have to make it occur. Individual human beings have to make it occur; otherwise, it doesn't come into existence, and this is not always easy. As a matter of fact, it's always hard, because Justice presents a threat to power; and, in order to make Justice come into being, you often have to fight power.

Mr. Dymond raised the question: Why don't we say it's a fraud, and charge the Government with fraud, if this is the case? Well, then, let me be explicit and make myself very clear on this point. The Government's handling of the investigation of John Kennedy's murder was a fraud. It was the great fraud in the history of our country. It was probably the greatest fraud ever perpetrated in the history of humankind. So, that's where I stand on that point. But that doesn't mean that we have to accept the continued existence of the kind of Government which allows this to happen. We can do something about it. We're not forced to either leave this country, or accept the authoritarianism that's developed, which tells us that in the year 2039 we can see the evidence about what happened to John Kennedy. Government does not consist only of secret police and domestic espionage operations and Generals and Admirals -- Justice consists of people. The Government consists of people, and our Government consists of juries; and cases of murder, whether of the poorest individual, or the most distinguished citizen in the land, should be looked at openly in a court of law, where juries can pass on them, and not hidden; not buried like the body of the victim, beneath concrete for 75 years.

Now, you men in the recent weeks, have heard witnesses that no one else in the world has heard, and you've seen the Zapruder film. You've seen what happened to your President, and I suggest to you that most of you know right now that in that area at least, a fraud has been perpetrated. That does not mean that our Government is entirely bad; and I want to emphasize that. It doesn't mean that the President is bad. It doesn't mean that the Supreme Court is bad. It does mean that in recent years, through the development of excessive power, because of the cold war, forces have developed in our Government over which there is no control, and these forces have an authoritarian approach to Justice, meaning, they will let you know what Justice is. Well, my reply to them, is we already know what it is. It is the Jury System. In the issue which is posed by the Government's conduct in concealing the evidence in this case. In the issue of humanity as opposed to power, I have chosen humanity, and I will do it without any hesitation, and I hope every one of you will do the same, and I do that because I love my country, and I want to communicate to the Government that we will not accept unexplained assassinations, with the casual information that if we live 75 years longer we may be given more data. In this particular case, our efforts to look into it, and it was our duty when we found out that part of the assassination finally occurred in New Orleans, massive power was brought to bear to prevent Justice from ever coming into this Courtroom as it has. The power to make authoritative pronouncements; the power to manipulate the news media by the release of false information; the power to interfere with an honest inquiry; the power to provide an endless variety of experts to testify in behalf of power, was demonstrated in this case. The American people have yet to see the Zapruder film. Why? The American people have yet to see and hear from witnesses about the assassination. Why? Because, today in our Government, we have a problem area in which too much emphasis is given to secrecy with regard to the assassination of our President, and not enough emphasis has been given to the question of Justice; to the question of humanity. These dignified deceptions will not suffice. We have had enough of power without truth. We don't have to accept power without truth, or leave the country. I don't accept that alternative. I don't intend to leave the country, and I don't intend to accept power without truth. I intend to fight for the truth, and I suggest that not only is this not un-American, but it is the most American thing we can do, because if the truth does not endure – then our country will not endure – not in the way it was supposed to. In our country the worst of all crimes is when the Government murders truth.If it can murder truth, it can murder freedom. If it can murder freedom, it can murder your own sons, if they should dare to fight for freedom, and then announce that they were killed in an industrial accident, or shot by the enemy, or God knows what. But, in this case, finally it has been possible to bring the truth about the assassination into a Court of Law; not before a Commission composed of important and powerful and politically astute men, but before a Jury of citizens. Now, I suggest to you that yours is a hard duty, because in a sense what you're passing on is equivalent to a murder case. It has the same essential characteristics, and the difficult thing about passing on a murder case is that the victim is out of your sight, and buried a long distance away, and all you can see is the Defendant, and it's very difficult to identify with someone you can't see; and sometimes it's hard not to identify to some extent with the Defendant and his problems. In that regard, every Prosector who is at all humane, is conscious of feeling sorry for the Defendant in very case he prosecutes. But, he is not free to forget this victim who lies buried out of sight, and I suggest to you that if you do your duty, you also are not free to forget the victim who is buried out of sight.

You know, Tennyson once said that authority forgets a dying king. This was never more true than in the murder of John Kennedy --

the strange and deceptive conduct of the Government after his murder began while his body was warm, and has continued for five years. In a sense, you have even seen in this Courtroom indications of the interest of some part of the Government power structure, in keeping the truth down; in keeping the grave closed. We presented a number of eye witnesses, as well as an expert witness, as well as the Zapruder film, to show that the fatal wound of the President came from the front. A plane landed from Washington, and out stepped Dr. Finck for the Defense, to counter the clear and apparent evidence of a shot from the front. I don't have to go into Dr. Finck's testimony in detail for you to see that it simply did not correspond with the facts. He admitted that he did not complete the autopsy, because a General told him not to complete the autopsy. Now, in this conflict between power and Justice -- to put it that way – just where do you think Dr. Finck stands? A General, who was not a Pathologist, told him not to complete the autopsy, so he didn't complete it. This is the way I don't want my country to be. When our President is killed, he deserves the kind of autopsy that the ordinary citizen gets very day in the State of Louisiana. We can't have Government power suddenly interjecting itself and preventing the truth from coming to the people; but in this case, before the next morning when the sun rose, power had moved into the situation, and the truth was being concealed. And, five years later, in this Courtroom, it's continuing in the same way. We presented eye witnesses who told you of the shots coming from the grassy knoll. A plane landed from Washington, and out came ballistics expert Frazier for the Defense.

MR. DYMOND:

Object to this, if the Court please. Mr. Frazier was subpoenaed here as a State witness.

THE COURT:

He testified for the Defense. He was called by the Defense, Mr. Dymond.

MR.DYMOND:

He was subpoenaed here from Washington as a State witness.

THE COURT:

Makes no difference who subpoenaed him it's who put him on the stand.

MR. DYMOND:

We didn't have anything to do with his coming here on a plane from Washington.

MR. GARRISON:

Now, the issue I'm sure every one of you understands, is whether or not the Government has created a fraud, and I call to your attention that Mr. Frazier's explanation of the sound of shots coming from the front, which was heard by eye witness after eye witness and after eye witness – his explanation is that Lee Oswald created a sonic boom in his firing. Not only did Oswald break all of the world's records for marksmanship, but he broke the sound barrier as well. And I suggest to you, that if any of you have shot on a firing range, and most of you probably have in the Service, you were shooting rifles in which the bullet traveled faster than the speed of sound, and I ask you to recall if you ever head a sonic boom. If you remember when you were on the firing line, and they'd say, "Ready on the left; ready on the right; ready on the firing line; commence firing;" you heard the shots coming from the firing line, to the left of you and to the right of you, and if you had heard, as a result of Frazier's fictional sonic booms, firing coming at you from the pits, you would have had a reaction, and you would still remember. It simply doesn't exist. It's a part of the fraud -- a part of the Government fraud -- and the best way to make this country the kind of country it's supposed to be, is to communicate to the Government that no matter how powerful it may be, we do not accept fraud. We do not accept false announcements. We do not accept the concealment of evidence with regard to the murder of President Kennedy. Who is the most believable -- a Richard Randolph Carr, seated here in a wheelchair, and telling you what he saw and what he heard, and how he was told to shut his mouth – or Mr. Frazier, with his sonic booms? Do we have to actually reject Mr. Newman and Mrs. Newman and Mr. Carr and Roger Craig, and the testimony of all those honest witnesses -- reject that and accept the fraudulent Warren Commission, or else leave the country? I suggest to you that there are other alternatives; and one of them has been put in practice in the last month in the State of Louisiana; and that is to bring out the truth in a proceeding where attorneys can cross-examine; where the Defendant can be confronted by testimony against him; where the rules of evidence are applied, and where a Jury of citizens can pass on it, and where there is no Government secrecy. Where you do not have evidence concealed for 75 years in the name of National security. All we have in this case are the facts -- facts which show that the Defendant participated in the conspiracy to kill the President, and that the President was subsequently killed in an ambush. The reply of the Defense has been the same as the early reply of the Government in the Warren Commission; has been authority, authority. The President's Seal outside of the volume of the -- each volume of the Warren Commission -- made necessary because there's nothing inside of these volumes. Men of high position and prestige sitting on a Board, and announcing the results to you, but not telling you what the evidence is, because that has to be hidden for 75 years. You heard in this Courtroom in recent weeks, eye witness after eye witness after eye witness, and, above all, you saw an eye witness which was indifferent to power -- the Zapruder film. The lens of the camera is indifferent to power, and it tells what happened, and that is one of the reasons 200,000,000 Americans have not seen the Zapruder film. They should know exactly what happened. They should know what you know now. Why hasn't this come into being, if there hasn't been Government fraud? Of course, there has. But, I'm telling you that I think we can do something about it. I think that there's still enough Americans left in this country to make it continue to be America. I think that we can still fight authoritarianism – the Government's insistence on secrecy; Government force used in counterattacks against an honest inquiry -- and when we do that, we're not being un-American -- we're being American, because it isn't easy, and you're sticking your neck out in a rather permanent way, but it has to be done, because truth does not come into being automatically. Justice does not happen automatically. Individual men, like the members of my staff here, have to work and fight to make it happen, and individual men like you have to make Justice come into being, because otherwise it doesn't happen. And, what I'm trying to tell you is that there are forces in America today, unfortunately, which are not in favor of the truth coming out about John Kennedy's assassination. As long as our Government continues to be like that; as long as such forces can get away with these kind of actions, then this is no longer the country in which we were born. The murder of John Kennedy was probably the most terrible moment in the history of our country. Yet, circumstances have placed you in the position where not only have you seen the hidden evidence, but you are actually going to have the opportunity to bring Justice into the picture for the first time. Now, you are here sitting in judgment on Clay Shaw; but you, as men, represent more than jurors in an ordinary case, because of the victim in this case. You represent, in a sense, the hope of humanity against Government power. You represent humanity which yet may triumph over excessive Government power, if you will cause it to be so, in the course of doing your duty in this case. I suggest that you ask not what your country can do for you, but

what you can do for your country. What can you do for your country? You can cause Justice to happen, for the first time in this matter. You can help make our country better by showing that this is still a Government of the people; and if you do that, as long as you live nothing will ever be more important than that.
Thank you.

Endnotes

Certain abbreviations and conventions have been used when referencing the most commonly cited works used in this volume. The *Report of the President's Commission on the Assassination of President John F. Kennedy* (Washington, D.C: U.S. Government Printing Office, 1964), commonly referred to as the *Warren Report* is abbreviated as WR. The twenty-six volumes of testimony, documents, and exhibits that accompany the report are cited by volume and page - for example, WC XVI, p. 23. References to Warren Commission exhibits are designated "CE" and the Commission documents are designated "CD."

The *Report of the Select Committee on Assassinations*, U.S. House of Representatives (Washington, D.C: U.S. Government Printing Office, 1979) is hereafter referred to as HSCA Report. The accompanying twelve volumes are cited by volume and page - for example, HSCA X, p.130. Documents from the Select Committee likewise carry the designation, HSCA.

Documents originating from the New Orleans District Attorneys Office bear the designation, NODA.

The National Archives and Records Administration is hereafter referred to as NARA.

Introduction

1. For some reason, on this date Banister was drinking much more heavily than usual. This is evidenced by Banister's bar tabs Garrison had obtained from the Katz and Jammer both on and prior to November 22nd.
2. HSCA X, p.130
3. Affidavit of Jack Martin and David Lewis, February 20, 1968.
4. Ibid.
5. New Orleans Police Report # K-1263-63, dated 11/22/63.

Chapter 1: Swept Up In The Gales Of History

1. The title for this chapter is taken from Jim Garrison's interview in the October 1967 issue of *Playboy* magazine. The full quote from Garrison is, "Ferrie could have quoted as his epitaph the last words of the Serb partisan leader Draja Mikhailovitch before Tito shot him for collaboration: "I was swept up in the gales of history.""

2. Unless otherwise noted Ferrie background material is taken from FAA investigative report on Ferrie dated December 13, 1963.

3. Ibid., p.7.

4. HSCA X, p. 115, *n*. 19.

5. FAA Report, p.7.

6. Ibid.

7. Ibid.

8. Ibid. p.9.

9. Ibid.

10. Ibid., p.10

11. Ibid., p.11

12. Ibid., pp.10-15. The four cadets who joined the Marines were Joe Pratrini, Ivy Rodriguez, Jerry Walker and Joe Howard.

13. Ibid., p.10.

14. HSCA X, p.115, *n*.20.

15. The cadets recollections are taken from NODA memo from Garrison to File, April 18, 1967, re: CAP cadets under David Ferrie; NODA statement of John Espenan, October 6, 1967; NODA memo from Kent Simms to Louis Ivon, no date, re: Interview of Lawrence Marsh; HSCA interview with Fred O'Sullivan, December 15, 1978; HSCA interview with George E. Boesch, Jr., October 5, 1978; HSCA IX pp. 103-115; G. Robert Blakey, and Richard Billings, *The Plot to Kill the President* (New York: New York Times Books, 1981), pp. 346-348.

16. HSCA interview with Jerry Paradis, December 15, 1978, document # 014374.

17. HSCA interview with Anthony Atzenhoffer, January 2, 1979, document # 014373.

18. Ibid.

19. NODA statement of Thomas Lewis Clark, March 15, 1967.

20. Gerald Posner, *Case Closed* (New York: Doubleday, 1994), p.142.

21. Frontline, *Who Was Lee Harvey Oswald?* November 16, 1993.

22. FAA Report, December 13, 1963.

23. HSCA IX, p. 112.

24. Robert Groden, *The Search For Lee Harvey Oswald* (New York: Penguin,1995), p.21.

25. Ibid. p. 29.

26. Ferrie's troubles with Eastern from FAA Report, December 12, 1963.

27. Ferrie's physical appearance from many sources; Garrison, Summers,

Flammonde, HSCA, et al.

28. Ferrie's interests also from many sources including Garrison, Summers, Flammonde, HSCA, et al. Ferrie's interest in medical research, specifically cancer research, is from Edward Haslam, *Mary, Ferrie, and the Monkey Virus* (Albuquerque: Wordsworth, 1995), passim.

29. Warren Hinckle, William Turner, *Deadly Secrets* (New York: Thunder's Mouth Press, 1992), p.232 and Richard Popkin, "Garrison's Case," *New York Review of Books*, September 14, 1967,p. 28.

30. Ibid., p.233.

31. NODA interview with Al Landry, March 23, 1967.

32. Author's interview with Carl McNabb, May 30, 1996. McNabb would later become an investigator for Jim Garrison adopting the alias of Jim Rose.

33. HSCA interview with Robert Boylston, October 17, 1978.

34. Ibid.

35. HSCA interview with Jack Martin, December 5, 1977. The ONI liaison was Guy Johnson who we will examine in a later chapter.

36. CIA memo, October 30, 1967, re: Frente Revolucionario Democratico, released 1993.

37. Letter from Arcacha to Eddie Rickenbacker, July 18, 1961.

Chapter 2: A Most Frighteningly Violent Person

1. Background information taken from 3 page autobiographical "sketch" by Guy Banister found in the Banister file at the Assassination Archives in D.C.

2. NODA memo re: "Guy Banister's Associations", September 30, 1968.

3. Hinckle & Turner, p. 229.

4. The Banister/Kohn relationship was an unusual one. According to the memo referenced in the previous footnote, Banister twice "bagged" the offices of Kohn, who he considered a member of the Jewish underground movement. On Banister and the police scandals, see Edward F. Haas, *DeLesseps S. Morrison and the Image of Reform* (Baton Rouge: Louisiana State University Press, 1974), p.209.

5. *New Orleans Times Picayune* , March 23, 1956.

6. Anthony Summers, *Official and Confidential* (New York: G.P. Putnam's Sons, 1993), pp. 322-323.

7. Banister barroom incident from *New Orleans Times Picayune*, March 3 & 4, 1957.

8. Wegmann, along with his brother Edward, also represented Clay Shaw during his conspiracy trial.

9. The Balter Building was named after its owner, Colonel Buford Balter, another notorious right-wing reactionary.

10. HSCA interview with Joseph Oster, January 27, 1978, document #005207.

11. NODA memo, re: "Guy Banister's Associations," September 30, 1968.

12. HSCA interview with Joseph Oster, January 27, 1978, document #005207.

13. Ibid.

14. NODA interview with Vernon Gerdes, October 30, 1968.

15. Jim Garrison's interview of I. E. Nitschke, January 17, 1967.

16. CIA memo for file from Marguerite D. Stevens, March 8, 1967, document # 1338-1052.

17. Ibid.

18. FBI memo from SAC, New Orleans to Director, March 1, 1967. # 89-69-1530.

19. Author's interview with Joe Newbrough, April 3, 1995 confirming statements made to Scott Malone in a previous interview.

20. This incident commonly referred to as the "Bolton Ford Incident" has been covered in several books on the assassination as well as the author's own article in *Back Channels* magazine, Volume 3, No. 1&2, Fall/Winter 1993-94. Unless otherwise noted this information is taken directly from the New Orleans District Attorney's files, memos dated May 9, 1967 and February 14, 1968, titled, "Interview with Fred Sewell."

21. This form is reprinted in Anthony Summers, *Not In Your Lifetime*, p.293 and the original is available from the FBI files at the National Archives.

22. This report was later released as part of CD 75, pp. 677-678.

23. NODA memo, April 1, 1967, "Interview With Betty Parrott." Parrott, who was the landlady and lover of Friends of Democratic Cuba member William Dalzell also revealed that the FBI and the CIA had liaisons to the FDC. The FBI representative was Regis Kennedy, who along with Warren DeBrueys, was Hoover's point man with the anti-Castro community in New Orleans.

24. NODA statement of Martin L. McAuliffe, Jr., May 9, 1967. McAuliffe is no doubt the "Martin McCullah" mentioned in a 1976 "affidavit" by Oswald's former Marine buddy, Kerry Thornley. If so, McAuliffe's ties to the anti-Castro intrigues of New Orleans may be deeper than he let on. According to Thornley, McAuliffe met Thornley in the Bourbon House in the summer of 1961 where they discussed Thornley's work-in-progress, *The Idle Warriors*, his fictionalized portrait of Marine life with its central character modeled after Oswald. A short time later McAuliffe introduced Thornley to Guy Banister who, according to Thornley, expressed great interest in Thornley's foray into the literary arts. In a NODA memo dated February 6, 1968, from Assistant D.A.Sciambra to Garrison regarding Thornley there is a handwritten note (presumably by Sciambra) which reads, "Thornley called me after his second Grand Jury appearance and told me that Dave Lifton told him that McAuliffe was affiliated with the Friends of Democratic Cuba and other anti-Castro groups." It is also significant to note that in McAuliffe's 1967 statement to the New Orleans D.A.'s office he tells of meeting David Ferrie in a coffee house in the French Quarter. McAuliffe apparently was never questioned about Thornley.

25. Not to be confused with the French Quarter restaurant, Tujague's, which,

according to the New Orleans Metropolitan Crime Commission, "had a reputation as a longtime gathering place for various racketeers and underworld figures." In an interview with the HSCA, Gerard Tujague's successor, Frank DiBenedetto stated that Gerard Tujague was in no way related to the Tujagues who owned the restaurant. See HSCA IX, pp. 101-102.

26. NODA memorandum, December 18, 1967, "Interview with B.P." In this memo the CIA liaison is believed to be a man named "Logan". This is was a nickname for Lloyd Ray, the head of the New Orleans Domestic Contacts office, who describes himself as an acquaintance of Grady Durham. See Memorandum for File from Lloyd Ray, dated November 15, 1960. No identifying number, but part of a 1993 CIA release and on file at the National Archives. Also Gus Russo, *Live By The Sword* (Baltimore: Bancroft Press, 1998), p.544 *n*. 85.

27. In fact, when questioned by Congressional investigators Dalzell admitted he worked for the CIA. HSCA document #064559, December 9,1977.

28. Ibid.

29. FBI document # 62-10960-5144, April 28, 1967.

30. FBI document # 62-109060-5240, May 7, 1967.

31. Gus Russo, *Live By The Sword* (Baltimore: Bancroft Press, 1998), p.137.

32. CIA document #F82-0277/33, January 12, 1968, released December 28, 1983.

33. Memo to Garrison from confidential informant, undated, part of HSCA materials on Guy Banister, document #002215.

34. Hinckle & Turner, p. 231.

35. Ibid. Also author's interview with Joseph Newbrough, April 3, 1995.

36. HSCA document #002215.

37. Ibid.

38. Hinckle & Turner, p.231. Also part of this global family was the American Friends of the Anti-Bolshevik Bloc of Nations whose Secretary-General was one Spas T. Raikin. As a representative of the Traveler's Aid Society, Raikin was the first to greet Oswald upon his return from Russia. See Peter Dale Scott, *Deep Politics and the Death of JFK* (Los Angeles: University of California Press, 1993), pp. 58-59.

39. Hinckle & Turner, p.232.

40. Ibid.

41. Gatlin in Cuba and his association with Castorr is from NODA report from Bill Boxley to Garrison, undated but circa 1968. Castorr's association with Cuban exiles is from CE 3108. Castorr and Ruby from Flammonde, p.126.

42. CIA memo, January 18, 1968. No identifying number, but part of 1993 release.

43. Ibid.

44. Ibid.

45. Scott, *Deep Politics and the Death of JFK*, p.109 and Robert Sam Anson, *"They've Killed the President"* (New York: Bantam Books, 1975), pp. 124-125.

46. CIA memo, January 18, 1968.

47. Novel deposition, Novel v. Garrison et. al. May 7, 1969, pp. 421-422.

Chapter 3: Cold War in the Big Easy

1. After *Playboy* magazine published an interview with Garrison in their October 1967 issue, Novel sued both Garrison and HMH Publishing claiming defamation and libel. In May of 1969 Novel gave a sworn deposition. That testimony serves as the basis for most of this section. For the information on Butler, see Novel v. Garrison, et al, p.384.

2. Novel v. Garrison, et al, pp. 394-399.

3. Ibid., p. 406.

4. David Atlee Phillips, *The Night Watch* (New York: Atheneum, 1977), pp. 34-36.

5. Gaeton Fonzi, *The Last Investigation* (New York: Thunder's Mouth Press, 1993), p. 265.

6. For Hunt and relationship to CRC, see E. Howard Hunt, *Give Us This Day* (New York: Arlington House), 1973, pp. 182-183.

7. Martin's statement re Hunt and 544 Camp from HSCA interview with Jim Garrison, August 6, 1977, HSCA #002097, 5 audiocassettes. It does not seem unreasonable that Hunt would visit the offices of the CRC and therefore be acquainted with Banister, especially in light of Gatlin's and Banister's association with the Anti-Communist League of the Caribbean and their peripheral (at a minimum) role with Hunt and Phillips in the CIA's 1954 ouster of the Arbenz government of Guatemala.

8. Phillips, p.85.

9. Fonzi, p.265.

10. Ibid., pp. 261-267.

11. HSCA X, p. 41.

12. Novel v. Garrison, et al, p. 552.

13. David Wise and Thomas B. Ross, *The Invisible Government* (New York: Bantam, 1964), pp. 79-80.

14. Unless otherwise noted, Houma raid background from Novel v. Garrison, et al, pp.441-490.

15. Although the CIA has denied any connection with the events in Houma, it could not so easily deny their connection with Schlumberger. At least five of their executives and officers were approved for contact use in the 1950's and 1960's. See CIA report titled, "Schlumberger Well Surveying Corporation," December 12, 1967, released (but still heavily redacted) in 1993. Prior to the "burglary" at Houma, Banister was overheard talking with the manger of Schlumberger in a conversation that seemed to be firming up the details for the upcoming raid. See affidavit of Jack Martin and David Lewis, February 20, 1968.

16. Stephen Schlesinger and Stephen Kinzer, *Bitter Fruit* (New York:

Doubleday, 1990), p.115. Banister operative, Jack Martin presented a different origin of the weapons cache at Houma. The weapons, according to Martin, were left over from anti-Gaullist operations in Guadeloupe and Martinique. See affidavit of Jack Martin and David Lewis, February 20, 1968.

17. Hinckle and Turner, pp. 84 & 230.

18. Ibid.

19. Ibid., pp. 93-94.

20. Novel v. Garrison, et al, p.490. Arcacha's attorney confirmed that the Houma weapons transfer was a CIA operation. It was setup so that Schlumberger could report the raid as a burglary to their insurance company. Arcacha's attorney later confirmed that the CIA reimbursed the insurance company. See Gus Russo, *Live By The Sword* (Baltimore: Bancroft Press, 1998), p. 152.

21. Milton Brener, *The Garrison Case* (New York: Clarkson N. Potter, Inc., 1969), p.183.

22. Ibid.

23. Ferrie Grievance hearing, August 5, 1963, p. 841.

24. HSCA, X, p.111.

25. NODA interview with Al Landry, March 23, 1967.

26. Ibid.

27. Russo, *Live By The Sword*, p.146.

28. NODA deposition of Herbert Wagner, December 6, 1967.

29. L. Fletcher Prouty, *JFK: The CIA, Vietnam and the Plot to Assassinate John F. Kennedy* (New York: Carol Publishing Group, 1996), pp.167-168.

30. Arthur Krock, "The Intra-Administration War in Vietnam," *New York Times*, October 3, 1963, p.34. Some have theorized that the "high level administration official" Krock quotes in the article was President Kennedy himself.

31. Anthony Summers, *Conspiracy* (New York: McGraw-Hill, 1980), p.329.

32. Ferrie Grievance Hearing, p.858.

33. Ibid.

34. NODA memo from Ward to Garrison, re: Emile Stopper, December 30, 1966.

35. Author's interview with Joe Newbrough, April 3, 1995.

36. Jim Garrison, *A Heritage of Stone* (New York: G.P. Putnam's Sons, 1970), p.126. Ferrie's godson, Morris Brownlee, recalled the maps of Cuba and the presence of several Cubans at Ferrie's, apparently preparing for a re-invasion of Cuba. See Russo, *Live By The Sword*, p. 187.

37. Interview with Robert Tannenbaum, *Probe*, July-August, 1996, p.24.

38. Ibid.

39. HSCA interview with John Irion, October 18, 1978, document #012754.

40. Ibid.

41. CIA memorandum for Chief, CI/R&A, "Garrison Investigation: Belle Chasse Training Camp," October 1967, document # WH/C 67-336.

42. Ibid.

43. FBI # 89-69-1637, March 8, 1967.
44. FBI # 89-69-1455, February 21, 1967.
45. FBI # illegible, but from SAC, Miami to Director, dated July 23, 1960.
46. Ibid.
47. Hunt, *Give Us This Day*, p. 64.

Chapter 4: The Return of Lee Harvey Oswald

1. For Reily's support of Crusade to Free Cuba, see Brener, p. 47 and for his support of INCA see Arthur Carpenter, "Social Origins of Anticommunism: The Information Council of the Americas," *Louisiana History* #30, Spring 1989, p. 128.
2. HSCA Report, pp. 193-194. Alba's recollection came several years after the incident and should be regarded with a measure of skepticism. However, corroboration of Oswald's association with the FBI was offered by the Cuban proprietor of the Habana Bar located on Decatur Street in New Orleans. Orest Pena alleged that he saw Oswald and FBI agent, Warren deBrueys talking on a number of occasions. According to an interview Pena gave to author Mark Lane, he said "the CIA was aware of the relationship; deBrueys had introduced Oswald to contacts known by Pena to be CIA through his service to the Agency in providing lodging for Cuban defectors." Pena claims that deBrueys threatened him with physical harm if he revealed this to the Warren Commission. DeBrueys has denied Pena's Claims. See Mark Lane, *Plausible Denial* (New York: Thunder's Mouth Press, 1991), pp. 55-56.
3. Jim Garrison, *A Heritage of Stone* (New York: G.P. Putnam's Sons, 1970), p.150.
4. Ibid.
5. NODA memo from Alcock to Ivon, March 6, 1967 and NODA memo from Alcock to Garrison, March 6, 1967.
6. NODA "Roundtable Discussion" with Garrison, Bill Turner, Bud Fensterwald, et. al. September 21, 1968. Transcript available at AARC.
7. Ibid.
8. CIA memo to file from M.D. Stevens, dated January 31, 1964, document # 1307-475.
9. Ibid.
10. NODA interview of Gerald Patrick Hemming, May 8, 1968.
11. In early 1961, the CIA ran a domestic destabilization operation against the FPCC under the direction of David Atlee Phillips and future Watergate conspirator, James McCord. After the CIA's operation wound down, the FBI picked up the reigns and ran their own operations to infiltrate the FPCC. See John Newman, *Oswald and the CIA* (New York: Carroll and Graf, 1995), pp. 236-244.
12. NODA statement of John Irion, January 30, 1967.
13. According to William Walter, the security clerk on duty at the time of

Oswald's request, Quigley asked Walter to check the security indices to determine if there was an existing file on Oswald. Walter did indeed find a file on Oswald, which he recalled carried an *informant* classification. He also recalled that Special Agent Warren deBrueys' name was on the jacket of that file. Amazingly, Walter would testify that he had also seen a Telex shortly before the assassination, warning that a "militant revolutionary group may attempt to assassinate President Kennedy on his proposed trip to Dallas." Since no other FBI employee could (or would) corroborate Walter's revelations, the HSCA chose to disregard his testimony. But the HSCA could not provide any motive for Walter's supposed subterfuge. He had no ax to grind with the FBI, he left the Bureau on good terms, and started a career in banking. He also did not seek notoriety or financial gain and believed the Warren Commission's conclusions. Walter summed up nicely for the HSCA his thoughts about his colleagues' silence, "I had gotten the [gut] feeling from everybody I talked to that "we know it is true, but we are not going to talk about it."" From Walter's Executive Session testimony to the HSCA, March 23, 1978, HSCA document #014029. As for Special Agent Quigley, he quit the FBI in early 1964 to go work for a wealthy Dallas right-winger named A.W. Cullum. Remarkably, in 1966, both Quigley and his wife left for a two-month trip behind the Iron Curtain. See NODA memo from Gary Sanders to Jim Garrison, December 11, 1967.

14. Summers, *Conspiracy,* p. 303.

15. James DiEugenio, *Destiny Betrayed: JFK, Cuba, and the Garrison Case* (New York: Sheridan Square Press, 1992), pp. 218-219.

16. One of the individuals was a local Tulane student named Charles Steele. The other, a young man of apparent Latin extraction, has yet to be identified.

17. David Chandler, "The Assassin's Trail," *Westword,* November 25-December 1, 1992, p. 15.

18. Ray and Mary La Fontaine, *Oswald Talked* (Gretna, LA.: Pelican, 1996), p. 162.

19. Ibid.

20. Letter and enclosure from Roy Jacob to William Gurvich dated April 15, 1967. According to the results of the polygraph, Quiroga also lied when he answered "No" to the following questions:

- You have said you were in Lee Oswald's company only on one occasion. Isn't it a fact that you were in Oswald's company on a number of occasions?

- In the late Summer and early Fall of 1963, Lee Oswald is often seen in the company of a stocky, unusually powerful man of Latin descent. Do you think you know the name of this man?

- Is it not a fact that at that time Oswald was in reality a part of an <u>anti-Castro</u> operation?

- According to your own knowledge, did Sergio Arcacha know Lee Oswald?

- Did Guy Banister?

- Did any other persons whom you know of?
- Prior to the assassination of the President, did you ever see any of the guns which were used in the assassination?

21. Interview with Delphine Roberts, August 27,1978, HSCA document #011196 and Summers, *Conspiracy*, p. 324.
22. Summers, *Conspiracy*, p.324.
23. Ibid., p. 325.
24. Hoke May's interview of Bill Nitschke, May 11, 1967, from Hoke May's files.
25. Ibid.
26. James DiEugenio's interview with Dan Campbell, September 3, 1994.
27. Ibid.
28. Ibid.
29. Ibid.
30. Ibid.
31. Ibid.
32. DiEugenio interview with Allen Campbell, September 6, 1994.
33. Summers, *Conspiracy*, p. 324.
34. Ibid.
35. NODA interviews with George Higginbotham, April 12, 16, 17, 1968.
36. Salvatore Panzeca interview with Vernon Gerdes, April 7, 1967, from the Wegmann Collection.
37. Ibid.
38. Summers, *Conspiracy*, pp. 364-365.
39. Ibid.
40. NODA statement of Jack Martin, December 26, 1966.
41. NODA interviews with Mary Banister, April 29 & 30, 1967.
42. Interview with Tommy Baumler by Bud Fensterwald and J. Gary Shaw, dated December 30, 1981. Baumler also revealed that Banister and Shaw were "close" and was clear that "Oswald worked for Banister."
43. Johnson background information taken from CIA memo from Marguerite D. Stevens to Deputy Chief, SRS, dated September 12, 1967. Document number unknown, released in 1993.
44. Indeed Johnson may have been involved in a covert CIA project. According to the above referenced CIA memo, a "second" Guy Johnson, also from New Orleans, was granted a covert security clearance on January 12, 1954. The clearance was required for Johnson's use in a project codenamed QK/ENCHANT. As we shall see later, Clay Shaw and others were also given covert security clearances for use in the same project. In addition, in 1954 Johnson was considered for use by the CIA as contract agent in Guam but the request was canceled, possibly because Johnson was "already in liaison with the Agency." CIA memorandum, Subject: Guy Persac JOHNSON (201-207873), April 23, 1968, released in 1993.

45. Letter from Guy Banister to Guy Johnson, January 5, 1959. It is interesting to note, that the National Student Association mentioned in the letter had been infiltrated and used by the CIA. This was revealed in a 1967 expose' in *Ramparts* magazine and subsequently confirmed by the CIA.
46. CIA RIF # 1993.06.25.14:08:25:280800, Box # OSW16, Volume 56, from the National Archives collection.
47. Affidavit of Jack Martin and David Lewis, February 20, 1968.

Chapter 5: The Ides of November

1. Virtually all of the doctors and medical personnel at Parkland Hospital and Bethesda Naval Hospital described a large, gaping wound in the occipital parietal region of Kennedy's head, indicative of a shot originating from the front of the President. From many sources, but for example see Robert Groden, *The Killing of a President* (New York: Penguin Books, 1993), pp. 86-88 and Gary L. Aguilar, MD and Kathleen A Cunningham, "How Three Investigations of the Medical Autopsy Evidence Got It Wrong: Part Two," *Probe*, pp. 18-25.
2. Gill was one of Marcello's many attorneys. Ferrie worked directly for Gill, not Marcello. In addition to the Marcello case, Ferrie assisted Gill on other less controversial cases as Garrison revealed in the documentary work-in-progress by Richard Cohn and Carol Kachmer, *Rough Side of the Mountain*.
3. NODA interview with Melvin Coffey, February 18, 1967.
4. NODA statement of Alvin Beauboeuf, December 15, 1966.
5. NODA interview with David Ferrie, December 15, 1966.
6. Ibid.
7. Testimony of Rowland Charles Rolland, *State of Louisiana v. Clay L. Shaw*, February 12, 1969.
8. Ibid.
9. Garrison, *A Heritage of Stone*, p. 117.
10. Ibid.
11. Ferrie phone bills from Gill's office from the NODA's files.
12. Jim Garrison, *On the Trail of the Assassins* (New York: Sheridan Square Press, 1988), pp. 111-113. Garrison commented on this in his earlier volume as well writing, "Here we have Ferrie, Oswald's mentor and associate in New Orleans, calling a telephone number which has a factual correlation with the patriotic nightclub owner who killed Oswald in Dallas. There is a time correlation as well. Ferrie placed the call to Chicago on the exact day Oswald left New Orleans. The owner of the Chicago telephone went to Dallas the day before the assassination with a man who then met with Jack Ruby. There are millions upon millions of telephones in America. The arm of coincidence is not so long that it can be plausibly regarded as responsible for the interconnecting relationship of one Chicago telephone to David Ferrie in New Orleans and Jack Ruby in Dallas before the assassination." From Garrison, *A Heritage of Stone*, pp. 124-125.

13. NODA interview with Thomas Compton, March 10, 1967.

14. HSCA X, p. 113.

15. Ibid.

16. Ibid., p. 114.

17. Ibid., p. 113.

18. NODA interview with Jack Martin, December 14, 1966.

19. Letter from Jack Martin to Richard Robey, November 25, 1963.

20. Andrews testimony from WC XI, pp. 325-339.

21. FBI document # 105-8255-Not Recorded. This document can be found in the HSCA FBI Investigative File on Lee Harvey Oswald, Record number 1801003010064, Box 2, Section 8. This is a 24-page document that consists of several FBI reports.

22. WC XI, pp. 325-339.

23. Ibid.

24. HSCA FBI Investigative File on Lee Harvey Oswald, Box 2, Section 8.

25. Ibid.

26. Ibid.

27. Ibid.

28. Ibid. Davis also recalled that when Andrews returned to this office, he found that someone had broken into the office and rifled his files, but nothing of value had been taken. Also, when questioned later by Garrison's investigators, Davis admitted he had seen Oswald and the "gay kids in the office." NODA interview with Davis, March 9, 1967.

29. HSCA FBI Investigative File on Lee Harvey Oswald, Box 2, Section 8.

30. Ibid.

31. Ibid.

32. Ibid.

33. Unless otherwise noted, all Cheramie material is taken from HSCA X, pp. 199-205.

34. HSCA deposition of Francis Fruge, April 18, 1978, JFK document #014570, p.29.

35. NODA interview of Emilio Santana, February 14, 1967.

36. Ferrie friend, Perry Russo, in an August 30, 1994 interview with the author, remembered Santana as a visitor to Ferrie's apartment.

37. HSCA Contact Report, April 7, 1978, Bob Buras interview of Francis Fruge, document # 014141, p. 7.

Chapter 6: Origins of an Investigation

1. Letter from Joseph M. Rault, Jr. to Jim Garrison, September 14, 1966. Available in the New Orleans Public Library microfilm collection.

2. James A. Autry, "The Garrison Investigation: How and why it began," *New Orleans,* April 1967, p. 8., and author's interview with Senator Russell Long, December 29, 1998. Senator Long also stated in our interview that he never

regarded Garrison as a "nut" or "a wild man" as he has so often been portrayed.

3. Letter from Lorraine G. LeBouef to U.S. Government Printing Office, December 6, 1966.

4. Garrison state of mind, *Heritage*, p.16.

5. Banister Autopsy Protocol, Orleans Parish Coroner's Office, #CW64-6-45, June 7, 1964.

6. NODA interviews with Mary Banister, April 29 & 30, 1967.

7. Ibid.

8. Card listing from the NODA's Banister file.

9. From the Wegmann collection, part of the special collections at the National Archives.

10. Memo from Lloyd Ray, Chief, New Orleans Office to Director, Domestic Contact Service, April 6, 1967, # NO-133-67.

11. Newman, *Oswald and the CIA*, p. 325.

12. CIA memo, "Garrison Investigation of Kennedy Assassination: Allegations of Involvement, CIA and Cuban," February 23, 1968. This document refers to the "DRE Animus" memo, but it appears that particular memo was not included in the same release. Also, all references to the memo's author have been redacted.

13. CIA memo, "Cubans and the Garrison Investigation," March 7, 1968.

14. NODA interview with Jack Martin, December 13, 1966.

15. NODA interview with David Ferrie, December 15, 1966.

16. The informant was Jimmy Johnson who would submit several reports to the NODA's office over the course of the following weeks.

17. Tom Bethell, *The Electric Windmill: An Inadvertent Biography* (Washington: Regnery Gateway, 1988), pp. 60-71.

18. See Bethell's diary, from the Wegmann collection, p. 23.

19. HSCA interview with Barbara Reid, January 21, 1978, NODA's affidavits of Barbara Reid and Peter Deageano, both from 1968.

20. Bill Wynn, "3,300 Guns For Hire: The Booming Business in Private Police," *New Orleans Courier,* 1973, Volume X, Issue 24.

21. Novel v. Garrison, et. al., p.879.

22. Ibid., p. 869. Novel certainly aided the FBI in their investigation. In his deposition, Novel describes how the FBI was waiting for him at his apartment one night. The FBI asked him, "What's the giant (Garrison) got on his mind tonight?" Novel's response to the agents was "Well come listen and I'll tell you." Novel v. Garrison et. al., pp. 941-943.

23. Memo from Ray to Director, DCS, dated February 6, 1967, #NO-43-67. It is also interesting to note that Garrison was looking into the activities of Tracy Barnes at this early date. According to Novel, Garrison had some sort of "fascination" with Tracy Barnes. From Novel v. Garrison, et. al., p. 929. At the time of the assassination Barnes was CIA chief of Domestic Operations Division. One of the most clandestine branches of the CIA, the DOD was

sometimes called the "dirty tricks" division. It is intriguing that Garrison was "on to" Barnes at this early juncture. It has been alleged that Barnes had some sort of clandestine involvement in the assassination of JFK. See Dick Russell, *The Man Who Knew Too Much.* New York: Carroll and Graff, 1992, passim.

24. Garrison, *On the Trail of the Assassins*, p. 85.

25. NODA interview with Clay Shaw, December 23, 1966.

26. CIA memo from Marguerite D. Stevens, dated March 16, 1967 re: J. Monroe Sullivan, document #1337-1051.

27. *New Orleans Times-Picayune*, March 2, 1967.

28. Written correspondence introduced as evidence at Shaw's trial confirmed this.

29. Sullivan's recollections from letter to author from Bill Turner, October 17, 1995. Shaw's statements from NODA interview with Shaw, December 23, 1966 and Shaw's trial testimony, February 27, 1969.

30. NODA interview with J.B. Dauenhauer, February 10, 1967.

31. Novel v. Garrison, et. al., *passim.*

32. Steve Tyler, *He Must Have Something*, a video documentary, 1991.

33. Ibid. Also author's interview with Jack Dempsey, September 2, 1994.

34. Author's interview with Lou Ivon, April 7, 1995.

35. Decatur Street was the location of Carlos Bringuier's clothing store as well as Orest Pena's Habana Bar. It has been alleged that both Ferrie and Shaw frequented Pena's bar. An incident at the bar where Oswald (or a look-alike) and a Cuban companion created a disturbance has been adequately covered in several books. For example. see Henry Hurt, *Reasonable Doubt* (New York: Holt, Rinehart & Winston, 1986), pp. 360-361.

36. Curiously, the last person to supposedly see Ferrie alive was the *Washington Post's* reporter on the intelligence community, George Lardner who had been interviewing Ferrie into the wee hours of the morning.

37. Eric Norden, "Interview with Jim Garrison," *Playboy,* October 1967, p. 165.

38. Quote is from Flammonde, *The Kennedy Conspiracy*, pp. 41-42.

39. Tyler, *He Must Have Something*.

Chapter 7: Humble Origins

1. Tangipahoa Parish earned its gory appellation because of the degree of violence of the local feuds.

2. Unless otherwise noted, Shaw biographical information is taken from the notes of New Orleans reporter, Hoke May or from Shaw's biography in the *Who's Who in the South and Southwest* (Chicago: The A.N. Marquis Company, 1950), p.832.

3. *Who's Who*, p. 832. Shaw wrote most of his plays under the pseudonym, "Allen White," a name derived from the maiden names of Shaw's two grandmothers.

4. Kiddick was a member of the Rockefeller based, Foreign Policy Association.

In 1961, Shaw would introduce CIA Assistant Director, Charles Cabell at a Foreign Policy Association function in New Orleans. See Donald Gibson, "Establishment Radicals and Kennedy," *Probe,* November-December 1998, p.14.

5. Ibid.

6. Shaw military medical record from NODA's files.

7. James Bacque, *Other Losses* (New York: Prima Publishing, 1991), pp. 92-96.

8. Shaw received the Croix de Guerre from France and the Bronze Star and Legion of Merit from the US. Shaw also apparently developed a close friendship with General Thrasher. An FBI source in Fort Riley, Kansas reported that the General's daughter, Frances L. Thrasher, had quit her job as a court reporter in April of 1967 because "Miss Thrasher became emotionally upset over the prosecution of Clay L. Shaw, inasmuch as Shaw and her father, Brig. Gen. Thrasher, were close friends during World War II. Her resignation was based partly on her desire to be free to pursue the Shaw-Garrison dispute, which became an obsession with her." FBI memo from SAC, Kansas City to Director, dated July 14, 1967, document # 62-109060-5550.

9. Shaw's Justice Department "rap sheet" is on file in the Shaw/FBI file at the National Archives.

10. Command and General Staff College Special Text, "Military Intelligence, Operational." Fort Leavenworth, Kansas ST 30-6-2. p. 158.

11. Ibid. p. 161.

Chapter 8: With A Little Help From His Friends

1. John Wilds, *Ochsner's* (Baton Rouge: Louisiana State University Press, 1985), p. 67.

2. From notes of Hoke May. Also author's interview with Joe Newbrough, April 3, 1995.

3. Wilds, p.68.

4. Notes of Hoke May, undated but circa 1967.

5. Ibid.

6. The FBI had reports about Shaw as far back as 1954. An informant for the Bureau described Shaw as "a brilliant and powerful man, given to sadism and masochism in his homosexual activities." FBI memorandum from Branigan to Sullivan, March 2, 1967, #62-109060-4608.

7. Testimony of Dean Andrews, WC XI, pp. 325-339.

8. The number of people identifying Shaw as Bertrand is well into the double digits. I will be citing several of these throughout the course of this book. I was personally told by a veteran New Orleans police detective that Shaw's use of this alias was an open secret. Author's interview with L.J. Delsa, April 5, 1995.

9. New Orleans District Attorney's Office memorandum from Lorraine LeBouef to Jim Garrison, dated August 9, 1967.

10. Wilds, p. 68. Also Carpenter, Arthur, "Social Origins of Anticommunism:

The Information Council of the Americas." *Louisiana History* #30, Spring 1989, pp. 117-143. Hecht would later be approved for "limited contact" use by the CIA in 1950. See CIA memo from CI/R&A to John Greaney, OGC, March 18, 1968, released in 1993.

11. Donald Gibson, "Clay Shaw, Freeport Sulphur, and the Establishment," *Probe,* November-December 1996, p.17.

12. Ibid.

13. Ibid.

14. Ibid. p. 18.

15. Ibid. As Gibson notes, Martin actively opposed President Kennedy's low interest rate policies.

16. NODA's office memorandum from William R. Martin to Jim Garrison, dated May 24,1967. The author of this memo admitted to Garrison that he (Martin) was himself a former CIA employee. Also, it is interesting to note that after Shaw's arrest Baldwin wrote a letter to Shaw stating, "With my own CIA connections, I may be seeing you sooner than you think. I would be delighted to tell Garrison what an idiot I think he is." Letter from Baldwin to Shaw, May 31, 1967. From the Papers of Clay Shaw Collection at the National Archives.

17. CIA document #1344-1056, dated September 11, 1967 and attachment. Core was also an informant for FBI Special Agent Warren deBrueys. See CD 1114, deBrueys report on Fair Play For Cuba Committee, dated October 25, 1963.

18. Handwritten investigative notes of William Gurvich, ca. 1966, NODA's files. See also Edward F. Haas, *Delesseps S. Morrsion and the Image of Reform.* (Baton Rouge: Louisiana State University Press, 1974), *passim.*

19. For example in the *New Orleans Times-Picayune* Sunday Supplement of January 17, 1965 titled "Report to the People," Aaron Kohn commented on Garrison's use of padlocking strip joints that were engaged in prostitution and fleecing their customers, "The District Attorney of the Parish of Orleans cut off the flow of these crimes through the civil - not criminal - action of "padlocking." The law wisely provides the District Attorney with both the authority and the responsibility of taking this action. Jim Garrison, the present District Attorney, is the only one who has made persistent use of this power and responsibility." p.12. Kohn concludes his praise by writing, "The District Attorney for Orleans Parish is the most powerful, and most important, single official in the City's processes of law enforcement. The vitality with which this authority has been used by the Garrison administration has been an unprecedented deterrent to crime and organized racketeering in New Orleans." p. 16. This issue will be dealt with in greater detail in a later chapter.

20. James DiEugenio. "New Orleans Aristocracy and the JFK Assassination." *Back Channels*, Spring 1993, p. 1.

21. Carpenter, pp. 125-126.

22. When Brent died in 1953, he bequeathed over a million dollars to the Ochsner Foundation. In his honor, Ochsner re-named the clinic's hotel, Brent

Endnotes

House. See Wilds, p. 68.

23. Carpenter, p. 119. Also, Jane Wolfe, *The Murchisons*. (New York: St. Martin's Paperbacks, 1989). pp. 319-320. Ochsner also held positions on several boards including Tulane Medical School. Additionally, he did classified work for the Air Force "on the medical side of subversive matters." See Peter Dale Scott, *Deep Politics and the Death of JFK*. (Los Angeles: University of California Press, 1993). p. 97.

24. Interview with Evan Thomas, C-SPAN, "BookNotes," December17, 1995. Also, E. Howard Hunt, *Undercover*, (New York: Berkley Publishing Corp), 1974, p.99.

25. CIA memorandum from James R. Murphy to Chief, CI/R&A and Director, Domestic Contact Service, dated May 23, 1968. Released in 1994.

26. Arthur Carpenter, *Gateway to the Americas: New Orleans's Quest for Latin American Trade, 1900-1970*, diss., Tulane University, 1987 (New Orleans: UMI Dissertation Services, 1987), p.184.

27. CIA project # OO-32-51, document number unknown, but available from the AARC. Also in 1953, Gaudet's security clearance was upgraded to allow him to "be given information classified up to and including Secret." Memo from Chief, Security Division to Chief, Contact Division, dated July 20, 1953.

28. The garage in question was undoubtedly Adrian Alba's Crescent City Garage located one block from Banister's office and next door to Oswald employer Reily Coffee Co.

29. Summers, pp. 362-365.

30. Ibid.

31. Carpenter, *Gateway*, p. 128. As previously noted, a newly released CIA memo, states that "this firm [Reily's] was of interest as of April 1949." Reily's was assigned a CIA number, EE-334. CIA memo from M.D. Stevens to file, January 31, 1964, document # 1307-475.

32. CIA memo dated May 23, 1968, part of the JFK collection at the National Archives.

33. Carpenter, *Gateway*, p.236.

34. The Alton Ochsner Papers, The Historic New Orleans Collection, Box 105, Folder 4. Apparently these records contained some of the late Guy Banister's files. See Edward Haslam. *Mary, Ferrie & the Monkey Virus*. (Albuquerque: Wordsworth. 1995), pp. 145-170.

35. Letters from Ochsner to Butler, June 29, 1967 and July 12, 1967, Ochsner Papers, Box 105, Folder 4. As we have seen, William Gurvich was a New Orleans private eye who volunteered to be part of Garrison's probe. He later "defected" from the staff and devoted his energies to attacking Garrison and his investigation. Gurvich had, in fact, told the press that Garrison was about to arrest "a number of people in New Orleans, including a doctor, a coffee man, and a hotel owner." Gurvich was referring to Ochsner, a member of the Reily family, and hotel executive, William Monteleone, who headed the "Crusade To

Free Cuba" campaign.

36. Ochsner Papers, Box 121, Folder 7.

37. Minutes of this meeting are in the Guy Banister file at the AARC.

Chapter 9: The Cuban Problem

1. Report of the Select Committee on Assassinations. U.S. Government Printing Office, 1979. pg. 105. For CIA sentiment re: Kennedy see E. Howard Hunt, *Give Us This Day*. (New York: Arlington House, 1973); David Atlee Phillips, *The Night Watch*. (New York: Athenaeum, 1977); Warren Hinckle and William Turner, *Deadly Secrets*, (New York: Thunder's Mouth Press, 1993). Kennedy, of course privately blamed the CIA for the Bay of Pigs and vowed to "splinter them into a thousand pieces." As I noted in Chapter 3, CIA funded rebels were planning a dangerous attack on U.S. forces at Guantanomo in order to provoke Kennedy into a full scale military invasion of Cuba.

2. Carpenter, *Social Origins of Anti-Communism*, pp. 118-119.

3. Ibid., p. 119.

4. Ibid.

5. Ibid., pp. 119-120.

6. NODA memoranda from Andrew J. Sciambra to Jim Garrison, October 9, 1968 and from Andrew J. Sciambra to Jim Garrison, October 23, 1968.

7. NODA memo from Sal Scalia to Jim Garrison, June 27, 1967.

8. Interview with Dean Andrews and Richard Townley by Robert Wilson, April 19, 1967, from the Wegmann Collection, National Archives.

9. NODA memo from Andrew J. Sciambra to Jim Garrison, October 9, 1968.

10. Newman, *Oswald and the CIA*, p. 124.

11. Tim Weiner, *Blank Check: The Pentagon's Black Budget* (New York: Warner Books, 1991), pp. 28 & 126.

12. Kai Bird, *The Chairman* (New York: Simon & Schuster, 1992), p. 497.

13. For example, Augustus Long, longtime chairman of Texaco, Jean Mauze, third husband of Abby Rockefeller, and Benno C. Schmidt, business partner of David Rockefeller. Also on the board was Godfrey Rockefeller, second cousin to Nelson and David.

14. Lisa Pease, "David Atlee Phillips, Clay Shaw and Freeport Sulphur," *Probe*, March-April, 1996, p.17. This is a groundbreaking, two-part article that this author highly recommends.

15. Ibid.

16. Ibid.

17. Thomas G. Paterson, *Contesting Castro* (New York: Oxford University Press, 1994), p. 160.

18. HSCA Outside Contact Report, re: James J. Cogswell III, from Gaeton Fonzi, July 6, 1978, document # 009812.

19. Ibid.

Endnotes

20. Ibid.

21. Phillips, *The Night Watch*, passim.

22. NODA's office statement of Jules Ricco Kimble, October 10, 1967.

23. CIA memo, March 3, 1967, author unknown. Document id # 1993.06.28.15:29:52:780280, JFK Box # JFK1, Volume F, Folder 7, on file at the National Archives. At this time it is still unknown what Project ZR/CLIFF was. A four-year-old FOIA request by the author has yielded nothing.

24. B. Bugge, *The Mystique of Conspiracy*. 1978 (?) pp. 121-122. Cienfuegos died a few months later in a mysterious airplane crash in Cuba.

25. CIA memo from David Atlee Phillips to JMWAVE, January 2, 1968 and CIA Memorandum Number 8, January 12, 1968.

26. FBI memo from SAC, Houston to Director, FBI, August 24, 1966, document # 62-109060-4176.

27. NODA interview with Rudy Spremich, December 13, 1966.

28. NODA interview with Rudy Spremich, January 11, 1967.

29. Author's interview with Steve Tyler, April 4, 1995.

30. NODA memo from Tom Bethell to Garrison, Re: Clay Shaw's Property, January 22, 1968.

31. Fowler background material taken from CIA memoranda dated April 6, 1967 and May 8, 1967 located in JFK Box # JFK1, Volume F, Folder 7 at the National Archives. Also Anthony and Robbyn Summers, "The Ghosts of November," *Vanity Fair*, December 1994, p. 110.

32. Richard Billings, "The Case for a Conspiracy - The Garrison Hypothesis." Unpublished article for *LIFE* magazine, March 1967. Taken from NODA interview with Mrs. Carlos Marquez, February 14, 1967. Shaw's secretary would testify at his trial that Shaw would allow certain Cuban exile groups free space at the ITM. See Shaw trial testimony of Goldie Naomie Moore, February 21, 1969.

33. Ibid., Marquez interview.

34. Coincidentally, Cabell's brother, Earl, was the mayor of Dallas at the time of Kennedy's ill-fated trip to that city.

35. FPA press release, April 27, 1961 located in Shaw's CIA file.

36. The Girnus information is from NODA interview with Girnus, document dated December 7, 1967.

37. Flight plan is available as HSCA document # 006795. To an untrained eye, the handwriting on the flight plan does seem to resemble Ferrie's.

38. Author's interview with Edward Joseph Girnus, February 24, 1996.

39. Blakey, who took over as Chief Counsel after Richard Sprague was fired, was an advocate of the "Mafia did it" theory.

40. Author's interview with Joe Newbrough, April 3, 1995.

41. Author's interview with Jack Dempsey, September 2, 1994.

42. DiEugenio interview with Dan Campbell, September 3, 1994.

43. CIA memorandum, "Garrison and the Kennedy Assassination: Cubans and

other Latin Americans Allegedly Involved," March 7, 1968.

44. HSCA memo from S. Jonathan Blackmer to G. Robert Blakey, Gary Cornwall, Ken Klein & Cliff Fenton dated September 1, 1977, HSCA document #002209.

Chapter 10: PERMINDEX: Trade Organization or Assassination Bureau?

1. Many of these documents were released in 1982 as a result of FOIA suit initiated by the late Bud Fensterwald. These cables serve as the basis for most of this chapter.

2. State Department cables dated February 1, 1957 and November 7, 1958.

3. S. Menshikov, *Millionaires and Managers* (Moscow: Progress Publishers, 1973), p. 297.

4. DiEugenio, p. 371, *n*.7.

5. Burton Hersh, *The Old Boys* (New York: Charles Scribner's Sons, 1992), p. 368.

6. Ibid. p. 73.

7. State Department cable re: PERMINDEX, February 1, 1957.

8. Ibid.

9. State Department cables re: PERMINDEX, April 9, 1958 and July 18, 1958.

10. State Department cable, November 7, 1958.

11. DiEugenio, p. 211.

12. All of this material is covered in Flammonde's book and I would refer the interested reader to that volume.

13. Executive Intelligence Review, *Dope, Inc.*, (Washington D.C: Executive Intelligence Review, 1992.), p. 528, *n*.4. NOTE: I use this reference with much reluctance. I cannot, in all honesty, support most of the wild conclusions in this book. Therefore, I urge caution on the part of the reader. If there are any researchers with access to French newspaper archives, tracking this down would be a worthy project.

14. Soustelle background information is taken mostly from Andrew Tully, *CIA: The Inside Story* (New York: William Morrow, 1962) and Flammonde, p.217.

15. Ibid.

16. Chicago Tribune, June 15, 1975.

17. NODA memorandum, from Andrew Sciambra to Jim Garrison, April 1, 1967.

Chapter 11: East Louisiana Intrigue

1. Edwin Lee McGehee's recounting of his meeting and conversation with Oswald is taken from his deposition before the House Select Committee on Assassinations, April 19, 1978, HSCA document #008506 and his testimony in the State of Louisiana vs. Clay L. Shaw, February 6, 1969.

2. In McGehee's testimony and deposition he mentions seeing a green car containing a woman and a baby bassinet that seemed to arrive at the same time as Oswald. At no time does McGehee ever testify that he saw Oswald either enter or exit this car. McGehee told me that he felt this car was associated with someone who was using the laundromat across the street and was just coincidental to Oswald's arrival. Author's interview with Ed McGehee, August 26, 1994.

3. Reeves Morgan's recollections are taken from his HSCA deposition, April 19, 1978, HSCA document #008501 and State of Louisiana vs. Clay L. Shaw, February 6, 1969.

4. To date no record of Morgan's call has been produced by the FBI.

5. Indeed, Jim Garrison would later recall that the New Orleans D. A.'s office interviewed some 300 witnesses from East Feliciana Parish, see Garrison, *On The Trail Of The Assassins*, p. 108). Louisiana State Policeman, Francis Fruge, remembers seeing a pared down list of 45+ witnesses from assistant D.A., Andrew Sciambra, see Fruge interview with HSCA, document #015044. Many of these interviews are now available at the National Archives.

6. Affidavit of Corrie Collins, November 7, 1978, HSCA document #013007. Also State of Louisiana vs. Clay L. Shaw, February 6, 1969.

7. Deposition of William Dunn, April 18, 1978, HSCA document #008497. Also State of Louisiana vs. Clay L. Shaw, February 7, 1969. Dunn's identification is a little problematic. Although he has always maintained Shaw was in the car, he also once placed Banister operative, Thomas Beckham, in the front seat. Another witness, Andrew H. Dunne (apparently no relation) placed Shaw, Banister and Jack Ruby (!) in the car. However, the number of credible witnesses placing the three principals (Shaw, Ferrie and Oswald) in Clinton *and* Jackson cannot be ignored.

8. Henry Earl Palmer's recollection of these events and conversations are taken from his HSCA deposition dated April 19, 1978, HSCA document #008499 and from State of Louisiana vs. Clay L. Shaw.

9. There was actually another white man attempting to register that day named Estes Morgan. However, Morgan was a local, and was known to most residents.

10. From *Rough Side of the Mountain*, a documentary work-in-progress by Richard Cohn and Carol Kachmer.

11. Ibid.

12. NODA memo from Simms and Ruiz to Ivon, January 29, 1968.

13. NODA memo from Simms and Ruiz to Ivon, January 31, 1968.

14. Affidavit of Henry Burnell Clark, September 12, 1967, HSCA document #006795.

15. Ibid.

16. Executive Session testimony of John Manchester, March 14, 1978, HSCA document #008503.

17. Palmer deposition, HSCA document #008499. This bit of corroborating testimony could not be elicited during the Clay Shaw trial due to the hearsay rule.
18. Billings journal, pp. 81-82, on file at the AARC.
19. Medical staff records, East Louisiana State Hospital, HSCA document #006098. Silva, a Cuban exile formerly associated with Tulane Medical School, is now a prominent psychiatrist in Baton Rouge. According to Cuban intelligence, Silva was active in the anti-Castro cause and is believed to be related to Frank Bartes. Bartes took over as the Cuban delegate to the CRC from Sergio Arcacha Smith. He was also a close associate of Carlos Bringuier, the head of the DRE who engaged in the street brawl with Oswald in August of 1963. As for Dr. Pierson hospital records show Pierson was a former narcotics offender who listed Silva as a reference on his job application. Either choice of doctor by Oswald is compelling, as is his selection of hospitals. As we will see, several former employees have recalled experiments with psychedelic drugs, incidents of torture, and a general loose atmosphere in the hospital at that time. It is interesting to note that Tulane had an outreach program at the hospital.
20. Ms. Wilson died in 1965, before the Garrison investigation started.
21. Researchers Paul Hoch, Peter Dale Scott, Dick Russell, Phil Melanson, Henry Hurt, and Anthony Summers have all expressed this view at some point.
22. Ward Churchill and Jim Vander Wall. *The COINTELPRO Papers*, (Boston: South End Press, 1990), pp. 92-93. It should also be noted that the purpose of Oswald's visit was to find employment at the hospital in Jackson, NOT to disrupt the CORE drive in Clinton.
23. State of Louisiana vs. Clay L. Shaw, February 6, 1969.
24. Palmer deposition, HSCA document #008499.
25. HSCA Report, pp. 142-145.
26. G. Robert Blakey & Richard Billings, *The Plot to Kill the President* (New York: Times Books, 1981), p. 170.
27. HSCA memo from Kenneth Klein to file, April 4, 1977, HSCA document # 008269.
28. HSCA interview with Ronald Johnston, March 10, 1978, HSCA document # 006499.
29. By noting the days of the week Palmer kept the registrar's office open - Thursday, Friday, and a half day Saturday, it is possible to pinpoint the days of the week these incidents took place (assuming the events occurred sequentially). Oswald first arrives in Jackson in the early evening (see McGehee and Morgan). The following day Oswald et al arrive in Clinton and stay all day. A third day is required for the return trip to Jackson. By working back from this point, it becomes clear that Oswald's visit to the Jackson hospital was on a Friday (assuming their personnel department was not open on Saturdays). Therefore the Clinton visit took place on Thursday and the arrival at McGehee's and Morgan's on Wednesday.

30. Deposition of Bobbie Dedon, May 19, 1978, HSCA document #008498. Also State of Louisiana vs. Clay L. Shaw, February 7, 1969.

31. HSCA interview with Maxine Kemp dated February 16, 1978, HSCA document #006101. Also State of Louisiana vs. Clay L. Shaw, February 7, 1969.

32. Ibid.

33. Alan Scheflin and Edward Opton, Jr., *The Mind Manipulators* (London: Paddington Press LTD, 1978), p.192.

34. Ibid., p. 336-337.

35. Ibid.

36. Dr. Butterworth's revelations are from James DiEugenio's interview with Butterworth, August 29, 1994.

37. NODA interviews with Pete Reeche, January 10, 1968 and January 22, 1968.

38. Ibid.

39. NODA interview with Rudy Spremich, December 13, 1966.

40. Author's interviews with Edwin Lea McGehee and Reeves Morgan, August 26, 1994.

41. Undated interview of Erick Crouchet by Shaw's defense team. From the Wegmann files at the National Archives.

42. Ibid.

43. Shaw testimony, State of Louisiana vs. Clay L. Shaw, February 27, 1969.

44. NODA memo, undated, titled "Notes from Alberto Fowler."

45. Ibid.

46. CIA document dated June 5, 1968 from 1994 CIA Segregated Collection, Box 24, Folder L.

47. HSCA interview with Joseph Oster, January 27, 1978.

48. HSCA interview with McGehee, April 19, 1978, HSCA document #008506.

49. HSCA interview with Morgan, April 19, 1978, HSCA document #008501.

50. HSCA interviews with McGehee and Morgan.

51. HSCA interview with Henry Earl Palmer, April 19, 1978, HSCA document # 008499.

52. NODA interview with Lawrence Howard, February 26, 1968.

53. Author's interview with Reeves Morgan, August 26, 1994. Morgan also said that not long after his appearance at the Shaw trial, someone blew out the windows of his truck with a shotgun. Morgan was not in the truck at the time.

54. Author's interview with Edwin Lee McGehee, August 26, 1994.

55. HSCA interview with Francis Fruge, December 19, 1978, HSCA document #015044.

56. Kirkwood, pp. 220-223.

57. Ibid., p. 220. According to Shaw juror, Bill Ricks, the jury found the Clinton people most convincing. See *Rough Side of the Mountain*. The court reporter, Helen Dietrich, expressed similar views on the Clinton testimony. See *He Must Have Something*.

58. Gerald Posner. *Case Closed.* (New York: Anchor Books, 1994), p. 144. The documents Posner cites were in the possession of the late Edward Wegmann, one of Shaw's defense lawyers. Since there were no discovery laws in Louisiana at the time of the Shaw trial, one should ask how Garrison's files ended up in the possession of Shaw's lawyer.

59. Author's interview with Edwin Lea McGehee, August 26, 1994. Back issues of *The Councillor* are on file at the Northwestern State University Library, Louisiana.

60. State of Louisiana vs. Clay L. Shaw, February 6, 1969.

61. Ibid.

62. Ibid.

63. Ibid.

64. Testimony of Rex L. Kommer, State of Louisiana vs. Clay L. Shaw, February 21, 1969.

65. State of Louisiana vs. Clay L. Shaw, February 6, 1969.

66. Author's interviews with Reeves and Van Morgan, August 26, 1994 and Mary Morgan Jenkins, September 4, 1994.

67. Author's interview with Mary Morgan Jenkins, September 4, 1994.

68. Author's interview with Reeves and Van Morgan, August 26, 1994.

Chapter 12: Fourth Estate or Fourth Reich: The CIA/Media Attack on Jim Garrison

1. Garrison, *On The Trail of the Assassins*, pg. 85. An early entry in the investigative notes of *Life* magazine reporter Richard Billings reads, "Evidence that Shaw is actually Bertrand is popping up everywhere." See the Richard Billings Papers, Georgetown University, Box 2, Folder 22.

2. NODA interview of William Morris by William Boxley and William Martin, July 12, 1967. Gene Davis was later accused by an obviously scared Dean Andrews, of being Clay Bertrand. Andrews was subsequently convicted of perjury for his efforts. Morris was introduced to Bertrand in 1958 and believed Shaw "resembled" this person.

3. NODA interview of David Logan by James Alcock, April 13,1968.

4. Ibid.

5. FBI memo from New Orleans office to Director, February 25, 1967, document # unknown. Available at the National Archives.

6. Russo's description of an unshaven, disheveled Oswald dovetails with the description of Oswald as reported to the Warren Commission by Sylvia Odio. During the last week of September of 1963, Odio, a Cuban exile living in Dallas, was visited by two Latin men and a white man they introduced as "Leon Oswald," a perfect match in both appearance and name to Russo's "Leon." Later, one of the Latinos called Odio on the phone and told her Oswald was "kind of nuts" and that Oswald said "the Cubans don't have any guts because President Kennedy should have been assassinated after the Bay of Pigs." See

WR, pp.321-322. Pushing the envelope of coincidence even further is the fact that Odio's uncle, Agustin Guitart, lived at 3694 Louisiana Avenue Parkway, three blocks on the same street as Ferrie. He also attended Oswald's court hearing after his street scuffle with Carlos Bringuier. See Peter Dale Scott, *Deep Politics*, (Los Angeles: University of California Press, 1993), p.119.

7. Russo testimony, various sources. Ferrie, after returning from Texas on the weekend of the assassination, did indeed end up at the campus in Hammond. As noted previously, Shaw arranged to be on the West Coast, and subsequently gave several conflicting stories about that trip.

8. Details from the Russo/Sciambra controversy are taken from the Shaw trial testimony of Perry Russo (February 10 & 11, 1967) and Andrew Sciambra (February 12, 1967), as well as author's interviews with Perry Russo, August 31, 1994 and April 7, 1995. For Phelan's status as FBI informant, see FBI documents # 62-109060-5113, 62-109060-5060, 62-109060-5092 and 62-109060-5093.

9. James Kirkwood, *American Grotesque* (New York: Simon and Schuster, 1970), p.162.

10. William Turner, *The Garrison Investigation* (Unpublished manuscript). 1968, p.52.

11. Ibid.

12. For an excellent treatment of the Habighorst issue, see DiEugenio, pp. 198-202.

13. Interview with Tommy Baumler by Bud Fensterwald and J. Gary Shaw, dated December 30, 1981. Baumler also revealed that Banister and Shaw were "close" and was clear that "Oswald worked for Banister."

14. The State also called the police officer who arrested Oswald, various Cubans, the coroner's photographer who photographed Ferrie's autopsy and the police photographer who took the photos of Ferrie's house.

15. Bundy testimony from Shaw preliminary hearing March 17, 1967.

16. NBC White Paper, *The Case of Jim Garrison*, June 19, 1967.

17. Torres background from the personal notes of Richard Billings.

18. NBC White Paper, 1967.

19. NODA interview with Vernon Bundy, March 16, 1967.

20. Ibid.

21. Ibid.

22. Author's interview with Perry Russo, August 31, 1994.

23. There are no less than 23 references to Sulzer in James Kirkwood's, *American Grotesque*, all favorable towards Shaw.

24. NOPD statement of Arthur King, May 22, 1967.

25. NODA statement of Samuel Davis, Jr., May 22, 1967 and statement of Vernon Bundy, May 23, 1967.

26. NODA memo from Boxley to Garrison, undated, on file at the AARC.

27. Letter from Dymond to Wegmann, August 29, 1967.

28. Kirkwood, p. 647.
29. Gerald Posner, "GARRISON GUILTY: Another Case Closed," *New York Times Magazine,* August 6, 1995.
30. NODA memo from Gurvich, Jonau and Navarre to Garrison, March 16, 1967.
31. NODA memo from Volz to Garrison, March 16, 1967.
32. Author's interview with John Volz, August 30, 1994. Volz made it clear in the interview that he believed that Shaw and Oswald were associated but had not engaged in an assassination conspiracy. While in New Orleans in 1994, the author attempted to locate Vernon Bundy. His father, Vernon, Sr., informed the author that Vernon had passed away five years earlier.
33. Author's interview with Irvin Dymond, August 29, 1994 and FBI document # 62-109060-5090. For more on Wackenhut's extensive intelligence connections see Jim Hougan, *Spooks,* (New York: William Morrow), 1978.
34. These revelations came as a result of investigations by the Pike and Church Committees. Their findings were incorporated into a groundbreaking article by Watergate reporter, Carl Bernstein for *Rolling Stone* magazine, October 20, 1977.
35. Carl Bernstein, "The CIA and the Media," *Rolling Stone,* October 20, 1977, pp.56-67.
36. Ibid.
37. Ibid.
38. Ibid., p.59.
39. Ibid.
40. Interview with Victor Marchetti by Bud Fensterwald April 22, 1975 also published in *True,* April 1975. Also author's interview with Marchetti, April 26, 1995. In the Fensterwald interview, Marchetti added: "...this guy Ferrie came up,...and I was given a similar kind of explanation, that he's been involved in the Bay of Pigs and been a contract agent or contact at the time."
41. New Orleans Police Report, June 12, 1967.
42. Ibid.
43. Unless otherwise noted, Aynesworth's background is from the CIA's biographical data sheet on him, document # 100-300-17, dated October 10, 1963.
44. Ibid.
45. Ibid.
46. CIA memorandum on Aynesworth, dated January 25, 1968.
47. FBI memo from SAC, Dallas to Director, FBI. Document number illegible but dated December 15, 1966.
48. Using a purloined trial brief, Aynesworth and William Gurvich went to Clinton and Jackson, Louisiana and attempted to intimidate those witnesses. See DiEugenio, *Destiny Betrayed,* p.367, *n.* 21.
49. The amount of correspondence between Aynesworth and Shaw and his

lawyers is voluminous. See the Wegmann collection at the National Archives.

50. CIA memorandum from Chief, Houston Office to Director, DCS, December 27, 1967.

51. Gurvich's interview, August 29, 1967, from the Wegmann Papers at the National Archives.

52. CIA memorandum from Chief, Houston Office to Director, DCS, December 27, 1967 and CIA memorandum titled, "Garrison and the Kennedy Assassination, Memorandum Number 8," January 12, 1968. Note, the DDP is the ultra-secret Plans Division, which includes the Clandestine Services.

53. Roger M. Williams & Michael Parks, "The Clay Shaw Trial: Reporter-Participants," *Columbia Journalism Review*, Spring, 1969, pp. 38-41.

54. Ibid., p. 41.

55. Ibid.

56. Novel v. Garrison, p. 534.

57. Ibid.

58. Regarding the recording studio, Andrews is quoted as saying, "I can get the equipment here all I have to do is make a phone call, I'll have open credit, I can pay off on any terms. Look, Bobby Sarnoff promised me those facilities and he'd better pay off, baby." From NODA memo from Gary Sanders to Ivon, dated January 11, 1968. Bobby Sarnoff was, of course, Robert Sarnoff, NBC president and later chairman of the board of its parent company, RCA. Russo's inducement is from Turner, *The Garrison Investigation* pp. 73-74 and author's interview with Russo, August 31, 1994.

59. CIA memo, dated December 1, 1967 released in 1993.

60. CIA memo from Ray Rocca to ADDP, dated May 12, 1967.

61. FBI memo from New Orleans office to Director, May 18, 1967, document # 89-69-3075.

62. For an excellent analysis of the broadcast, see Flammonde, Chapter 12.

63. "Gurvich Blasts Investigation," *New Orleans Times-Picayune*, June 23, 1967.

64. CIA memo from Donavan E. Pratt, dated September 26, 1967.

65. NODA affidavit of Fred H. Leemans Sr., dated January 6, 1969.

66. FBI memo from SAC, New Orleans to Director, April 12, 1967, document # 62-109060-5090.

67. CIA memo for file from Lloyd A. Ray, dated May 28, 1968.

68. Ibid.

69. CIA memo from Lloyd Ray to Director, DCS, dated June 4, 1968.

70. FBI memo from DeLoach to Tolson, April 4, 1967, document # 62-109060-5075.

71. Ibid.

72. CIA Propaganda Notes, May 15, 1967. CIA document number 1081-963.

73. Ibid.

74. Ibid.

75. Ibid.

76. CIA memo from Donovan Pratt to A/DCI, October 2, 1967.

77. Ibid.

78. CIA memo from Donovan Pratt for Raymond Rocca to General Counsel and ADDP, June 6, 1967.

79. CIA dispatch to Chiefs, Certain Stations and Bases, July 19, 1968. CIA document number 1127-987.

80. Brener would go on to write an anti-Garrison tract entitled, *The Garrison Case: A Study in the Abuse of Power* (New York: Clarkson N. Potter, Inc, 1969).

81. Letter from Quaid to Helms, dated May 15, 1967.

82. Jim DiEugenio, "The Wegmann Files Part II," *Probe,* July-August, 1997, p.18.

83. CIA Memo from Richard H. Lansdale, Associate General Counsel, dated May 11, 1967.

84. CIA Memo for the record from Richard H. Lansdale, May 1, 1967.

85. CIA Memo for the record from Richard H. Lansdale, May 8, 1967.

86. Ibid.

87. "Garrison Interview," *Playboy,* October, 1967, p.64.

88. CIA Memo from Lansdale, May 11, 1967.

89. DiEugenio, "The Wegmann Files II," *Probe* July-August 1997, p.21.

90. Letters from Miller to Lansdale, dated March 21, 1968 and March 26, 1968, CIA Segregated Collection, National Archives.

91. Novel letter to Dulles, March 14, 1968 available from the Wegmann papers at the National Archives.

92. Novel's Answers to Interrogatories, dated April 16, 1969.

93. NODA memo from William Martin to Jim Garrison, re: Central Intelligence Agency Connections In The City Of New Orleans, May 24, 1967.

94. Jim Hougan, *Spooks* (New York: William Morrow & Company, 1978), p.270.

95. Ibid.

96. HSCA interview with Joseph Oster, January 27, 1978, document #005207.

97. Hougan, pp. 270-271.

98. Letter from Maurice Gatlin to William Martin, November 21, 1961.

99. CIA memo from Chief, New Orleans Office to Director, Domestic Contact Service, January 3, 1968.

100. Ibid.

101. Ibid.

102. For the definitive treatment of Nagell see Dick Russell, *The Man Who Knew Too Much* (New York: Carroll & Graf, 1992).

103. CIA memo from Chief, New Orleans Office to Director, Domestic Contact Service, January 3, 1968.

104. CIA memo from Chief, New Orleans Office to Director, Domestic Contact Service, January 19, 1968.

105. Boxley biographical data from CIA memoranda dated April 26, 1968 and May 8, 1968, released in 1993 and available at NARA.

106. Garrison, *On The Trail of the Assassins*, p.191.

107. Ibid.

108. Garrison also suspected Boxley of attempting to set him up in a compromising position in the men's room at L.A. Airport. See Garrison, *On The Trail*, pp. 187-190.

109. HSCA memo from Fonzi to Tannenbaum, May 17, 1977, document #014582.

110. Ibid.

111. NODA memo from Ivon to Garrison, February 26, 1967.

112. Jim DiEugenio, "What Harry is Hiding," *Probe*, September-October 1996, p.20.

113. Ibid.

114. HSCA memo from Fonzi to Tannenbaum, May 17, 1977, document #014582; HSCA memo from Fonzi and Gonzales to Blakey, November 8, 1977, document #014602 and HSCA summary of deposition of Gerry Patrick Hemming, March 21, 1978.

115. HSCA memo from Fonzi to Tannenbaum, May 17, 1977, document #014582.

116. From HSCA document, "Request For Immunity For Bernardo De Torres," March 10, 1978 and HSCA summary of de Torres testimony, May 18, 1978, document # 008532.

117. HSCA memo from Fonzi to Tannenbaum, May 17, 1977, document #014582.

118. Ibid. Also Donald Freed and Fred Landis, *Death in Washington* (Westport, Conn.: Lawrence Hill & Company, 1980), p.195.

119. FBI memo from SAC, New Orleans to Director, January 4, 1967, # 62-109060-4366.

120. Ibid.

121. Ibid.

122. John Davis, *Mafia Kingfish* (New York: Signet, 1989), p.369.

123. John Davis, *The Kennedy Contract* (New York: Harper Paperbacks, 1993), p.180.

124. Davis, *Mafia Kingfish*, p.220.

125. Ibid.

126. Author's interview with Bill Triplett, October 7, 1994.

127. HSCA Executive Session Testimony of Carlos Marcello, January 11, 1978.

128. Ibid.

129. Garrison, *Heritage*, p. 127 citing NODA's office interview with Herbert Wagner, August 6, 1969.

130. G. Robert Blakey & Richard N. Billings, *Fatal Hour: The Assassination of President Kennedy By Organized Crime* (New York: Berkley, 1992), p.xxxix.

131. Ibid.

132. "Letters to the Editor," *The Washington Post,* April 6, 1993.

133. Sandy Smith, "The Mob, Part 2," *LIFE,* September 8, 1967, pp.94-96.

134. Garrison answers some of these charges in *On The Trail,* p. 164. Other writers have tried to make the case that Garrison also met with West Coast Mafiosi, Johnny Roselli in Las Vegas just after Ferrie's death. The source of that information is the CIA, hardly a credible source on the subject of Garrison. See CIA Inspector General's Report, *Report on Plots to Assassinate Fidel Castro,* April 25, 1967.

135. *The New Orleans Times-Picayune,* January 9 & 13, 1963, March 29, 1964, April 11, 1964.

136. *The New Orleans Times-Picayune,* January 9, 1963.

137. Bob Greene, "Garrison Probe Is One for (Spy) Books," *Newsday,* March 7, 1967, pp. 7 & 53.

138. NODA memo from Garrison to Staff, December 24, 1967.

139. Novel v. Garrison, et. al., p. 713.

140. FBI memo, June 10, 1967, document number illegible.

141. David Chandler, "The Devil's D.A." *New Orleans,* November 1966, pp.31-32 & 90-91.

142. David Chandler, "The Assassin's Trail," *Westword,* November 25 - December 1, 1992, pp. 13-23.

143. James Phelan, "The Vice Man Cometh," *Saturday Evening Post,* June 8, 1963, 67-71.

144. Bill Davidson, "New Orleans: Cosa Nostra's Wall Street," *Saturday Evening Post,* February 29, 1964, pp.15-20.

145. Fred Cook, *Mafia!* (Greenwich, Conn: Fawcett Gold Medal, 1973), p.111.

146. Davidson, *Saturday Evening Post,* February 29, 1964, pp. 15-20.

147. Garrison letter to Donald V. Organ, April 17, 1968 and Kohn's own admissions to the *New Orleans Times-Picayune,* September 13, 1967 and December 14, 1967.

148. NODA interview of Aaron Kohn, June 29, 1967.

149. Transcript of Orleans Parish Grand Jury testimony of William Monaghan, June 28, 1967, p.3. It is worth noting that Monaghan was Oswald's direct supervisor at Reily Coffee Company.

150. Materials Relating to the Investigation of the Assassination of President John F. Kennedy, the Trial of Clay Shaw and Related Matters, 1966-1973. 3 boxes of 16mm microfilm on file at the New Orleans Public Library.

151. "Kohn Is Placed in N.O. Prison," *The New Orleans Times-Picayune,* December 15, 1967, p.10.

152. William C. Sullivan, *The Bureau* (New York: W.W. Norton & Company, 1979), p.93.

153. Anthony Summers, *Official and Confidential* (New York: Putnam, 1993), p.208.

154. Ibid., p.209.
155. Ibid., p.210.
156. Ibid.
157. Ibid.
158. Sandy Smith, "The Fix," *Life,* September 1, 1967, p.45.
159. Summers, *Official and Confidential*, p.211.
160. Ibid.
161. Ibid., p.212.
162. Ibid.
163. Ibid.
164. William Turner, *Hoover's FBI* (New York: Thunder's Mouth Press, 1993), pp.121-122.
165. Ibid. Smith's close relationship with the FBI was apparently quite well known as it was the subject of Oval Office discussions during President Nixon's administration. See Summers, *Official and Confidential*, p.445, *n.*6.
166. Ibid.
167. Ibid.
168. Turner had the last laugh, however. *The Nation* magazine published the article under the title, "Crime Is Too Big For The FBI" and the more widely read *Pageant* magazine reprinted it in their May 1966 issue.
169. Summers, *Official and Confidential*, p.213.
170. Ibid.
171. Frank J. Donner, *The Age of Surveillance* (New York: Alfred A. Knopf, 1980), p.271.
172. Walter's information is from Garrison's notes from his interview with Walter, January 26, 1977.
173. A representative sample would be FBI document 62-109060-1501, dated February 20, 1967, FBI document 62-109060-4613, dated February 28, 1967 and FBI memo dated May 4, 1967 but there are many more.
174. Congressional Record - House, April 5, 1977, H 3074.
175. Davis, *The Kennedy Contract*, p. 181.

Chapter 13: Trial and Error

1. FBI memo of September 21, 1967 conference sent as an attachment to September 24, 1967 letter to Lawrence Houston of the CIA.
2. Ibid.
3. Ibid.
4. This was the defense's fourth such motion for a change of venue. The previous three having been overruled by the presiding judge, Edward Haggerty. This motion was also overruled.
5. Shilstone information from CIA memorandum from Chief, New Orleans Office to Director, DCS, June 27, 1967 and CIA Memorandum Number 8, January 12, 1968.

6. Ibid.

7. Transcript of New Orleans "Roundtable" discussion, September 21, 1968, p.142.

8. Bethell affidavit, January 16, 1969, on file at the New Orleans Public Library. In addition to many of the witnesses who did testify at the Shaw trial, this trial brief contained several who did not. The most notable exclusion was that of Clyde Johnson. In 1963, Johnson was a candidate for governor of Louisiana and was campaigning in New Orleans. Sometime in July or August of that year, Johnson was paged in the lobby of the Roosevelt Hotel, where he was staying. The party who paged him introduced himself as Alton Bernard and the two sat down and conferred for about a half-hour. Bernard told Johnson he had seen him on television several times and encouraged Johnson to keep up with his current anti-Kennedy harangues. Bernard was particularly angry at Kennedy's Cuban policies, expressing rage over the Bay of Pigs affair. To assist Johnson, Bernard "contributed" $2,000 to Johnson. After this, Johnson received several telephone calls from Bernard, always supportive of Johnson's anti-JFK rhetoric. In early September, Bernard asked Johnson to meet him at the Capitol House Hotel in Baton Rouge. When Bernard arrived, he was accompanied by a man introduced as "Leon." Johnson's description of Leon was identical to Perry Russo's identification of the grubby, erstwhile Ferrie roommate, Leon Oswald. Bernard, Johnson, and Leon were subsequently joined by an unidentified, mustachioed Cuban and a man known as Jack. Johnson recalled, "I left the room to go to the bathroom in the other room and while in there I overheard a conversation among the three men. One of them said, to the effect that he would get him. I heard Alton Bernard say there was some others working on this. I thought they were talking about me so I went and got my pistol out of my briefcase and a thought flashed through my mind to either go out the door and get to a telephone when I heard one say, "Well, he's got to come down from Washington the pressure is on. He's got to come back." So I knew that they weren't talking about me then and I came back into the room and Jack said, What about him?" and pointed toward me. Alton Bernard said, "That's alright. He's one of my boys."" Later Johnson would identify Jack as Jack Ruby, Leon as Lee Harvey Oswald and Alton Bernard as Clay Shaw. Partial corroboration of Johnson's story came from his running mate, Edward McMillan. He recalled a post-election celebration in January of 1964 at the Monteleone Hotel where Johnson was staying. Among the crowd of revelers in Johnson's room, was a man McMillan would identify as Clay Shaw. (NODA's office statement of Edward McMillan, April 11, 1967). Whether Johnson was a kook or the genuine article we'll never know. The jury never got the opportunity to decide on his credibility. In February of 1969, he was severely beaten and never testified. Five months later he was killed in a shotgun attack near Greensburg, Louisiana.

9. Bethell affidavit, January 16, 1969.

10. Kirkwood, p. 462.

11. CIA memo from CI/R&A to Sara Hall, Security, February 11, 1969.

12. CIA memo from Angleton to Hoover and Papich, February 28, 1969.

13. Kirkwood, pp. 231-248.

14. Ibid. An interesting footnote to the Spiesel episode is a CIA memo concerning Spiesel's father. According to the CIA, Boris Spiesel did undercover work for the FBI spying on "USSR personnel" in the United States. CIA memo for the record, February 12, 1969.

15. Kirkwood, p.360.

16. The National Archives released what was available of the transcript in 1993. The Assassination Archives and Research Center in Washington, D.C. (202) 393-1917 also has the transcript on file where it can be purchased either in part or in its entirety.

17. Posner, p.447.

18. Ibid.

19. Ibid.

20. Transcript of address, August 20, 1969.

21. NODA affidavit of Jessie Parker, September 12, 1967.

22. NODA memo from Alcock and Duffy to Garrison, November 17, 1967.

23. Leake's attendance at party and conversation with Moran from CIA memorandum from Chief, New Orleans Office to Director, DCS, November 15, 1967.

24. CIA memo from Donovan Pratt to Director, DCS, November 24, 1967.

25. CIA memo to George Musulin, November 29, 1967.

26. CIA memo from Office of General Counsel to New Orleans, November 30, 1967.

27. Ibid.

28. CIA memo from Pratt to Director, DCS, November 24, 1967. Apparently doctoring 201 files was standard operating procedure. The HSCA produced notes from CIA agent, William Harvey who was in charge of the Agency's program of assassination called ZR/RIFLE. One of Harvey's notations regarding the recruitment of a potential assassin was "should have phony 201 in RI to backstop this. All documents therein forged and backdated." HSCA IV, p.200.

29. CIA memo titled, "Garrison and the Kennedy Assassination, Memorandum Number 8," January 12, 1968.

30. CIA memo from New Orleans to Office of General Counsel, December 13, 1967.

31. CIA memo from Leake to Director, DCS, January 23, 1969.

32. Ibid.

33. CIA memo from Office of General Counsel to New Orleans, November 30, 1967.

34. Shaw trial, February 28, 1969.

35. Shaw trial, February 25, 1969.

36. Undated CIA memo re: Cobb from 1993 release. On file at the AARC.

37. Curt Gentry, *J. Edgar Hoover: The Man and The Secrets* (New York: Plume, 1992), pp.73 & 148.

38. Ludovic Kennedy, *The Airman and The Carpenter* (New York: Viking, 1985), p.201.

39. CIA background sheet from Angleton's Counter-Intelligence unit to the Office of General Counsel, March 18, 1968.

40. Ibid.

41. Weisberg investigative notes, February 23, 1969.

42. Weisberg letter to Garrison, March 4, 1969.

43. CIA memorandum from David Atlee Phillips to Director, March 18, 1969.

44. Ibid.

45. HSCA interview with Joseph Oster, January 27, 1978, document #005207.

46. Ibid.

47. Shaw trial, February 24 & 25, 1969.

48. Letter from Edward Wegmann to Elmer Gertz, March 12, 1969.

49. Tyler video, *He Must Have Something*.

50. Answer to Motion to Dismiss Complaint, filed January 18, 1971.

51. Shaw trial, February 27, 1969.

52. Answer to Motion to Dismiss.

53. Ibid.

54. One wonders if Garrison would have used two witnesses who placed Oswald with Shaw. In "Destiny Betrayed" Jim DiEugenio writes of his interview with researcher and Garrison consultant, Vincent Salandria. He revealed that a psychiatrist, who had treated a friend of Shaw's, told him he saw Oswald at Shaw's house. This ties in with a report Garrison's office received in 1969 concerning a plumbing contractor who had worked on Shaw's apartment on 906 Esplanade. Sometime in 1956, this plumber was working in Shaw's apartment for two days. During that time, two teenage boys were always hanging around. He identified Oswald as one of the teenagers. (NODA's office memo from Andrew Sciambra to Jim Garrison, April 3, 1969).

55. Letter from Caroline Christenberry to Clay Shaw, March 9, 1969, from Shaw's personal papers at the National Archives.

56. Reprinted in Harold Weisberg, *Whitewash*, Vol. IV (self-published, 1974), p.143.

57. James DiEugenio, "The Wegmann Files, Part II," *Probe*, July-August, 1997, p.32.

58. Shaw medical diagnosis from police report of Shaw's death, August 28, 1974.

59. Ibid.

60. Dooty background from Dooty interview by Jim Garrison and James Alcock, March 23, 1967.

61. *Times-Picayune*, August 20, 1974.

62. Police report of Shaw's death, August 28, 1974.

63. Statement of William Acosta, August 16, 1974. Coincidentally, the Bultmans were major backers of Shaw during his trial.
64. Ibid.
65. DiEugenio, pg. 375 *n*.72.
66. *Times-Picayune*, August 17, 1974.
67. *Times-Picayune*, August 18, 1974.
68. HSCA Report, p.145.
69. Ibid., p.143.
70. Ibid., p.145.
71. Ibid., p.115.
72. That movie is, of course, Oliver Stone's, *JFK*. Stone's film contained a tag line about the number of documents classified until the year 2037. The resultant public outcry led to hearings in both the House and the Senate. Congress then passed the JFK Records Act, which was signed into law by President Bush in 1992. The act provided for the creation of the Assassination Records and Review Board.

Chapter 14: The Hidden Record

1. *New York Times*, March 3, 1967.
2. Ibid.
3. Ibid.
4. Ibid.
5. *New York Times*, June 3, 1967.
6. FBI memo from DeLoach to Tolson, March 2, 1967, FBI document # 62-109060-4635.
7. Ibid.
8. Undated interview with Ramsey Clark from Personal Papers of Ramsey Clark, Box 70, folder, "Garrison," LBJ Library.
9. Ibid.
10. FBI memo, author unknown, March 2, 1967, FBI document # 62-109060-4720.
11. FBI memo, from Los Angeles office to Director, March 22, 1967, FBI document # 62-109060-4907.
12. Ibid.
13. Ibid.
14. Coincidentally, deBrueys was transferred to Dallas just after the assassination to assist in the investigation of Oswald. A recent CIA release indicates deBrueys was part of a covert operation named Project SEAL. Curiously, the CIA document reveals another Project SEAL member - New Orleans anti-Castro activist, Sergio Arcacha Smith. (CIA SRS file, no date or number, probably prepared by Marguerite D. Stevens. Document was part of 1993 CIA segregated file release).
15. Shaw trial, February 17, 1969.

16. FBI memo dated March 21, 1967, document # 62-109060-4874.

17. Ibid.

18. FBI memo from New Orleans office to Director, March 4, 1967, document # 89-69-1569.

19. CIA memo, author unknown, circa March, 1967, no document number but part of 1992 release on file at the AARC. As with my FOIA request for files on ZR/CLIFF, my request for QK/ENCHANT information has likewise been on hold. CIA Information and Privacy coordinator, John Wright, has written to the author that information on QK/ENCHANT is still classified. Yet, an admitted ex-CIA employee has published on the Internet that QK/ENCHANT involved routine debriefing of people in the trade industry. Either this person has violated his/her secrecy agreement by revealing classified information or is deliberately spreading false information. Time will tell.

20. Marchetti interview with Bud Fensterwald, April 22, 1975 and author's interview with Marchetti, April 26, 1995.

21. Author's interview with Marchetti, April 26, 1995.

22. Ibid.

23. Ibid.

24. CIA memo dated October 27, 1970 from 1993 CIA release. Available at the AARC, no box number.

25. 1994 CIA release on Clay Shaw.

26. CIA Information Report, December 13, 1948. 1994 CIA release available at NARA. All documents used in this section are from the 1994 release, unless otherwise noted.

27. CIA memo from William P. Burke to Chief, Contact Branch, dated June 7, 1946.

28. CIA Information Report, June 14, 1949.

29. CIA Information Report, June 14, 1949.

30. CIA Information Report, June 29, 1951.

31. Wilds & Harkey, pp. 123-124.

32. CIA Information Report, January 23, 1952.

33. CIA memo from William P. Burke to Chief, Contacts Division, August 9, 1955.

34. Ibid. The report mentioned in this memo was not included in the 1994 release. It is interesting to note that Shaw reported on an international fair at Basel, Switzerland. In less than a year, Basel would be the home to the mysterious PERMINDEX project. See Chapter 10. Basel was also the headquarters of Sandoz, the chemical firm that was the CIA's sole supplier of LSD for their nefarious MKULTRA experiments. See Marks, *The Search for the Manchurian Candidate*, p.3.

35. CIA memo from William P. Burke to Chief, Contacts Division, May 25, 1956.

36. CIA memo from William P. Burke to Chief, Contacts Division, June 4,

36. CIA memo from William P. Burke to Chief, Contacts Division, June 4, 1956.

37. Anonymous and undated handwritten note included in the CIA's 1994 Shaw file release. Another anonymous handwritten note by someone on the HSCA staff alludes to a CIA document the HSCA had just seen where, some critics have alleged, it was noted that Shaw was an *unwitting* contact for Project [Redacted] in December of 1962. It is possible that this could be a reference to Project QK/ENCHANT. There is some question whether this memo actually refers to Shaw or San Francisco Trade Mart Director, J. Monroe Sullivan. Since a CIA memo on Sullivan exists and makes reference to Sullivan being security approved for QK/ENCHANT on December 10, 1962, and because the HSCA memo refers to the Executive Director of the San Francisco Trade Mart, the HSCA memo is undoubtedly referring to Sullivan. (See CIA Memo for File, March 16, 1967, re: SULLIVAN, J. Monroe, document # 1337-1051). However, without seeing the <u>unredacted</u> CIA memo in question it makes it difficult to tell definitively.

38. CIA memo from Lloyd A. Ray to Director, Domestic Contact Service, April 6, 1967.

39. CIA memo from James R. Murphy to Director, Domestic Contact Service, et. al., March 4, 1970.

40. CIA memo from J. Walton Moore to Chief, Domestic Collection Division, et. al., June 3, 1976.

41. Ibid.

42. Moore/ de Mohrenschildt relationship from Summers, *Conspiracy*, pp. 226-228.

43. CIA memo for the record, dated February 20, 1964, document # 1272-1028, released in 1993.

44. HSCA interview with J. Lee Rankin, May 31, 1978. HSCA document #008815.

45. FBI memorandum from Deloach to Tolson, April 4, 1967, document # 62-109060-5075.

46. For an excellent expose' of the inner workings of the Committee, see Gaeton Fonzi, *The Last Investigation* (New York: Thunder's Mouth Press, 1993).

47. HSCA memo from Blackmer to Blakey, et al, September 1, 1977, HSCA document # 002220. When the HSCA first released their files in 1992, this document was originally restricted and put in "referred" status. The agency that withdrew this file was the CIA.

48. HSCA Executive Session interview with "John Scelso," May 16, 1978, document #001891, p. 109.

49. Ibid, document #001910, p. 128.

50. Ibid, document #'s 001910 & 001911, pp. 128-129.

Bibliography

Agee, Phillip, *Inside the Company: CIA Diary* (New York: Bantam Books, 1976).

Anson, Robert Sam, *"They've Killed the President"* (New York: Bantam Books, 1975).

Bacque, James, *Other Losses* (New York: Prima Publishing, 1991)

Bethell, Tom, *The Electric Windmill: An Inadvertent Biography* (Washington: Regnery Gateway, 1988).

Bird, Kai, *The Chairman* (New York: Simon & Schuster, 1992)

Blakey, G. Robert and Billings, Richard, *The Plot to Kill the President* (New York: Times Books, 1981).

Brener, Milton E., *The Garrison Case* (New York: Clarkson N. Potter, 1969).

Carpenter, Arthur, *Gateway to the Americas* (Ann Arbor: UMI Dissertation Services, 1996).

Churchill, Ward & Vander Wall, Jim, *The COINTELPRO Papers* (Boston: South End Press, 1990).

Colby, Gerard with Dennett, Charlotte, *Thy Will Be Done* (New York: Harper Collins, 1995).

Cook, Fred J., *The Warfare State*, (New York: The MacMillan Company, 1962).

_____*Mafia!* (Greenwich, Conn: Fawcett Gold Medal, 1973)

Corson, William R., *The Armies of Ignorance* (New York: Dial Press, 1977).

Davis, John H., *Mafia Kingfish* (New York: Signet, 1989).

_____, *The Kennedy Contract* (New York: Harper Paperbacks, 1993).

DiEugenio, James, *Destiny Betrayed* (New York: Sheridan Square Press, 1992).

Donner, Frank J., *The Age of Surveillance* (New York: Alfred A. Knopf, 1980).

Fensterwald, Bernard, Jr., *Coincidence or Conspiracy* (New York: Zebra Books, 1977).

Flammonde, Paris, *The Kennedy Conspiracy* (New York: Meredith Press, 1969).

Fonzi, Gaeton, *The Last Investigation* (New York: Thunder's Mouth Press, 1993).

Freed, Donald with Landis, Fred, *Death in Washington* (Westport, Conn: Laurence Hill & Company, 1980).

Garrison, Jim, *A Heritage of Stone* (New York: G. P. Putnam's Sons, 1970).

_____, *On the Trail of the Assassins* (New York: Sheridan Square Press, 1988).

Gentry, Curt, *J. Edgar Hoover: The Man and the Secrets* (New York: Plume, 1992).

Gibson, Donald, *Battling Wall Street* (New York: Sheridan Square Press, 1994).

Groden, Robert J., *The Killing of a President* (New York: Penguin Books, 1993).

_____, *The Search for Lee Harvey Oswald* (New York: Penguin Books, 1995).

Haas, Edward F., *DeLesseps S. Morrison and the Image of Reform* (Baton Rouge: Louisiana State University Press, 1974).

Haslam, Edward, *Mary, Ferrie and the Monkey Virus* (Albuquerque: Wordsworth, 1995).

Hersh, Burton, *The Old Boys* (New York: Charles Scribner's Sons, 1992).

Hinckle, Warren and Turner, William, *Deadly Secrets* (New York: Thunder's Mouth Press, 1992).

Hougan, Jim, *Spooks* (New York: William Morrow and Company, 1978).

Hunt, E. Howard, *Give Us This Day* (New York: Popular Library, 1973).

____, *Undercover* (New York: Berkley Publishing Corp., 1974).

Hurt, Henry, *Reasonable Doubt* (New York: Holt, Rinehart & Winston, 1985).

James, Rosemary and Wardlaw, Jack, *Plot or Politics?* (New Orleans: Pelican Publishing House, 1967).

Kantor, Seth, *The Ruby Cover-Up* (New York: Zebra Books, 1978).

Kennedy, Ludovic, *The Airman and the Carpenter* (New York: Viking, 1985).

Kirkwood, James, *American Grotesque* (New York: Simon and Schuster, 1970).

Krock, Arthur, *In the Nation: 1932-1966* (New York: New York Times Company, 1966).

LaFontaine, Ray and Mary, *Oswald Talked* (Gretna, Louisiana: Pelican Publishing Co., 1996).

Lane, Mark, *Rush to Judgment* (New York: Holt, Rinehart & Winston, 1966).

_____, *A Citizen's Dissent* (New York: Holt, Rinehart & Winston, 1968).

_____, *Plausible Denial* (New York: Thunder's Mouth Press, 1991).

Mangold, Tom, *Cold Warrior* (New York: Simon & Schuster, 1991).

Marchetti, Victor and Marks, John D., *The CIA and the Cult of Intelligence* (New York: Dell Publishing Co., Inc., 1975).

Marks, John D., *The Search for the Manchurian Candidate* (New York: Times Books, 1979).

Meir, August & Rudwich, Elliott, *CORE: A Study in the Civil Rights Movement* (Chicago: Illini Books, 1975).

Menshikov, S., *Millionaires and Managers* (Moscow: Progress Publishers, 1973).

Newman, John, *Oswald and the CIA* (New York: Carroll & Graf, 1995).

Oglesby, Carl, *The Yankee and Cowboy War* (New York: Berkley Medallion Books, 1977).

Patterson, Thomas G., *Contesting Castro* (New York: Oxford University Press, 1994).

Phillips, David Atlee, *The Night Watch* (New York: Athenaeum, 1977).

Posner, Gerald, *Case Closed* (New York: Anchor Books, 1994).

Powers, Thomas, *The Man Who Kept The Secrets* (New York: Pocket Books, 1981).

Prouty, L. Fletcher, *The Secret Team* (Englewood Cliffs, New Jersey: Prentice-Hall, 1973).

_____, *JFK: The CIA, Vietnam and the Plot to Assassinate John F. Kennedy* (New York: Citadel Press, 1996).

Russell, Dick, *The Man Who Knew Too Much* (New York: Carroll & Graf, 1992).

Russo, Gus, *Live By The Sword* (Baltimore: Bancroft Press, 1998).

Sahl, Mort, *Heartland* (New York: Harcourt Brace Jovanovitch, 1976).

Scheflin, Alan and Opton, Edward Jr., *The Mind Manipulators* (London: Paddington Press, LTD., 1978).

Schlesinger, Stephen and Kinger, Stephen, *Bitter Fruit* (New York: Anchor Books, 1990).

Schotz, E. Martin, *History Will Not Absolve Us* (Brookline, Massachusetts: Kurtz, Ulmer & DeLucia Publishers, 1996).

Scott, Peter Dale, *Deep Politics and the Death of JFK* (Los Angeles: University of California Press, 1993).

Seldes, George, *Facts and Fascism* (New York: In Fact, Inc., 1943).

Sheridan, Walter, *The Fall and Rise of Jimmy Hoffa* (New York: Saturday Review Press, 1972).

Smith, Dwight C., Jr., *The Mafia Mystique* (New York: Basic Books, Inc., 1975).

Stone, Oliver and Sklar, Zachary, *JFK: The Book of the Film* (New York: Applause Books, 1992).

Sullivan, William C. with Bill Brown, *The Bureau* (New York: W. W. Norton & Company, 1979).

Summers, Anthony, *Conspiracy* (New York: McGraw-Hill, 1980)

_____, *Official and Confidential* (New York: G. P. Putnam's Sons, 1993).

_____, *Not in Your Lifetime* (New York: Marlowe & Company, 1998).

Tully, Andrew, *CIA, The Inside Story* (Greenwich, Conn: Crest Books, 1963).

Turner, William W., *The Garrison Investigation*, 1968, unpublished volume, furnished by author.

_____, *Power On The Right* (Berkeley, California: Ramparts Press, 1971).

_____, *Hoover's FBI* (New York: Thunder's Mouth Press, 1993).

Weiner, Tim, *Blank Check* (New York: Warner Books, 1990).

Weisburg, Harold, *Oswald in New Orleans* (New York: Canyon Books, 1967).

Who's Who in the South and Southwest (Chicago: The A. N. Marquis Company, 1950 & 1964).

Wilds, John, *Ochsner's* (Baton Rouge: Louisiana State University Press, 1985).

Wilds, John and Harkey, Ira, *Alton Ochsner, Surgeon of the South* (Baton Rouge: Louisiana State University Press, 1990).

Wise, David and Ross, Thomas B., *The Invisible Government* (New York: Bantam Books, 1965).

Wolfe, Jane, *The Murchisons* (New York: St. Martin's Paperbacks, 1989).

INDEX

323

Index

Index

and Ray, 62-63, 90, 138, 172
and Reily, 36
and Republican circles, 140
and Robertson, 172
and Rocca, 201
and Rusk, 141
and safe house, 147
and Santana, 54
and *Saturday Evening Post*, 129
and Schlumberger, 284n15, 285n20
and Schroder Banking Corporation, 96, 97
and Schroder Trust, 96
  secrecy agreement, 80
and security clearances, 113, 195-196, 288n44, 295n27
and Shaw, 66, 76, 94, 98, 100, 130, 139, 150, 170, 173, 178-179, 180, 185, 195-201, 288n44
and Shaw's security number, 195
and Sheridan, 135-136
and Shilstone, 172
and Soustelle, 99
and Southern Air Transport, 88
and Soviet Bloc, 142, 199
and Spain, 199
"Special Counsel," 127
and Spiesel (Boris), 311n14
station chiefs, 142, 172
and Stevens, 195, 313n14
and Sullivan (J. M.), 195
and Sulzberger, 129
and Switzerland, 199
and Tofte, 143
and trade fairs, 197, 198-199
training, 87, 130
training camps, 29-31
and Truth and Consequences, Inc., 172
201 file modification, 179, 200, 311n28
and United Kingdom, 199
and USIA
and Vietnam, 28-29
and Wackenhut, 129, 304n33
and Walter, 163
and Warren Commission, 139, 187
and *Washington Post*, 129
and weapons supplier, 148
and Wegmann, 170
and Weissberg, 142
and Werbell, 148
and Western economies, 199
and White, 196
and withdrawing of file, 315n47
and Wright, 314n19
and Zicarelli, 161
see also Bay of Pigs invasion

Chandler, David, 127, 154, 156
Chandler, Jeff, 105
Charity Hospital, 2
Cheramie, Rose, 53-54, 55, 102
Chetta, Nicholas, 121, 131
Chicago, Illinois, 11, 46, 77
Chicago Tribune, 99, 162
Chief Justice, 141
Chilean leader, 148
Chittenden, Alfred, 17
Christenberry, Herbert, 186, 187
Christenberry, Caroline, 186
Christian, George, 133
Cienfuegos, Camillo, 88, 297n24
Ciravolo, John B., Jr., 6
Citizen's Council Program, 42
Civil Air Patrol, 4-6, 7, 8, 47, 48, 113
Civil Service exam, 102
Clark, Henry Burnell, 104-105
Clark, Ramsey, 161, 187, 191-192
Clark, Thomas, 5-6
classified medical research, 295n23
Claude, Alfred, 36
Cleveland, Ohio, 3-4
Clifford, Clark, 140
Clinton, Louisiana, 42, 102, 103-110, 113-115, 175, 181, 299n7, 300n29, 301n57, 304n48
CMC, *see* Rome World Trade Center
Cobb, Alvin, 113, 182
Cobb, Lloyd J. 59, 112, 113, 181-182
Cobos, Arturo, 148
coffee imports, 84
Coffee, Melvin, 45-47
Cogswell, James III, 87
Cohn, Roy, 160, 162
COINTELPRO, 107-108
CORE, *see* Congress of Racial Equality
Collins, Corrie, 103, 104
Columbia Journalism Review, 134-134
Columbia University, 72
Communist Party, 7, 12
Compton, Thomas, 47
Congress of Racial Equality (CORE), 103-104, 107-108, 300n19
Connally, John, 166
Connick, Harry Sr., 187, 204
Cook, Fred, 156
Core, Jesse R., 38, 77, 294n17
Cornwell, Gary, 202
corporations, covert use of, 86-87
Cosa Nostra, La, 155-156
Cosimo's, 63, 119
Council on Foreign Relations, 86
Councillor, The, 115

Index

Index

331

Index

Index

Miller, Herbert J., 143, 144, 145
Miller, McCarthy, Evans and Cassidy, 143
mineral trade, 85
Minneapolis, Minnesota, 11
Minyard, Frank, 67, 189
Miranda rights, 174-175
Miro Cardona, Jose. 27
Mitchell, John, 194
missile bases, 59
Mississippi, 12, 71, 107, 112
Mississippi Shipping Company, 75, 76
Moa Bay Mining Company, 87
Moisant Airport, 6, 178, 185
Moisant Civil Air Patrol, 6
Monaghan, William, 36, 308n149
Monroe & Lemman, 127
Monroe, Louisiana, police 11
Monteleone, William, 296n35
Monterey, 89
Montreal, 88
Moore, J. Walton, 201
Moore, Joseph, 16
Moore, Goldie Naomie, 297n32
Moran, Alfred, 178
Morgan, Estes, 299n9
Morgan family, 76, 117
Morgan, Mary, 117
Morgan, Reeves, 102-103, 113, 114, 116-117, 301n53
Morgan, Van, 117
Morrell, Robert E., 5
Morris, William, 120
Morrison, deLesseps "Shep", 12, 77
MRR, 26
Murchison, Clint, 79
Mussolini's cabinet, 98

Nagy, Ferenc, 95, 96, 97, 98, 99
narcotics, 123, 124, 125
Narcotics Bureau, 161
Nashville Banner, 81
Nation magazine, 309n168
National Aeronautics and Space Administration (NASA), 36
National Archives, 133, 164
National Guard, 82
National Security Action Memorandum, 28
National Security Agency, 135
National Security Council, 86
National Students Association, 42, 289n45
National Trial Lawyers Association, 165
Nazis, 96, 97, 98
NBC (National Broadcasting Company), 77, 90

Special on Garrison, 78, 124, 125, 131, 135-137, 143, 144, 171, 172, 177
New Jersey, 160
New Orleans
    Anderson in, 138
    Bolton Ford incident, 15-16
    Banister in, 82
    Banister's operatives in, 39-42
    Brent in, 75-76
    CIA in, 18, 31, 39-42, 62-63, 76 79, 81, 83, 90, 149, 172, 197, 200
    Cuban exiles settle in, 83
    elite, 80-81, 84
    FRD in, 9,
    French Quarter of, 49, 61, 119, 120, 154, 174
    gay bars in, 120
    Girnus in, 91-92
    homosexual FBI sources in, 193
    homosexual underground in, 75
    House investigators in, 94
    Howard in, 114
    imports, 84
    international relations director, 89
    and Latin American trade, 84
    Ochsner in, 82
    Oswald in, 35-36, 61, 80
    police, 2, 12, 49, 77, 132, 148, 156, 160
    Russo in, 121
    Santana in, 54
    Shaw in, 71, 75-77, 91-92
    Sheridan in, 135, 136
    Thornley in, 61
    Triplett, Bill, 151
    Turkish bath house in, 137
    vice in, 154
    see also International House; International Trade Mart; Metropolitan Crime Commission; organized crime
New Orleans Academy of Trial Lawyers, 175
New Orleans Athletic Club, 51
New Orleans Board of Trade, 76
New Orleans Criminal Bar Association, 51
New Orleans District Attorney, *see* Garrison, Jim
New Orleans magazine, 156, 200
New Orleans Public Library, 78
New Orleans States Item, 39-40, 64-65, 66, 94
New Orleans Stevedores Union, 17
New Orleans Times-Picayune, 63, 154, 156-157, 180, 294n19
New York, 37, 103
New York City, 57, 139, 173
    police, 161, 174
New York Rackets Bureau, 161

335

Index

and Raikin, 283n38
at Reily Coffee Company, 35-36, 81, 308n149
and Ruby, 54, 289n12, 310n8
and Russo, 121
and rifle purchase, 14
and Shaw, 64, 76, 103-104, 109, 110, 121, 185, 189, 195, 310n8, 312n54
and Silva, 107
and taped debates, 81
at Texas School Book Depository, 43
and Thornley, 61, 282n24
and Tujague, 17
and TV watching, 7
and Walter, 163, 286n13-287
and wife's citizenship petition, 50, 76
Oswald, Marguerite, 6
Oswald, Marina, 50, 126, 175, 177
Oswald: Portrait in Red, 81
Oswald Speaks, 81
Oster, Joseph, 13-14

Paesa Sera, 98
Pageant magazine, 309n168
Palmer, Henry Earl, 104, 105, 106, 107, 108-109, 114, 300n29
Paley, William, 129
Panzeca, Sal, 122, 173
Paradis, Jerry, 5
Parent, Ed, 163
Paris, France, 199
Parker, Jessie, 178
Parkland Hospital, Dallas, 45, 289n1
Parks, Michael, 134-135
Parrott, Betty, 282n23
Payne, Ruth, 177
PBS (Public Broadcasting System), 6
Peace Corps, 82
Pena, Orest, 286n2, 292n35
Penkovsky, Oleg, 59
Perdido Building, 60
PERMINDEX, 95-100, 143
Peron, Evita, 198
Peron, Juan, 79, 198
Phelan, James, 122, 131, 134
Philadelphia, 147, 164
Philbrick, Herbert, 7
Phillips, David Atlee, 22-24, 30, 31, 87, 142, 182, 286n11
Piedra, Orlando, 18-19
Pierson, Malcolm, 107, 108
Pipes, Chico, 90
Planer, Ed, 138
Playboy, 140, 144, 155, 162, 284n1
Plot to Kill the President, The

(Blakey/Billings), 109, 152, 153
Plotkin, Stephen, 41, 127, 145
police corruption, 12
Port Nickel, Louisiana, 85
Posner, Gerald, 5, 115, 116, 128, 175, 302n58
Pratini, Joe, 280n12
privacy, 159-160
Probe magazine, 187
Project CLIP, 31-33
propaganda, Red, 72
prostitution, 53, 54, 294n19

QK/ENCHANT, Project, *see* CIA and
Quaid, James, 143
Quaker directory, 126
Quakers, 126, 127
Quigley, John, 37, 287n13
Quiroga, Carlos, 38-39, 59, 287n20-230

Rabenet, Dr., 112
racist views, 79
Ragano, Frank, 165
Raikin, Spas T., 283n38
Ramparts magazine, 203, 289n45
Rankin, J. Lee, 201-202
Rarick, John, 115
Rault, Joseph M., 57, 172
Rault Petroleum Corporation, 57
Ray, Lloyd, 62-63, 90, 138, 172, 283n26
RCA, 305n58
Registrar of Voters, 102, 103, 104, 176
Reily Coffee Company, 35-36, 81, 157, 308n149
   CIA number, 295n31
Reily, Eustis, 36, 81, 157
Reily, William B., 35, 36, 81
Remington Rand Corporation, 145
Reynolds, Warwick, 61
Rheims, France, 72
Rickenbacker, Eddie, 9
Ricks, Bill, 301n57
RICO statute, 152
Robbins, J. Stanton, 76
Roberts, Delphine, 2, 39
Robertson, Willard, 62
Robertson, Wilmot, 78-79
Robey, Richard, 48
Roberts, Charles, 139
Robertson, Willard, 172
Rocca, Ray, 201
Rockefeller, Abby, 296n13
Rockefeller, David, 296n13
Rockefeller family, 86
Rockefeller, Godfrey, 296n13

337

Index

DiEugenio on case against, 187
and Dooty, 188
and FBI, 191-195, 293n6
fear of flying of, 88
and Ferrie, 85, 86, 87-88, 93, 94, 103-104, 109, 185-186, 189, 194-195
firing of, 182
in Foreign Policy Association, 90
and Fowler, 89, 149, 200
and Freeport Sulphur, 85-86, 88
and Garrison case against, 63-64, 78, 91, 119-120, 121-122, 130 –167, 169-187, 200, 203, 299n5
in gay bars, 120
and Girnus, 91-92
Grand Jury indictment of, 129
and gun-running, 94
and Habana Bar, 292n35
home of, 91-92
and homosexuality, 293n6
and injunction to stay trial, 186
intelligence background of, 73, 200
and Johnson, 123, 310n8
and Justice Department, 191-192
and Kennedy assassination, 64
and Kimble, 87-88
and Kohn smear, 78
as "Lambert", 93
Latin American travel of, 197-198
and Logan, 120
and *Look* magazine, 159
and McMillan, 311n8
and Manchester, 105-106
and Marichini, 36
and Marquez, 90
medals awarded to, 293n8
military service of, 71-73, 200
and Moore (Goldie), 297n32
and Morris, 120
in New Orleans, 71, 75-77, 90, 119-120
in New York, 72
and Ochsner, 78, 90
and Oswald, 64, 76, 103-104, 109, 110, 121, 185, 189, 195, 310n8, 312n54
and Palmer, 107
and Parish Prison social workers, 126
and perjury, 185
and PERMINDEX, 97, 98, 100
plays of, 71, 292n3
and polygraph test offer, 122
preliminary hearing of, 123, 124, 129
and Rabenet, 112
and Ruby, 310n8
and sadomasochism, 293n6

and Sciambra, 120
San Francisco/West Coast trip of, 185, 303n7
and Sterns, 77, 78
and Sulzer, 125
and Thomas, 194-195
and the Thrashers, 293n8
trial of, 103, 107, 115-117, 124, 129, 134-135, 173-187
and trial jury , 173, 301n57
and trial transcript, 166, 175
and trial witnesses, 173-174, 175, 177-178, 185, 186, n299n5, 301m57, 303n14, 304n48, 310n8, 312n54
at Western Union, 71, 72
and "White" pseudonym, 292n3
and Wright, 85-86
and Wingfield, 76-77
see also International House; International Trade Mart
Sheridan, Walter, 78, 124, 125, 135-137, 142, 143, 144
CIA on, 135-136, 144
in NSA, 135
Shilstone, Cecil, 172
Sho-Bar, The, 154
Shreveport, Louisiana, 115, 182
Siegman, Edward, 3-4
Silva, Francisco, 107, 112
Silver Slipper, The, 53, 54
Sinopoli, Frank, 154
Sky Tech Airway Service, 4
Smith, Richard A., 82
Smith, Sandy, 154, 162, 163, 167, 309n165
"Social Origins of Anticommunism" (Carpenter), 78-79
social workers, 126, 127
sodium penthothal, *see* truth serum
Somoza, Anastosio, 19, 79, 198
Soule, Mr., 29
Soustelle, Jacques, 99
South Central Airlines, 89, 113
Southeastern Louisiana University, 47, 121, 166
Southern Air Transport, 88
Southern Research, 164
Soviets, 95-96, 99, 199, 310n14
Spain, 199
Spears, Eddie Lee, 104
Spicer, Henry C., 180
Spiesel, Boris, 311n14
Spiesel, Charles I., 173-174, 175, 185
Sprague, Richard A., 164-165
Springer, Eva, 51, 52
Standard Fruit, 36

Index

Vea, Peter, 196
Veciana, Antonio, 24, 87
Venezuelans, 180
Voebel, Edward, 5
Volkswagen dealership, 172
Volz, John, 61, 128-129, 152, 304n32
Voorhees, John, 152
voter registration drive, 103-104

Wackenhut Corporation, 129,163, 164, 304n233
Wagner, Herbert, 186
Walker, Edwin A., 59
Walker, Jerry, 280n12
Wall, Breck, 46
Walter, William, 163-164, 286n13-287
war strategy, 86
Ward, Hugh, 40
Warren, Earl, 141
Warren Commission, 6, 16, 36, 38, 49, 50-51, 63, 76, 119, 133, 142, 169, 187, 286n2
 and CIA, 139, 187, 201-202
 cover-up, 52
 and oaths, 187
 report, 55, 57, 58, 139, 169
Warren Eastern High School, 71
Washington County, 164
Washington, D.C., 148
Washington Post, 80, 138, 152
Wackenhut Corporation, 129, 163, 164
Watson, Marvin, 202
Watson, William, 16
WCBS, 139
WDSU TV, 77, 78, 86, 127, 136, 138
weapons, 14
Webb, Harry A., 4
Wegmann, Edward, 59, 169-170, 185, 188, 189, 281n8, 302n58
Wegmann Papers, 133-134, 302n58
Wegmann, William, 13, 59, 281n8
Weiner, Jerry, 145
Weisberg, Harold, 55, 142, 182
Weisman, Lawrence, 160
Weiss, Victor, 53, 54
Werbell, Mitch, 148
West, Jean, 46
West Virginia, 132
Western Union, 71, 72
"What's My Line?", 141
"White, Allen," 292n3
White, Victor R., 196
Whitney, John Jay "Jock", 86
Whitten, John, 203-204, 315n48, 315n49, 315n50

Who's Who in the Southwest, 100
Wilds, John, 75
Williams, Roger, 134-135
Wilson, Bill, 163
Wilson, Gloria, 107
Wingfield, Edmund Duane, 76-77
Wise, David, 24
witness intimidation allegations, 131-132, 134, 304n48
WJMR TV, 42
Wood, William, 147, *see also*, Boxley, Bill
World War II, 72-73, 86, 96, 108, 293n8
Wright, Charles A., 85, 86
Wright, John, 314n19

Yablonski, Jock, 164
Yemen, 18
Ydigoras Fuentes, Miguel, 79
Yugoslavia, 201

Zelden, Sam "Monk", 51
Zetzmann, William, 76, 81
Zicarelli, "Bayone Joe", 160, 161

Compiled by Daniel C. Tsang

341